"Behold Generation Z—the first group of people that has never known life without cellphones, social media, or 24-hour news. What makes this cohort different? And how should the rest of us respond? In their incisive and important book, Elmore and McPeak deliver the answer. They explain why this generation is both the most empowered and the most anxious in history—and they show how to harness their special strengths. For educators, coaches, parents, and business leaders, GENERATION Z UNFILTERED is an invaluable book, with answers on how to lead today's young people."

**Daniel H. Pink**, Bestselling Author of *A Whole New Mind, Drive,* and *When*

"If you read just one book on leading today's youngest generation, make it this one. You'll be equipped to lead kids with hope and belief instead of fear and frustration."

**John C. Maxwell**, Bestselling Author; Founder of The John Maxwell Company.

"Gen Z is different—strikingly different from the Millennials just before them. Laying out nine challenges that face this digital generation and those who lead them, GENERATION Z UNFILTERED is a road map for motivating and helping today's young people, essential for parents, educators, and employers. Filled with inspiring stories, intriguing facts, and useful advice, GENERATION Z UNFILTERED is a must-read for anyone who wants to not only understand but lead this new generation with integrity and compassion."

**Jean Twenge**, Psychologist, San Diego State University, author of *iGen: Why Today's Super-Connected Kids Are Growing Up Less Rebellious, More Tolerant and Less Happy—and Completely Unready for Adulthood*

"Wow! What an amazing read! Tim Elmore has a gift for understanding and writing about the younger generations. Just like his previous books, Tim nails it with GENERATION Z UNFILTERED. As a school superintendent, a parent, and a grandparent, I can say this book is a MUST read for educators, parents, grandparents, business leaders, or ANY person who interacts with young people. Elmore articulates beautifully the challenges facing the young people today who have so much knowledge at their fingertips, yet so little guidance as to the accuracy of that information and how do to apply it in real-world situations to solve problems. The good news is that Elmore also provides today's more seasoned leaders with the skills and solutions needed to properly lead Generation Z."

**John Barge**, Former Georgia State School Superintendent

*"If you intend to lead young people, it is critical to read this book. The next generation offers tremendous opportunities in how they think and act. Great leaders understand how to connect those talents and skills to take advantage of the opportunities."*

**Gene Smith**, Vice President at The Ohio State University, Director of Athletics

*"People of all generations want to be well-led and Gen Z is no different! Tim Elmore has dug a deep well of insight, wisdom, and application for us all. For those a few years, or decades, down the road, our opportunity is simple: be intentional with the stewardship of our time and influence.* GENERATION Z UNFILTERED *provides concrete steps we can all take to literally shape the future."*

**Mark Miller**, Bestselling Author and VP of High Performance Leadership, Chick-fil-A

*"The foundation of this transformative book is that in order for our young people to thrive and grow, we who parent, teach and lead them must do a far better job. We need to believe in our children without fail, challenge them to become self-reliant and self-assured, and guide them to bravely face the new challenges our world brings. Anyone who guides young people needs the strategies taught in this book!"*

**Kathy Caprino**, Senior Forbes Contributor, Career Leadership Coach and Author

*"Tim Elmore nails it again in his new eye-opening, perspective-changing, purpose-driven book on inspiring our next generation of learners. I love how his research not only offers data on this next generation of students but solutions as well. If you are a parent, teacher, leader, coach or mentor of young people, you'll find how instilling hope and belief wins out over fear and frustration. The greatest investment we make is in the lives of others."*

**Joseph R. Castiglione**, Vice President and Director of Athletics, University of Oklahoma

*"Tim Elmore has been a pioneering agent in the field of leadership and education for emerging generations. This book offers data on today's students, but more than that it contains solutions to challenges they will face. As a parent, coach, or administrator* GENERATION Z UNFILTERED *is a must have resource to equip our youth for success."*

**David Tyree**, Director of Player Engagement, New York Giants, Author

"*The valuable insight Dr. Tim Elmore delivers in this book provides specific strategies to address the unique challenges of Generation Z. His passion for assisting leaders in transforming lives is a gift that will encourage you to develop others. Dr. Tim Elmore consistently delivers a research-based approach to addressing unique challenges facing Generation Z. The practical strategies provided in this book are valuable in developing not only youth but you.*"

**Jason Biles**, DPT, ATC, SCS, CSCS, FAFS, Head Athletic Trainer, Houston Rockets

"*Dr. Elmore, once again, knocks it out of the park with this brilliant, inspiring book!* Generation Z Unfiltered *is a compelling and timely argument against the attitudes and practices held by adults which are leaving an entire generation intellectually and emotionally ill prepared for the complex world they will soon inherit. It is a brave and necessary work providing insight on the challenges faced by young people, and most importantly, the tools needed to inspire, teach, and lead our young people to meet these challenges. Whether you are an educator, parent, or coach,* Generation Z Unfiltered *inspires us to become the bridge builders our young people so desperately need.*"

**Michelle McGrath**, Executive Director, Wisconsin Association of Student Councils

"*As a professor of higher education and mentor for the past 26 years, I have noticed changes in university students. At times it is difficult to know how to best help and challenge students to develop them. Dr. Tim Elmore offers concrete (actionable) ways to do this. He has reviewed the research on Generation Z as well as spoken with many of them and teaches us about how this generation wants to bring its best to the world.*"

**Dr. Mary Lynn Realff**, Assoc. Professor; Associate Chair for Undergrad Programs, Georgia Institute of Technology

"*As an educator who has spent several decades working with student leaders, I believe there has never been a more critical time to develop the next generation of leaders. Generation Z is similar to previous generations in their eagerness to learn and to find their place in this world. However, they are experiencing great difficulty in their journey as they encounter a world ill-equipped to understand them. Tim Elmore's book goes beyond defining this generation and describing the current crisis; it provides practical strategies for all leaders of students to use in guiding this generation towards discovering their "why" and to finding fulfillment. This book is one of the significant resources on Generation Z and a must read!*"

**Nancy Ward**, Executive Director, Gwinnett Student Leadership Team

"Dr. Elmore has done it again. His expertise and wisdom on how Gen Z thinks is uncanny. His practical, common sense approach provides a great guide for how to bring out the best in our youngest generation; a group who has only known a world of constant, unfiltered updates, likes and upgrades. I couldn't put this book down. I learned a lot about both my own young teenagers, as well as the early career employees I lead every day in the workforce. This book offers invaluable insights and advice. It is a must-have blueprint for navigating this new generation. Priceless!"

**Nicole Ashe**, Senior Vice President, Head of Human Resources, Iconex

"Keeping their fingers on the pulse of generational trends, Dr. Tim Elmore and Andrew McPeak have done it again! GENERATION Z UNFILTERED explains why our students face both challenges and opportunities in this age of emerging technologies and changing trends. But the book offers so much more: It confronts our tendencies as older generations to either overreact or fail to act in the face of uncertainties concerning our youth. It provides solutions on how we can motivate and guide our young leaders. It offers practical steps to help students discover and act on their amazing potential. This book is a rallying call to understand and respond to the realities facing Gen Z students. Our collective futures largely depend upon getting this right. This books gets it right."

**Will Parker**, Executive Director of Oklahoma Association of Secondary School Principals;  Founder, Principal Matters

"Tim Elmore has done it again. In this book, "GENERATION Z UNFILTERED— Facing Nine Hidden Challenges of the Most Anxious Population" Tim has given us practical advice to help align our expectations and actions. As a Principal, I am always looking for ways to meet the needs of my community and serve students. This synopsis fills my tool bag. If we don't know the characteristics of today's learner, how can we maximize their learning? Thank you, Tim."

**Gary Davison, PhD**, Principal, Lambert High School

"Tim Elmore's passion for helping today's youth become tomorrow's leaders fires me up – and helps me lead, coach, and parent better. What stands out most though is his optimistic belief in what today's youth can do rather than what they cannot do, his recognition that adults have significant responsibility in shaping the world they are living in, and his challenging nature in how we best help grow and develop them. Ultimately, our job is to prepare them for what is next, and this book is yet another powerful tool in assisting how we best do that."

**Kyle Stark**, Assistant General Manager, Pittsburgh Pirates

# GENERATION Z
## UNFILTERED

## *Facing Nine Hidden Challenges of the Most Anxious Population*

# TIM ELMORE | ANDREW McPEAK

**Poet Gardener**
PUBLISHING

Published in Atlanta, Georgia, by Poet Gardener Publishing in association with Growing Leaders, Inc.
www.GrowingLeaders.com

ISBN: 978-1-7320703-4-9
Printed in the United States of America

Library of Congress Cataloguing-in-Publication Data

# Contents

*We dedicate this book to two populations of people.*

*First, to the caring adults who genuinely want to discover how to lead this new generation of kids. They are teachers, parents, coaches, employers, youth workers and family members.*

*Then, to the members of Generation Z who genuinely want to mature into adulthood as leaders who will transform the world.*

ONE

# The Challenge of a New Generation

*Today's students need a new kind of leadership in order to flourish.*

If you've heard of Virgil Smith, it's not likely because of his incredible social media platform or his charismatic personality. He's actually just a quiet, unassuming, average teenager... until Hurricane Harvey hit the Houston area in August of 2017.

As a 13-year-old eighth-grader, this humble Generation Z kid was playing an online video game with his friend Keshaun who lived close by. When water began seeping into his home around 2:00 a.m., Virgil, along with his sister and his mother, grabbed some essentials and climbed to their apartment building's second floor for safety. They had hoped to wait out the storm there, protected from the hurricane. It was then that Virgil received a call from his friend asking for help. Keshaun and his family were trapped by rising floodwaters. Instead of waiting for an adult to do something or even waiting for authorization, Virgil quickly sprang into action.

He scampered downstairs to his own apartment, grabbed an inflatable mattress, and paddled to his friend's apartment to save him and his family. Once he secured them on a second level, Virgil began hearing noises from other parts of his lower-income neighborhood in Dickinson, Texas. They were the voices of neighbors crying for help. The entire neighborhood was rapidly submerging.

Virgil hopped on his makeshift raft again and paddled around the neighborhood near his apartment, pulling people out of dangerous, flooded homes. When all was said and done that night, he had saved seventeen lives. Virgil's mom, Lisa, was stunned as she watched her asthmatic son's heroic effort. The soft-spoken teen, who probably still doesn't see himself as a leader, intuitively modeled brilliant leadership and hardly spoke a word about it afterward. In the spring of 2018, Virgil Smith was awarded a Citizen Hero award from the Congressional Medal of Honor Society.[1]

Virgil Smith's story is a vivid case study, demonstrating the three unique qualities of those belonging to Generation Z when they are at their best.

First, Virgil did something *different* than others expected.

While it seemed everyone else was understandably stuck in survival mode, Virgil spent his time and energy risking his own life to save 17 people. He was in a different frame of mind—perhaps from his video game hours or the action movies he'd watched—but he was different. In all of the reports I've found about his heroic actions, it seems that no one else in his neighborhood was either willing or able to do such a thing. This is a picture of what we can expect from the students in Generation Z. They are going to be unique and will even pursue different aspirations with different methods than what older generations may deem conventional.

Second, Virgil did something *more* than what others expected.

You can tell what people are made of during catastrophic situations, like hurricanes. We've all witnessed heroic efforts by people of various ages in response to disasters in our country. The truth is that Virgil could have been a hero simply by helping his mom and sister get to safety. Or just his friend, Keshaun. But instead, he paddled to each voice he heard until he beat the odds and the job was done. In the research we've done and conversations we've had with the students of Generation Z, they are already showing signs that they will do more with opportunities than previous generations, through smart technology or pragmatic tactics.

Finally, Virgil did something *new* that others didn't expect.

Sometimes, it takes extreme circumstances to push folks into thinking new thoughts. Hurricane Harvey helped Virgil become a problem-solver as he transformed an inflatable mattress used for guests to sleep on—and leveraged it to save lives. He was unconventional, scrappy, and unworried about his youth and inexperience, his asthma, or his safety. For Generation Z, necessity really is the mother of invention. We can expect to see lots of new innovation as this generation of young people seeks to solve problems, some of which we've never seen before.

## ARE YOU READY FOR A NEW GENERATION OF KIDS?

Now, you may be thinking: Wait a minute. Virgil does not sound like the kids I know today. I see teens everywhere that are lazy and apathetic. They're gamers. They lack ambition. They're on their phones all day long.

I know those kids, too. Those are kids who represent the other side of Generation Z. Too many of them have not been led well; they've not been equipped to become the best version of themselves. I'll bet that even Virgil has exhibited some of these characteristics. As

 Ultimately, it drove Virgil to solve problems and serve people.

our non-profit, Growing Leaders, has worked in partnership with more than 10,000 schools and organizations, we see students who are at their best along with those who aren't optimizing their potential. Perhaps the adults in their lives simply didn't know how to lead these "screen-agers"? The future snuck up on many of them, like it did millions of parents, teachers, coaches, and employers. The truth is that many of us were ambushed. This book is about how to lead today's emerging generation well, to equip them to look more like Virgil in the face of a great challenge.

Virgil didn't know what to do or what to say when others shared their gratitude for what he'd done. He's a boy of few words. He did admit through tears that it felt good. In saving 17 lives, this young leader influenced his entire school, quietly, boldly, and, at first, by acting alone. Essentially, this is where leadership begins. It's an inside job before it's ever an outside job. It usually begins with a negative emotion, a feeling of dissatisfaction with current conditions. Ultimately, it drove Virgil to *solve problems* and *serve people*.

What if all of Generation Z could do these two things as well? That's a goal they won't reach if we don't help them learn to be better—better even than we were. Ancient Hebrew and Chinese cultures told parents not to limit their children's knowledge to what they'd learned, since they grew up in different times. This advice has never been more relevant than it is today.

Elon Musk, who has been making headlines for years now with his Tesla self-driving smart car, colonies on Mars, spaceships for civilians, and other artificially intelligent devices, is a great example. In 2017, he became dissatisfied with his kids' private school, so he pulled them out of it and created his own. He called it *Ad Astra*, meaning "to the stars." It appears to be constructed around the notion that educators should "teach to the problem not the tools."[2] This simply means that instead of merely offering math equations to memorize or theories to digest, you begin with a problem and work backward. It's not that theories aren't helpful, just that incentive increases when students are actually *solving real problems* and *serving real people* not merely doing busy work. The world our kids will enter, as adults, will be drastically different from the ones we graduated into decades ago.

Journalist Benjamin Stetcher describes it as "a world filled with artificial intelligence, genetic engineering, automation, virtual reality, personalized medicine, self-driving cars, and people on Mars. A world where people might not even have jobs and where society itself may be arranged in fundamentally different ways. How are parents, and society for that matter, supposed to know how to prepare them to succeed in a world that we cannot predict?"[3]

**Educators, parents, coaches, professors, employers, and everyone who is invested in the success of Generation Z: May I whet your appetite for the rest of this book?**

**Educators:** What if education changed to match our world today? In the past, schools were basically storehouses of knowledge where the information resided. That's not true anymore. Information is online, wherever you are. The job of the school is to cultivate curiosity, to equip students to find solutions, and to blend them together in order to create new solutions for new problems, just like Orville and Wilbur Wright blended bicycles and birds to create an airplane.[4] They originated an entirely new industry by combining two existing realities. Virgil Smith took an air mattress, typically used to sleep on, and leveraged it to save lives.

**Parents:** What if parenting styles changed to match the culture in which we're raising our children? Today, most parents I meet fall into one of two categories:

- *Overwhelmed* (We give up trying to manage kids' high-tech lives.)
- *Over-functioning* (We do too much to control kids' lives and outcomes.)

But our kids actually need us to be neither. Our children need us to be intentional about equipping them to navigate smartphones and social media yet *laissez-faire* about letting them explore new places, skin their knees, and fail at projects, so they're not gripped by fear and anxiety as they enter adulthood.

**Coaches:** What if coaches approached their young athletes with a bigger picture in mind than merely winning games, matches, or meets? What if we began to see that the real value of sports is a platform for kids to perform at their best and learn life skills in the process? So while we don't have to stop keeping score, we must focus on developing habits in our athletes during the championship process, like discipline, focus, emotional intelligence, strategy, and leadership.

**Professors:** What if colleges no longer organized themselves based on "majors" but on problems that needed to be solved? This means that students would experience *customized learning.* Imagine students taking courses, for instance, in physics, psychology, math, and languages to solve a societal problem in Africa. It also may mean we blend departments and colleges based upon genuine dilemmas that require the perspective of multiple fields of study to address. Bringing together the young, enthusiastic minds of students with the brilliant, experienced minds of professors takes learning beyond the classroom.

**Employers:** What if we hired young team members and not only on-boarded them to their particular job but cast vision for the overall mission of the company—then we listened as they shared where they felt the future was heading? What if every supervisor practiced "reverse mentoring," where they both mentored and received mentoring from a Generation Z staff member who described how the latest social media platform could be leveraged to better achieve the mission? What if we allowed the students of Generation Z to weigh in on ideas to reach organizational goals?

## TODAY'S CULTURE IS SHIFTING AGAIN

I'm convinced we need to lead, parent, teach, and coach Generation Z differently because of these new realities we face. Generation Z is not merely a continuation of the Millennial generation. While there are definite similarities, today's kids who make up Generation Z have grown up in the 21st century, which is radically different from the 1980s and 1990s when Millennials were kids. But we've not adapted as we attempt to raise them, teach them, coach them, or employ them.

Let me offer you a picture.

In 1997, a young entrepreneur named Reed sold his tech company and decided to celebrate with his wife one evening. They drove down to the local Blockbuster video store, (You do remember those, don't you?) and they rented the movie *Apollo 13*. Afterward, Reed neglected to return the video. In fact, he lost it for quite some time. When he finally found it, he sped back to the store and turned it in only to find he owed a huge late fee. On his drive home, two thoughts flooded Reed's mind:

1. How do I tell my wife we've just been charged a big fine on a late video?
2. There's got to be a better way to experience home video entertainment.

Shortly afterward, on the way to his fitness center, Reed had an epiphany about a different way to handle memberships. His gym charged him one, flat fee regardless of how much he used the equipment there. What if a video store charged one monthly subscription and customers could rent as many videos as they wanted? And what if the customers never had to leave their homes? At this point, Reed Hastings created his original idea for Netflix. After some development, he shared the idea with Blockbuster, assuming they'd see the improvement on their business model. But, alas, they didn't. They believed they had a handle on the future of movie rentals and told Reed to take his idea somewhere else.[5]

And he did.

Netflix took the world of home entertainment by storm, mailing DVDs to consumers and, later, streaming videos on our televisions. And while they aren't the only "show in town," they control a large part of the market. In the meantime, Blockbuster shut down their last store in Alaska and is no longer a brand we buy from today. In less than three decades, Blockbuster went from entering the record books (with 9,000 stores) to entering our history books. Netflix is a 21st century approach to home entertainment, while Blockbuster was a 20th century method.

In many ways, I feel like we adults have a "Blockbuster" brand of leadership, while Generation Z is growing up in a "Netflix" world.

In May of 2019, the ABC network aired a special called "Screen Time" hosted by Diane Sawyer. For six months, Sawyer and her team toured the U.S. talking to doctors, families, teachers, and tech insiders in pursuit of answers to questions about how our smartphones are affecting us. I love one of the comments a pre-school child made to his mother. He was trying to talk to her while she scrolled social media sites, looking down at her phone, not at him. She replied once in a while with a nod as he spoke. Yet, clearly, she was preoccupied. The young boy finally took her face in his hands, moved it toward him, and said, "Mommy, I need you to listen to me with your whole face."

This young child was simply saying that the way his mother was leading him was not connecting with him. May I expand this thought? I believe the way our culture has conditioned all of us to parent, teach, coach, and lead is not working. Thankfully, there is a better way.

# TWO

# *Course Corrections: Two Narratives for Gen Z*

*We must change the way we see this digital generation.*

One of the saddest war stories you'll ever hear is a story of "friendly fire."

I will never forget hearing about Black Hawk Down in April 1994. It was a shootdown incident in which two U.S. Air Force F-15Cs shot down two U.S. Army UH-60 Black Hawk helicopters over northern Iraq, killing twenty-six military and civilian personnel. They were over the Iraqi "no-fly" zones, but both were from our U.S. military. Since the IFF (Identification Friend or Foe) system failed, our Air Force shooters could not tell they were firing on their own guys. It was a tragic and unnecessary loss of human life, coming from allies, not enemies.

The term "friendly fire" was officially adopted in World War I when we realized a significant percentage of our losses was due to our own military forces. Friendly fire is often a byproduct of the "fog of war"— the confusion inherent in the heat of battle. This "fog of war" happens both because the stakes are high and the emotions are high in the midst of battle. We mistake who the enemy is; we feel before we think; and we know how important what we're doing is to so many.

The same is true for leading our young today.

Most of the adults I meet who work with students are well-intentioned people. They are teachers, parents, leaders, and coaches who've committed their time to investing in the emerging generation. Sadly, too often, we are guilty of emotional "friendly fire." Because we know the stakes

are high and our emotions run high, we fire at our young unintentionally. We may aim poorly; we may get caught in the "fog" of all we're
doing; or we may mistake them for the enemy. However it happens,
ultimately, we're the ones who are actually doing most of the damage to
them. Let me explain.

## We Have Met the Enemy—and He Is Us

Over the last decade, I have spoken to over five hundred thousand
educators, parents, coaches, and employers. I began to see a pattern
regarding their attitudes toward young people. The two emotions they
expressed consistently to me were:

1. Frustration with their kids.
2. Fear for their kids.

The *frustration* is usually due to the rapid pace of change taking place
in our culture that kids embrace quickly and adults do not. The "generation gap" (begun sixty years ago with Baby Boomer teens) has widened.
A student can be present in a room with adults yet not present at the
same time if he or she has a smartphone in his or her hand. That student
can live in an entirely different world on a screen even while at home
with family. For millions, culture
and society influence them as much
as parents do. For example, when
social media app innovations transform teen lifestyles and language,
it's no wonder we become frustrated at our kids. We feel they're
mastering childish habits but not
adult disciplines.

Almost half of today's
kids are being raised
by adults who feel
concerned and even
fearful over their
children's futures.

The *fear* part usually stems from the 24/7 news cycle, broadcasting stories of terror, school shootings, drug abuse, cyber-bullying, abductions,
and human trafficking. It's not that these stories are "fake news," but
rather, we feel like they're happening all the time and everywhere. The
fear has grown amidst three-and-a-half decades of our rising awareness
of the need for child safety and protection. We began to make decisions
and to lead our kids out of fear. Clinical psychologist Wendy Mogel

explains this challenge most effectively saying that today's world offers us thousands of fears to worry about that we cannot control. So, many of us take all of those uncontrollable fears and reduce them to the one target we feel we can control: our children.[1] In fact, it is this fear that I believe has the most destructive effect on students.

## Survey Says Adults Are Concerned

I decided I needed to see if this picture was accurate, and if so, what it was doing to today's kids. Our organization, Growing Leaders, partnered with Harris Poll in the fall of 2018 to discover the most frequent emotions adults experience as they lead kids, including excitement, frustration, hope, apprehension, anger, concern, optimism, and others. We wondered what kind of leadership today's young people were receiving from their parents and teachers as they grew up. The poll was nationwide with 2,016 adults of varying ages and from a variety of locations participating across the U.S.[2]

What we discovered did not surprise me and, in fact, confirmed my suspicions. The top emotion that comes to Americans' minds when thinking about the future of today's youth is *concern* (46 percent), with older adults more likely than their younger counterparts to cite this emotion. Pause for a moment and just consider the ramifications of this reality.

Almost half of today's kids are being raised by adults who feel concerned and even fearful over their children's futures. Seventy-nine percent of adults agree with the following statement, "I am fearful of the future world we are leaving for today's youth." Nearly all Americans (98 percent) have at least one concern regarding today's youth, among them are the top concerns of:

- Social media or smartphone addiction (69 percent),
- Mental health issues (61 percent),
- School shootings (57 percent),
- Alcohol/drug abuse (56 percent).

Close to two-thirds of Americans (64 percent) have doubts about the abilities of today's youth when it comes to overcoming obstacles. We are both doubtful and afraid.

Want further evidence? According to a 2018 PDK Poll, one-third of parents worry that their children aren't even physically safe at school.[3] Yes, you read that correctly. Thirty-four percent of parents are afraid for their children at school, and only about one in four are very confident that their child's school can deter a gunman, according to that same poll.

Parents fears of school shootings, social media content (both sexting and bullying) and their child's future all top the concerns parents have for today's Generation Z kids. While all of these are legitimate concerns, they are also having a negative (and even damaging) effect on our children. When asked to select reasons why their children didn't spend more time playing outdoors, 82 percent of the mothers chose "safety concerns," including the fear of crime.[4]

So, what has this done to our leadership?

"Parents are going to ludicrous lengths to take the bumps out of life for their children. However, parental hyper-concern has a net effect of making kids more fragile," says Hara Estroff Marano who's been warning about this for fifteen years now and spoke about it brilliantly in her book *A Nation of Wimps*. "So many teens have lost the ability to tolerate distress and uncertainty, and a big reason for that is the way we parent them," says Kevin Ashworth, Clinical Director of the Northwest Anxiety Institute in Portland, Oregon.[5]

We adults actually make them fragile with our current leadership practices.

Some social scientists are calling today's style, "Paranoid Parenting." Lenore Skenazy began blogging about this damaging approach years ago on her site *Free Range Parenting*. When she allowed her nine-year-old son to ride a New York City subway alone, she was labeled the "World's Worst Parent," but it didn't deter her pursuit of getting parents to set their kids free from parental paranoia. Skenazy has noticed that today's Parents often use 'negative filtering' when thinking about the world around their kids. "Parents [say,] 'Look at all the food, activities, words, people that can harm our kids!' rather than 'I'm so glad we've finally overcome diphtheria, polio, and famine!'" She also notes how parents use dichotomous thinking: meaning, "if something isn't 100% safe, it's dangerous."[6]

The impact shows up early in children.

The truth is that kids are naturally anti-fragile. We adults actually make them fragile with our current leadership practices. Watch a toddler learn to walk; they fall and get up and fall and get up again. They bump their heads, their elbows, and their knees. But they just keep going. Why? Their ambition to explore uncharted territory. As they grow older, we begin to make them afraid. Watch a young child, just past the toddler age, bump his head or fall down. By this time, the child has learned to look to adults nearby to seek out their response. If adults panic and quickly rush to the child, they are conditioned to panic as well. They mirror our emotions. Kids do what kids see.

Now, consider the impact our fear and frustration have had on us.

## The Story We're Telling Ourselves

University of Houston Psychologist Brene Brown talks about "the story we are telling ourselves."[7] When we are in conflict, for instance, with a spouse or one of our kids, we may begin to suspect something other than the best and begin a narrative inside our minds that causes us to feel insecure, angry, distrustful, jealous—you name it. Dr. Brown suggests the best action to take in these moments is simply to acknowledge the story we are telling ourselves:

- I am failing as a wife.
- He's a horrible person.
- I am not a good father.
- He doesn't like me.

This story informs how we think, how we feel about a situation and even how we act. Our internal narrative significantly influences what we experience in life—positively or negatively—regardless of whether or not it is accurate. It impacts our happiness, our worry, and our level of satisfaction. The story we tell ourselves about the reality in front of us influences our life every bit as much as the reality itself.

More than 200 years ago, we learned this truth.

Elisha Perkins claimed to have discovered a treatment that cured all kinds of pains and ailments. In fact, people from all over the world were paying for his unusual cure, which amounted to him waving a thick metal rod that Perkins called a "tractor" over the place where their body felt pain—an arm, leg, lower back, etc. Perkins warned clients they'd feel a hot sensation (maybe even a burning feeling), and then the pain would begin to subside. Most people, once tortured by pain, received genuine relief.

When Dr. John Haygarth heard what was happening, he felt he had to investigate. In amazement, he observed the results of Perkins' "tractor" with several clients. He then took a long piece of wood and wrapped it in metal, creating his own fake tractor. In January 1799, with five distinguished doctors observing, he waved it over five people with chronic pain (including rheumatism), saying it might help them. The result? He wrote afterward, "Four of the five patients believed themselves immediately, and three remarkably, relieved by the false tractors." People were walking, stretching, and reaching items that were high above their heads without pain. Later, Haygarth requested other doctors to create their own fake tractors to see what might happen. The same results occurred. It didn't matter what the wand, stick or tractor was; people felt better.[8]

Over the last century, this phenomenon came to be known as the placebo effect. When a sugar pill (or something else) was given to a person and they believed it would help them, in most cases, it did. Haygarth proved "the story you tell yourself is often just as important as the drug." It actually impacts the outcomes. When anesthesiologist Henry Beecher ran out of morphine while operating on wounded soldiers during World War II, he feared performing surgery on them without any anesthetic. But, alas, he had none. So, he tried an experiment. He gave the wounded men a salt-water drip (with no pain killer) and discovered the same reality. "The patients reacted as if they had been given morphine. They didn't scream, or howl, and they didn't go into full-blown shock."[9]

Belief is quite a persuasive element.

## What's the Point I Am Making About Kids?

I believe most adults are walking around with an over-arching narrative about today's kids. It's the story we tell ourselves—whether it's based on fact or feeling—that informs the way we perceive, feel, and act toward them. In short, it informs how we lead them. Even if the story is based upon false assumptions, it is just as influential as reality.

My point is not that we should lie to ourselves or to our young people. Pretending something to be true is never enough. My point is to remind you of the power of your personal narrative. While we often look back at the discovery of the placebo effect with a smirk, we all know there are many occasions when what we believe about someone completely affects our reaction to him or her. Authors Jonathan Haidt and Greg Lukianoff put it this way: "We are not saying that the problems facing students, and young people more generally, are minor or 'all in their heads.' We are saying that what people choose to do in their heads will determine how those real problems affect them."[10]

Last year, a high school administrator told me the mother of one of his students asked if her daughter could change classes because her former boyfriend happened to be in her current class, and he was distracting and caused her stress. This mom's story was: "My daughter can't handle adversity."

This year, a college football coach said to me, "These kids today are wimps. I have to yell at them every day to get off their phones and do their work. They got no grit. I'm quitting at the end of the season." This coach's story is: "My student athletes can't learn life skills and don't deserve me to stick with them."

Recently, I met with a human resources executive who informed me that six times in the last two months she had made a job offer to a young professional and heard these recent graduates reply, "Thank you—but now my parents need to interview you to make sure you're a suitable boss for me." These parents' story was: "My kids are adults but still need my help to navigate decisions."

A college instructor told me a student confronted him after he handed back some graded papers to his class. This student had received a poor grade, but challenged his teacher saying his "parents paid full tuition to the school," so he "deserved an A in this class." Somehow this student had embraced the narrative: "If we just pay the money, we're entitled to the grades we want as a result."

I spoke to a university president who frowned as he told me a parent had called his office, saying, "I just noticed on the weather channel that it's cold up there where you are. Would you make sure my son wears his sweater today?" This person's story was: "My adult son needs my help to make even simple decisions during the day."

*In short, belief impacts (and even sometimes determines)*
*the reality we experience.*

So, as you begin this book, may I ask you: What is your narrative about kids today?

- Are you fearful for their future?
- Are you frustrated with them?

## WHEN DID THIS FEAR PARADIGM BEGIN?

If I'm honest, both the adults and the kids I meet these days are anxious. Students are stressed over scoring high enough on tests, getting accepted to the right college, bullying, school shootings, and getting a scholarship, among other things. Adult fears vary, but we're most afraid of what can happen on social media, drug abuse (vaping), school shootings, cyber-bullying, terrorism, and phone addictions. If we're honest, however, there have been sources of fear for many decades now. Since I see this everywhere, I decided to dig and discover how we became so deeply fearful.

How and when did our fear paradigm begin?

I believe several factors in the 1980s put us in our current frame of mind, including the Tylenol scare, drunk driving awareness, illegal drug awareness, etc. But I believe the modern "fear" movement has its roots at the beginning of that decade.

In 1981, John Walsh lost his six-year-old son (Adam) to a kidnapper and murderer. Adam was at a shopping mall with his mother when he left a video game kiosk and was abducted. This sent John on a mission to save other children from such a fate. It was understandable. Child abductions are horrifying. They are every parents' worst nightmare. What evolved, however, was a perfect storm for all of us in America. John created the Adam Walsh Child Resource Center, which advocated for legislative reform and eventually persuaded the government to launch a *Center for Missing and Exploited Children*. John helped create a television movie called *Adam*, which told his son's story and was watched by thirty-eight million viewers. Walsh then launched a television show,

*America's Most Wanted* (which most of us have heard of), and finally, Walsh was instrumental in getting pictures of missing children on milk cartons and other posters around the country. Throughout the 1980s, parents had begun to become fearful, even paranoid, about their children's safety.

If we are being honest, we must acknowledge that our fears are understandable but often exaggerated. And they have harmed our kids.

Centuries ago, Greek stoic philosopher Epictetus wrote, "What really frightens and dismays us is not external events themselves, but the way in which we think about them. It is not things that disturb us, but our interpretations of their significance."

Even though John Walsh was working to make our world safer, the unintended consequence of his work was that it made us all feel the world was becoming more dangerous.

## Follow My Sequence of Thought...

1. **American adults' top emotion regarding kids today is concern.**
   I mentioned earlier our 2018 Growing Leaders and Harris Poll survey of U.S. adults to discover what our most common "narrative" is regarding kids. What is the story we hold in our heads about Gen Z? Our discoveries confirmed my suspicions. Two of the top three words adults use to describe their attitudes regarding kids today are *concern* and *fear*. Our fear tends to govern our words and actions toward them. Because our kids are our "trophies" and are reflections of how well we teach and raise them, we (parents, teachers, coaches, and leaders) became focused on this fear they won't be safe, won't be happy, and won't reach their potential.

2. **When adults are fearful, we tend to try to seize control of our kids' lives.**
   Phase two in this sequence is our fears make us more prescriptive and more controlling with our young. Parents, coaches, and teachers all prescribe the steps students must take to succeed, and more importantly, to avoid failure. We have a ridiculous dread of failure. The greater our fear, the more we tend to seize control and ensure

everything gets done to get the grade, to get the acceptance letter, the scholarship, the position, you name it. We feel the best way to make sure it all happens is to monitor it ourselves. Kids experience more supervised time under adults now than at any point in modern history.

### 3. When we become controlling, kids feel out of control of their futures.

The natural third phase in this sequence is that when we take over their lives and control their inputs and outcomes, they like it at first, feeling a safety net underneath them. I believe most middle-class kids assume that if they fall or fail, some adult will swoop in and save them. It feels nice. Unfortunately, it also leads to a very negative feeling of being out of control. Kids hear mom nag them about the application, the quiz on Friday, their gym shorts, the permission slip that's due, grandmas' birthday, and more. They begin to both need mom's help and resent it. It's a love/hate relationship. There is a gnawing feeling that they are not even in control of their own lives.

### 4. When they feel this way, they assume an external locus of control.

The natural mental tendency at this point is to slip into an "external locus of control." Dr. Julian Rotter introduced this term to us over 60 years ago. We either tend to believe our success is up to us (internal locus) or it is up to someone or something else (external locus). When a kid constantly has adults control his life, he naturally spirals into an assumption that fate or external forces govern his outcomes. He can begin to blame others when things go wrong and feel entitled to benefits from others because he's come to expect them. Someone must do the work for him. He stops "owning" his life. (We'll examine this phenomenon more deeply in later chapters.)

### 5. When they experience an external locus of control, anxiety goes up.

Studies show that when a person assumes an external locus of control, he becomes more stressed, more anxious, even depressed.

Anytime someone else is in charge of our welfare—even if they're a good person—we can get anxious, especially when we are capable of caring for ourselves. Reflect for a moment: when you feel your fate is up to another person, doesn't that make you feel just a bit unsettled? It is out of your hands; you are not managing your day. While I don't believe our kids' anxiety issues are solely due to our leadership, I do believe we adults have added to the problem, unwittingly.

It is time to equip and release students to take responsibility for their own lives. In doing this, we express the belief that they are capable of leading themselves.

This is a huge step, however, for today's adults.

## THE BIGGEST CHANGES GENERATION Z BRINGS TO THE ADULT WORLD

Susan Sawyer, M.D. of the Murdoch Children's Institute confirmed something I have been saying for years now: *being an adolescent today is very different than it was even 20 years ago.* Certainly, different than when I was a teen.

The adolescent phase of human development now lasts much longer than it once did. In fact, adolescence, as a stage of life, is expanding on both sides. Kids are entering adolescence in elementary school, being exposed to information on teen websites and social media, getting something tattooed or pierced, and entering puberty earlier. At the same time, young people are staying in adolescence well into their twenties. They are not working jobs or leaving mom and dad until much later in life.

According to *MedPage Today's* writer Kristina Fiore, adolescence begins at age ten today (the onset of puberty) and extends until twenty-four years old.[11] Some educators would argue it continues to the ages of twenty-six to twenty-eight due to the delay of emotional maturation. What was once a doorway from childhood to adulthood has now become an elongated portion of life in today's young people. It's a fifteen-year window of time.

## How Is This Affecting Generation Z?

So, how is this reality impacting students today? The nationwide data may surprise you. They're avoiding certain adult temptations but also some adult responsibilities that once were "rites of passage" for young adults. It's both good news and bad news. Take a look.

### Avoiding Adult Temptations

Typically, teenage students begin to experiment with adult behaviors such as consuming alcohol, engaging in sex, and smoking. For example, according to a study among teens between 2010 and 2016, just 29 percent of eighth graders drank alcohol, down from 56 percent in the 1990s. And 67 percent of twelfth graders drank, down from 93 percent forty years ago. Engaging in sex dropped slightly from 68 percent in the 90s to 62 percent now. Smoking has seen a significant drop among high school students too. According to the *Center for Disease Control and Prevention*, just 8 percent of high schoolers smoked cigarettes last year. This number is a record low. The changes are seen in all economic groups and from all parts of the country.

This is all good news.

### Avoiding Adult Responsibilities

While the above numbers are encouraging, young adults today are also avoiding many of the responsibilities that accompany adulthood. For instance, the age teens begin driving, the age they begin working a job, and the age they begin living on their own are all rising. Thirty-two percent of eighth graders have worked for pay, down from 63 percent twenty-five years ago. About half of twelfth graders have worked for pay, down from 76 percent. When I was a teen, I remember a driver's licenses being a rite of passage for sixteen-year-olds. Today, not so much. Just 73 percent of twelfth graders even have their licenses today. Kids are fine with mom driving them around. In short, these teens are less likely to drive, work for pay, or live on their own until later in life.

Even dating without their parents has gone down. When I was a teen in 1976, 88 percent of twelfth-grade high school students dated. It was another rite of passage. Today, it's dropped to 63 percent. Instead, teens will actually go out on a date with their parents. There's obviously nothing wrong with this; I relish strong parent/teen relationships. The downside may just be, however, that these same young adults are not even able to live independently, moving out of the house much later than they did twenty-five years ago. Author Dr. Jean Twenge said, "The whole developmental pathway has slowed way down. Today's 18-year old is acting more like a 15-year old and today's young adult in their 20s acting more like a teen."[12]

This is not such good news.

## Changing Adult Norms

As these young Millennial and Generation Z populations enter the adult population, they are already introducing other changes, too. They look to do life differently than the past three generations. For better or worse:

- Their community is online, not in person. While their grandparents likely belonged to a civic club and spent time with neighbors, Generation Z prefers connecting virtually on a screen.

- Their beliefs are individual, not corporate. Many still claim to be spiritual, but they are less likely to participate in organized religious meetings.

- Their identification as a male or female is shifting. Gender is more fluid, and options for Generation Z are expanding beyond the binary ones of the past.

This is scary for some adults because the world feels so different.

As I've mentioned, when adults spot these shifts, we become fearful or frustrated. Teachers find that the pedagogies they learned in college may not work as well as they did a decade ago. Parents often find they can't raise their children the way they were raised as kids and see the same results. The athletic coaching climate today has been revolutionized by the expectations placed on them to win and to play every kid on the team. And employers tell me they're frequently baffled at how to onboard a young professional onto the work team—because they don't think like anyone else. Our leadership, however, is paramount to their success.

## A RELEVANT EXPERIMENT: OUR EXPECTATIONS MATTER

If you're still unconvinced regarding how much your approach influences the young people around you, allow me to share with you some experiments that made me think twice about how I lead them.

Over fifty years ago, Robert Rosenthal and Kermit Fode began to experiment with rats in a maze.[13] The goal for each rat was to reach the "gray end" of a T-shaped maze for an edible reward. The students who were assigned to work with them gave the rats ten chances to reach their goal: to reward them if they did and to record the results. In the end, it was the students, not the rats, who were the "study" in this experiment.

The students were told that through careful breeding, specialists had created a strain of genius rats and a strain of dummy rats. Half the students were told they had the smart ones, while the other half were told they had the remedial rats. In reality, no such selective breeding had happened. They were all average. The point of the experiment was to test the results of these interchangeable rats based on their handlers to see if the student's expectations biased the results. You can probably guess what happened.

Rosenthal and Fode discovered that the rats the students believed to be brilliant performed measurably better than the rats believed to be dumb. The researchers then asked the students about their behavior toward the rats and found a difference in the manner in which the two student groups related to their rodents. Those who believed they had genius rats, for instance, handled them more gently and spoke to them more kindly and with belief. In the end, their beliefs affected the rats' behavior.

Having published these results, another set of researchers repeated the experiment, this time admonishing the students to treat each rat identically, regardless of their perceived potential. But, although the students attempted to act impartially, alas they could not. They unconsciously delivered non-verbal cues based on their expectations, and the rats responded accordingly.

Rosenthal later decided to see if these experiments could be translated to humans.

He asked two sets of students to show a group of people photographs of human faces, asking them to guess what they were feeling. Although the faces depicted neutral emotions, the job of the student experimenter was to read a script and record the responses of their subjects. As with the rats, one cluster of students was told they were interacting with people who were failures in their careers and the other cluster with people who'd been wildly successful. To ensure their words could not impact the results, the students were told to follow the script and read it in a monotone fashion. Was there a difference? To make a long story short, every single student who had been led to expect high ratings from their "successful subjects" obtained higher ratings from their group than did any of those expecting low ratings.

The leadership and expectations of the experimenters impacted the results.

Dr. Rosenthal went on to focus his study on this issue: What do expectations mean for our children? His research later demonstrated that teacher expectations genuinely impact the academic performance of students. The faculty who were told they had gifted students ended up with significantly higher scores from their classrooms than those who were told they taught average-performing students. In fact, all the students in the study were average performers up until that point.

Of those who'd been identified as brilliant, 80 percent had an increase of at least ten IQ points. What's more, about 2 percent of the gifted group gained thirty or more IQ points. It was at this point that adults began to realize how labeling children as high performing proved to be a powerful self-fulfilling prophecy.[14]

Our expectations and belief are two of the most significant factors in determining the success of the Generation Z students we lead. I wonder, are you fearful or hopeful for Generation Z? Whatever your posture, you can bet they already know how you feel about them.

# THREE

# Who Are These Kids Anyway?

*How the children growing up in the 21ˢᵗ century are not like Millennials.*

In 2019, I learned about a 10-year-old boy named Ayush Kumar living in Menlo Park, California who offers yet another insightful case study on Generation Z. Each week, his parents allow him a strict thirty minutes of screen time, and Ayush fills that time with videos and games. Wanting to guard him from the negative impact of technology, his parents believe their fourth-grader is too young to have his own phone.

His parents noticed, however, that their son has loved coding since he was four years old. In fact, sometimes Ayush would use his thirty minutes of tech time to learn instead of be entertained. So, mom and dad stayed on the lookout for opportunities for their son to do something constructive with his skill. When his dad heard about Apple's Worldwide Developer's Conference, he told Ayush about it. He said, "Ayush, you're too young to enter their annual contest, but you could try to develop something and see what they say."

And that's exactly what Ayush Kumar did.

He developed a physics-based app with a catapult lever that enables users to release a projectile. It's quite impressive. Apple not only made an exception to let this 10-year-old into the contest, but Ayush also won the contest—against people who were much older than he is. He was awarded a college scholarship.[1]

So why is this a case study?

First, Ayush has grown up in a world lush with smart technology. It is his natural habitat. Trying new opportunities with artificial intelligence is natural. Creating something helpful with it is intuitive for many Gen Z kids like him.

Second, a caring adult made a difference in his life. (In this case, it was his dad.) Ayush's father was the one who cautioned him about the realities of the opportunity. (He told his son the contest was for people thirteen years old or older and that he probably couldn't get in.) But he challenged Ayush to give it a shot.

Third, Ayush broke the rules of the contest but delivered something superior to all of the older contestants' submissions. He was too young to be doing what he did, but he did it, nonetheless. He wasn't limited by precedents or confined by protocol.

The fact of the matter is everyone—including Generation Z—learned much about the impact of technology as the Millennials came of age while using it. Pause and consider. Young adults in the Millennial generation were coming of age as cell phones and smartphones became ubiquitous. Kids in Generation Z don't remember a day without smartphones. Many have had them all of their lives. These kids have witnessed the mistakes the Millennials made and have learned from them. Millennials were the guinea pigs, experimenting and learning both the benefits and consequences of smartphones over time. Generation Z, in so many ways, has raced out of the gate—portable device in hand and ready to do something new, something redemptive, and often something lucrative. Generation Z kids, as young pre-teens and teens, have been making money off of their innate and intuitive skills for years now.

Today, however, we are observing the outcomes of a generation who've grown up with such technology. The early data is in, and it is both positive and negative. We know enough to draw some conclusions that inform our leadership of these kids.

## CHARACTERISTICS OF GENERATION Z

What we've discovered in the first two decades of this century is that childhood has evolved. Being a kid today is very different from being a kid when we were kids. We will discuss the qualities that Generation Z can bring to the table in the proceeding chapters, but here, we want to introduce you to seven distinguishing characteristics they possess that collectively spell the word *PARTNER*. My challenge is to partner with these kids as they grow but to also give them ownership of their growth. Ten-year-old Ayush Kumar benefited from a father who empowered him to achieve a goal, but his dad didn't do the project for him. If we're going to *PARTNER* with kids in their development, I suggest we recognize who they are.

### 1. They are more *PRIVATE*.

Generation Z learned much from the Millennial generation before them. Because Millennials were the first generation of adolescents to experience social media, they were also the guinea pigs to all of its benefits and consequences. One of the many penalties of social media platforms is its allure for users to crave followers, likes, shares, views, and retweets. In their appetite for all of those, Millennials fell prey to stalkers, bullies, and even employers who saw their posts on Instagram or Facebook before a job interview and chose not to hire them because of those posts.

In response, Generation Z is more private than previous generations. According to *Global Web Index*, Gen Z kids are more private than Millennials about their information and profile, and nearly six out of ten are making a conscious effort to spend less time on social media sites. They are more individualistic and independent, with the majority preferring to learn alone and be alone than past generation of kids. They're more prone to share a vanishing message (like Snapchat) than older generations. They'll have an Instagram profile but may have several "Finsta" (fake Instagram) profiles. They have loads of content, photos, videos, and comments they'll never share with adults. In fact, many utilize the platform Calculator%, which is an app that looks like a calculator on their phone. When mom or dad see it, they assume that's what it is. In reality, it's a vault where users can store private content for certain eyes only.[2]

### 2. They are more *ANXIOUS*

We discussed this earlier and will suggest steps to take later in the book. But we'd be incomplete if we failed to list this element as a major factor in the life of most Gen Z kids. This generation of children and teens suffer from more mental health problems than any other generation of kids in American history. Both secondary schools and colleges report an insufficient number of counselors available to serve the students seeking help on campus. Many adults can't understand the angst Gen Z kids feel. We often say: "What have they to feel stressed about? This is the most convenient time in earth's history to be alive."

While that's true, Gen Z lives a life of paradox. These kids' lives are both easier and harder. It's easier and quicker to navigate technically but more difficult to navigate psychologically and emotionally. Let me illustrate. If I'd had a negative interaction at school or encountered a bully on campus, once I got home, I got relief. Today, Gen Z kids get no relief. The bullies remain on social media. The trouble stays in their faces. Further, because kids are exposed to world tragedies on a smartphone daily, they face information they may be unready to handle emotionally. At 14 years old, my biggest problems were the location of my baseball mitt and how to find a girlfriend. Today, kids may be preoccupied with the latest school shooting or a terrorist attack in California.

### 3. They are more *RESTLESS*

Gen Z's lifestyle and sense of identity are shifting consistently— based on the realities around them. They are a fluid generation. Our focus groups revealed that a large percentage of middle school students derive their senses of identity from social media, which destines them to be on an emotional roller coaster. Millions are restless at night, on a screen instead of sleeping, and restless during the day, always changing in response to circumstances. Eleven percent of Generation Z have been diagnosed with ADHD.[3] As a kid, my sense of identity came from my family, my sports team, and where I sat in the lunchroom. Today, it's online. In one sense, a shifting sense of identity is normal for teens. Hormones rage as their brains are pruning as they move from childhood to adulthood. What is concerning to me is their lack of congruency. I believe we as humans are at our best when we have a sense of integrity and congruency about ourselves—when we're not duplicitous. The good news and bad news about culture today is that there are so many options with which a kid can explore the world and their own identities. What's troubling is the stakes are high when it comes to a shifting and volatile self-image. We'll discuss this more in a later chapter.

### 4. They are more *TECH SAVVY*

This probably doesn't surprise you. Generation Z is more at home on a screen than previous generations. They spend the equivalent of a full-time job (nine hours a day) on their devices, not including school assignments. According to a 2018 study by the *National Institutes of Health*, kids who use smartphones, tablets, and video games more than seven hours a day are more likely to experience premature thinning of the cortex, the outermost layer of the brain that processes thought and action.[4]

According to marketing research from Sparks and Honey, Gen Z kids multitask on five screens, not two as the Millennials did.[5] As I mentioned earlier, they prefer to learn alone as opposed to being with others, which is a clear indication of their preferences for screens. They use various social media platforms, each for different reasons and sometimes for different audiences. Many have a girlfriend or boyfriend they've meet online but not face to face. This is, of course, where the text message code "LMIRL" came from: "let's meet in real life." We'll discuss this digital reality in depth later in the book. It has fostered an early entrance of skepticism and even cynicism.

### 5. They are more *NURTURED*

On the one hand, Gen Z is growing up in a world of ubiquitous information; millions of these kids are savvier about culture and world events than previous generations at their age. They know more about sex, alternative and illegal drugs, and human vices than we did as teens. Obviously, this is not inherently bad. My concern is that this awareness has caused caring adults to become preoccupied with the safety, self-esteem, and success of Generation Z kids. Parents became helicopters as they raised the Millennial generation. They have become Snowplows now that they're raising Gen Z.

As I mentioned earlier, dads and moms are consumed with the fears of school shootings, terrorism, and whether their kid will get into their top choice for college. This has caused a reciprocation on the part of the kids. Data relayed by Corey Seemiller and Meghan Grace reveals that teens are motivated by "not wanting to let others down," which can be positive but can also create a volatile trap of people-pleasing.[6] The 2015 Grammy award-winning song from Twenty One Pilots "Stressed Out" says it all: *"My name's Blurryface and I care what you think."*[7] The more kids take in information, the more protective and nurturing concerned parents become.

6. **They are more** *ENTREPRENEURIAL*

Generation Z has learned from the Millennials before them. Millions of Millennials simply believed what their parents told them about how going to college would result in a great job—and found that it wasn't true. Generation Z witnessed this reality check and now feels empowered to simply bypass climbing the corporate ladder and create their own company or freelance all through their twenties. A 2014 study from the consultancy Sparks & Honey found 72 percent of high-school students wanted to start a business and nearly one third of those ages sixteen to nineteen had already begun volunteering their time.[8] No doubt, some will be white-collar workers and others blue-collar workers, but a majority plan to be "no-collar" workers. They want to create something new from home as their expectations for work have been dashed by two recessions since 2000. Their problems with this paradigm are their struggles with confidence and their risk aversion. More on this later, as well.

7. **They are more** *REDEMPTIVE*

This characteristic is an identifying concept for Gen Z. They are more inclusive and accepting of different races, sexual orientation, backgrounds, or gender than any U.S. generation before them. Equality has become a top issue for kids today, just like global warming was for Millennials: racial equality, gender equality, and equality regardless of sexual orientation.[9] They want everyone to feel respected, no matter who they are.

For many, acceptance of the LGBTQ community is tightly linked to their innate individualism. Keep in mind that the first African-American president was elected during their childhood, gay marriage became legal, and the #MeToo movement was launched. They believe they can change the world because they've grown up in a world that is already changing. In March of 2018, over 400,000 teens participated in the March for our Lives across the country on behalf of gun control. In a 2017 global survey by *Universum*, Generation Z has a keener interest in leadership than the previous three generations.[10]

**Talk It Over:** What have you observed in students today?

## THE PARADOX OF THIS GENERATION

One reality I must remind myself of as our organization equips students is that they are growing up as a generation of paradoxes. In fact, paradoxes surround them:

- They are independent yet dependent on parents.
- They are trendy yet traditional in practices.
- They are both often alone yet never alone.
- They have it so good yet have it so difficult.
- They experience virtually no dramatic moments yet feel so much drama.
- They are cognitively advanced yet emotionally behind.
- Their life is both authentic and artificial.
- Their world is easy but very hard.

These paradoxes are the result of uncertain times. We are experiencing the aftershock of societal earthquakes over the last two decades, which we didn't see coming. In our previous book, *Marching Off the Map*, we suggest two simultaneous realities emerging in today's younger population:

*The Extinction of Childlikeness.*
*The Extension of Childishness.*

By this we mean that because children are exposed to information on devices so early, they become aware of life's harsh realities sooner. They lose their sense of wonder, their sense of innocence, and their sense of trust earlier than previous generations of kids. Because parents don't want their children to fall behind their peers, they enroll them in early learning programs, sign them up for teams, and supervise their days more than ever before. While this is understandable, we didn't see the downside of it all. Genuine childhood—with its freedom to play outside in autonomy, freedom to imagine what will fill a day, and control of personal time and what to think about—is evaporating. After all, as parents and leaders, we feel we know what's best for them.

At the same time, childishness is expanding across our nation. By this, I mean the entrance into adult responsibilities occurs much later than it has in the past. I've noted often that I've lost count of the number of university deans who've told me: "Twenty-six is the new eighteen." Teens are getting their driver's license later, getting jobs later, getting married later and moving out of the house later. While we're not implying that this is the end of the world, it is simply the end of the world *as we know it*. At the very time we need the members of Gen Zs' creativity and energy in the workplace, they are delaying their launch into both autonomy and responsibility. (When we fail to lead them well, they want autonomy without responsibility.) Too many of them desire to remain kids well into their twenties.

The question we need to ask ourselves as parents, educators, coaches, and leaders is, "Do they want to remain children as adults because we did not give them a true childhood?" An over-structured childhood will surely cause many to be unready to structure their own lives as young adults.

## Generation "Scapegoat"

In 2018, the *New York Times* asked members of Generation Z what they wanted to be called. Among the most popular responses was "Generation Scapegoat."[11] Why? They feel blamed for the wrongs society is enduring today. "It must be those lazy, apathetic slackers that are the source of society's ills," we muse. But, are kids really that bad, or are they growing up in a culture where adults have not been able to engage them, unable to cultivate the timeless life skills and values that sustained us in the past? Are we frustrated with them because they're "lazy slackers" or because they are adapting to a newer world than the one we grew up in and it's unfamiliar to us?

Those who blame the kids must remind themselves that these kids are growing up in the world that we (adults) created. They've been under our watch and our leadership. They are products of our making, by default or design.

I have a story to tell you about a young man who inspires me to continue my work with students. I invite you to relax for a moment and fasten your seatbelt for a short biography of an unlikely young leader, surviving in the slums of Tanzania, Africa. As you may already know, incredible young people live everywhere in the world, and many of the best leaders live in unpredictable places. Their difficult lives actually summon them to lead.

Their difficult lives actually summon them to lead.

## Picture Yourself as a Leader

Stephen has lived in the slum area of Arusha as long as he can remember. Tanzania (similar to Kenya or Uganda) contains some of the most impoverished areas of the world. Like thousands of others, he earns less than $1.50 a day. Most who live in this kind of scarcity don't see any way out of the poverty cycle. They're just doing time.

Stephen, however, is different.

It began when Robert and his LEAD Tanzania team began to cast a vision to Stephen and other teens like him that they are leaders and have great potential to influence their community, beginning by changing the trajectory of their own personal lives. Even though life is tough, these kids began to adopt hope instead of despair—and it all started by seeing themselves differently. Rather than being *passengers* (victims of their circumstances), they could be *drivers* of positive change.

The LEAD Tanzania team has been teaching *Habitudes®: Images That Form Leadership Habits and Attitudes* in this Arusha slum. Young Stephen decided to attend the course after one of the trainers gave him a shirt and pair of shoes to wear. These items were, in themselves, offerings of hope. Slowly, the trainers began to see Stephen's face light up as he associated the images with leadership principles that enabled him to live a different way.

According to LEAD Tanzania, Stephen's life was dramatically impacted when they discussed the image called "Opportunity Statue." It's all about the ancient statue in Greece called *Opportunity*. The statue had long, flowing hair coming down in front of the face but was completely bald in the back. It served as a reminder to Athenians that opportunity was something you could grab hold of when it was coming at you, but you could never get hold of it once it had passed.

Stephen suddenly saw some of the local challenges as opportunities to seize.

When he examined his community, he saw many young children on the streets with no place to go. Their parents were out looking for work or trying to find water or something to eat. Stephen then discovered an empty room that no one was using. To make a long story short, this poor teen took that empty room and those empty children and created a day care center for them with programs much like those he had gone through himself as a young teen.

The parents in the community were so impressed with what he'd done, they lobbied the local government to offer Stephen more resources. He now has an entire house with five rooms and provisional permission from the local government to start a school.

Young Stephen was transformed from a teen who needed help into a leader who had much to offer to help others. Someone from the emerging generation was serving the emerging generation. He went from being the "mission field" to being the "missionary." What's most exciting to me is stories like his take place thousands of times around the world every week when the narrative is changed. I believe young leaders like Stephen are waiting for you to help change the narrative for them.

# FOUR

# Two Huge Differences in Generation Z

*Students face realities today that kids never faced before.*

Another school shooting took place on May 7, 2019. Although youth violence has declined over the last four decades, it was the 116th mass shooting in the first five months of 2019. It took place just twenty minutes my former home, in Highlands Ranch, Colorado. The school is just eight miles away from Columbine High School.

Sadly, nine students were shot, one of them fatally.

"School shooting has become a cultural thing in the United States," says Mike Clumpner, president of Threat Suppression, who specializes in active-shooter response.[1] It appears to be a logical option for a generation of kids whose narrative centers around anxiety. *The Economist* referred to Generation Z students as:

- Stressed.
- Depressed.
- Exam Obsessed.

In the Fall of 2018, *Pew Research Center* surveyed 920 Americans ages thirteen to seventeen about the problems that they have seen among their peers. "The data shows that they are far less concerned about age-old teenage problems like unplanned pregnancy and binge-drinking than they are about mental health. Fully 70% of respondents thought anxiety and depression were a major issue among their peers."[2]

This is definitely the popular narrative on Generation Z we hear today.

## Two Narratives in This Tragic Incident

There is another narrative, however, that we don't hear enough about in our nation today. And it is also found in the tragic story above. One "STEM School Highlands Ranch student who was shot was 18-year-old Kendrick Castillo. His father, John Castillo, said his son was a hero and he wants people to know what a great kid he was."[3]

After studying the story, I have to agree. Kendrick is a hero. In fact, three teens were heroes on that day: Joshua, Brandon, and Kendrick. Reports say these students rushed the shooters in an attempt to thwart their plan. How incredible! Teenagers leading the response to this tragedy. Teens were the protagonists, not just the perpetrators.

Yes, there were two narratives that day: homicide and heroism.

I'd like to focus on the heroism of these students and see what we can learn from them. I believe they model a very real narrative I see in millions of Generation Z kids: heroism and leadership.

## FOUR INDICATORS OF LEADERSHIP

Being a hero and being a leader are not synonymous, but they have very similar characteristics. They're not "twins," but they are "cousins." I spotted some traits in these adolescents who were true first responders in the school shooting. They are indicators of potential leadership you can look for in students:

1. **They put sacrifice ahead of survival—in light of the bigger picture.**
   Kendrick's father said this kind of service was typical of his son. When in a frightening situation—one that made fellow students run from the gunfire—these three teens ran toward the shooters. Seeing the potential loss of human life, they sacrificed their own safety. In other words, because they saw the big picture, they were moved to take big action. Vision drove them to face fear instead of seeking survival, a natural human instinct.

2. **They took initiative without instruction—on behalf of other people.**
   Police responded to the STEM School Highlands Ranch call within minutes, yet witnesses say the students who immediately

responded likely saved this incident from becoming a worse trag-edy. They ran toward the shooters and attempted to take them down. It's this kind of initiative that is symptomatic of leadership. They didn't wait for someone to give permission; they didn't need some adult to empower them. They saw what needed to be done, and they pursued it instantly.

3. **They valued justice in the face of inequity—to protect those in danger.**

   As I listened to interviews, I noticed these young men had a strong sense of justice. Joshua acknowledged that the school shooting drills students had experienced taught them to run away from the gunshots. But he said when he witnessed the dangerous circum-stances expanding, he found himself running toward the shooters. What drove him? From his testimonial, I believe it was his sense of justice for those who were vulnerable. He couldn't stand by and do nothing.

4. **They were prepared for a problem—to circumvent potential damage.**

   Kendrick's father said in an interview that his son consistently readied himself for potential problems; he thought ahead and prepared himself for what he'd do, almost like a rehearsal before a show. This made decisions clearer and swifter to implement. Leaders embody the scout motto, "Be Prepared," which means you're always in a state of readiness, in mind and body, to do your duty. For these three teens, this was more than a motto for the program. Apparently, it was a lifestyle.

I will say it again—both negative and positive narratives follow Genera-tion Z. Their potential for both healthy and unhealthy lifestyles is real. I believe it's up to us to lead them into a positive one. And it begins with understanding them.

While the last four decades of students all have a propensity for technology and connecting on a screen, the kids born since the turn of the century would say those screens are an appendage to their bodies. The cell phone *changed* our lives, but the smartphone *transformed* them.

## THE MILLENNIAL GENERATION GIVES WAY TO GENERATION Z

Before we venture into what to do with the data on Generation Z, let's glance backward at where we've come from. It is very likely young adults from the Millennial generation had a different experience than today's kids have:

- **Their first gadget was likely an iPod**
  Steve Jobs called that personal device "a thousand songs in your pocket."

- **Their first trophy was likely for participating**
  It wasn't about winning but being present. Effort and results counted less.

- **Their first domestic memory was likely the introduction of a computer**
  Most families got a portable desktop device in the living room for all to use.

- **Their first global memories: Iron Curtain falling/Operation Desert Storm**
  They likely recall the Berlin Wall crumbling and winning the "100 Hour War."

- **Their first severe tragedy was likely the Columbine High School massacre**
  This was a frightening event, but it galvanized Millennials to stop the bullies.

The 80s and 90s were decades when the narrative was expansion and optimism. What happened inspired students, from iTunes to Columbine. Personal computers were introduced. Citizens felt sure of themselves; society was regaining its footing—its confidence. The economy was becoming strong again, and the dot.com era had begun. We were awesome.

But those are memories of the Millennials, the last generation to grow up during the 20th century. They are now young adults, professionals, even parents. It's time to turn our attention to the newest population being measured today: Generation Z.

Two significant changes in today's youth will be the focus of this chapter. They represent two vivid categories that shifted the way kids grow up and reveal that Generation Z is not just another batch of kids who will be just like previous generations. Jean Twenge, psychologist and author of *iGen*, explains that young people are breaking with the past: socially, vocationally, spiritually, sexually, and emotionally.[4] Over the course of this book, we'll look at the data on today's students and how cultural realities impact them for better and for worse. The two changes we'll survey in this chapter provide a backdrop for us to understand why kids today are different. Before we examine these two changes, let's compare and contrast Generation Z with the five previous generations who've grown up in the U.S.

It's time to turn our attention to the newest population being measured today: Generation Z

## The Last Century of Emerging Generations

This is my (Tim's) fourth book in which I've included a generational chart. The chart on the next page is a table allowing you to see the paradigms of five generations as they entered adulthood. We encourage you to scan the chart from left to right, in each of the categories we included. Pay special attention to their "life paradigm," which summarizes the perspective they brought with them as they shifted from backpack to briefcase. Then, notice the "attitude toward authority" and "sense of identity." These are our summaries after interviewing and observing people from each generation. Keep in mind, this is not about psychology. (There are clearly different temperaments in each person from every generation.) This is about sociology (the framework a generation carries with them into adulthood based on shared experiences, music, icons, tragedies, economies, etc. during their formative years). As you read through, remember each generation has a narrative.

## FIVE GENERATIONS COMING OF AGE

|  | **Builders**<br>Silent Generation | **Boomers**<br>Pig in Python Gen |
|---|---|---|
| **Birth years** | 1929-1945 | 1946-1964 |
| **Life paradigm** | Be grateful you have a job | You owe me |
| **Sense of identity** | I am humble | I am valuable |
| **Attitude toward authority** | Respect them | Replace them |
| **Role of work** | Means for living | Central focus |
| **Role of relationships** | Significant | Limited; useful |
| **Technology** | Hope to outlive it | Master it |
| **Market** | Goods | Services |
| **View of the future** | Seek to stabilize | Create it! |

| Busters<br>Generation X | Millennials<br>Generation Y | Homelanders<br>Generation Z |
|---|---|---|
| 1965-1982 | 1983-2000 | 2001-2018 |
| Relate to me | Life is a cafeteria | I'm coping and hoping |
| I am valuable | I am awesome | I am fluid |
| Endure them | Choose them | Not sure I need them |
| Irritant | Place to serve | It's my hobby |
| Central; caring | Unlimited; global | Utilitarian |
| Employ it | Enjoy it | Hack it |
| Experiences | Transformations | Reinventions |
| Skeptical | YOLO | FOMO |

## EXTERNAL AND INTERNAL CHANGES IN KIDS

The two reasons I'm convinced these kids are not just a continuation of the past are both inside and out. They've experienced external and internal changes that not only make them different but motivate me to look at them and lead them differently.

## External Changes: Culture and Environment

Change is happening at a faster rate than at any time in the past. In fact, Generation Z kids would tell you that even their fundamental beliefs and norms are changing.

Consider their childhood for a moment. While Millennials grew up in a time of expansion, Generation Z has grown up in a time of recession. Two economic downturns since 2000. Terrorism everywhere, including right here at home. Corporate scandals in major companies. Racial unrest in the streets. Political polarization, with both parties catastrophizing what the other does. Pluralism and complexities around the world. Is it any wonder why kids feel stressed? *Fast Company* Journalist Elizabeth Segran explains,

> *Millennials were internet pioneers. They invented Facebook, shopped from their smartphones, and smoothly transitioned from satellite TV to Hulu and Netflix. Generation Z, meanwhile, doesn't remember life without these basics of 21st century life. Millennials helped elect a black president and legalize gay marriage; many Generation Zers see these milestones as the norm. Millennials came of age during a time of economic growth and were shocked to find a diminished, unwelcoming job market after college; Generation Z has been shaped by the recession and is prepared to fight hard to create a stable future for themselves.[5]*

Social scientists vary on when Generation Z actually started. Some have them beginning as early as 1995. Others at 1997. Still others somewhere between 1999 and 2002. As I examined the rationale behind each start date, I felt the strongest case could be made for the turn of the century: 2001. While I respect each perspective, when we pause and consider history, so much of it shifted after Y2K. Reflect on the first eighteen years of this new Millennium.

## The First Eighteen Years of Generation Z

- The dot.com era bubble burst, and an economic downturn began.
- The September 11, 2001, terrorist attacks launched us into a "new normal."
- The ongoing war in the Persian Gulf (Iraq, Afghanistan) began and continues.
- Social media platforms became ubiquitous between 2005-2012.
- A second economic downturn, the Great Recession, occurred in 2008-2009.
- Unemployment remained high for twelve of the first twenty years of the century.
- Racial and gender polarization expanded, leading to shootings and protests.
- Mental health issues rose to "front and center" over the first two decades.
- Smartphones reached market saturation by 2011 and created a tipping point.
- Parenting styles moved from "helicopter" to "snowplow" and "lawnmower."

From my perspective, the most looming and bleak reality Generation Z kids have witnessed as they've grown up is the behavior of adults. We've actually hindered them from healthy maturation through our poor examples. After all, aren't we the generation of adults who created these difficult realities? I think we are. Let me give you a few examples.

One recent example is a club soccer game, where a coach went crazy on the sidelines after a play, setting a pitiful example for his young team of nine-year-olds. It was so bad that the referee threw him out of the game. After he left, two dads jumped from the bleachers to the bench to take the coach's spot. They were no better. A tirade of bad calls took place that day, and not one of them came from a referee. It was the adults who were supposed to be coaching and cheering. Across the country this banner has now been hung for parents to see at dozens of youth sports fields:

>*Remember...*
>
>>*These players are kids.*
>>
>>*This is a game.*
>>
>>*The coaches are volunteers.*
>>
>>*The referees are human.*
>>
>>*There are no scouts watching today.*

Too many adults today have lost sight of the big picture. Youth sports are about building future adults out of our children not living out our "unlived lives" through them. We've become shortsighted. Parents and coaches have failed to think long-term, see the big picture, and then take the high road, ultimately setting a pitiful example for kids. We're better at screaming expletives than setting examples. It's all about how we feel right here and now, not what we're building for the future.

And if we wonder why kids today seem to be slaves to their portable devices, take a look at the adults who raise them. One of the most common remarks we heard in our 2017-2018 focus groups with middle school students was: "I never talk to my mom. When I get home from school, she's on Facebook all afternoon; and even while she's making dinner, she's on her phone." In some cases, these students wanted more time with their parents, but, alas, those adults were preoccupied.

Additionally, while Generation Z has been growing up, sexual assault has taken the spotlight, with adults (mostly men) behaving badly. Kids watched as the #MeToo movement emerged, and these adults were found guilty of misusing their power for their own benefit. Not to mention lying to cover it up.

On top of this, those involved in politics have been poor models of conduct too. Both major parties have misbehaved, performing unthinkable acts from tax fraud to sexual misconduct to taking bribes to launching tirades on Twitter. In fact, social media has become one of the most embarrassing places to find childish behavior among adults.

We're often impulsive and illogical, becoming a miserable model for our teens. I believe, one reason so many young voters didn't make it to the polls to exercise their right to vote in 2016 is they didn't believe in either of the major candidates.

Finally, there has been a growing trend in schools that when in conflict a parent will side with their child instead of a fellow adult, be it a teacher, coach, or principal. This is nuts. We assume the problem *cannot* be our child, or that would be a poor reflection on us. It must be a bad educator that caused his failure. We've made our child our trophy, and his success is our success. It makes for miserable leadership at home. Faculty often say their greatest headache is not their students, it's the parents.

Faculty often say their greatest headache is not their students, it's the parents.

Following the March for Our Lives, which mobilized over four hundred thousand students to march for stricter gun control on March 24, 2018, one teen explained the current day we are in: "It feels like our leaders are acting like kids, and kids are acting like leaders." I would say that summarizes things pretty well.

## Internal Changes: Their Brains Are Rewired

In addition to societal shifts that have changed our young, they're also navigating internal changes in their brains. Growing up with pixels, computer screens, and streamed content "on-demand," Generation Z is actually different on the inside.

Two Australian researchers recently made a bizarre discovery while examining hundreds of X-rays of human skulls, finding a large percentage of them had bone growths. "The study, which was published last year in the journal *Scientific Reports*, indeed found bony growths on the bases of skulls of around four hundred adults ages eighteen to eighty-six. And younger people were found to have larger growths."[6]

"The development of these growths," the researchers found, "may be attributed to, and explained by, extensive screen-time, the researchers said. Sustained 'forward head flexion,' or bending the head down, and poor posture could be the reasons for these physiological changes."[7]

Technology has altered human physiology. It's affected all of us, not just our kids. But our young have grown up in this new world, shaped by these very realities. It makes them think differently, feel differently, even dream differently. It affects memory, attention spans, reading habits, and sleep cycles. This is attributed to a scientific phenomenon known as neuroplasticity or the brain's ability to alter its behavior based on new experiences. In this case, it's the abundance of information provided by the Internet and interactive screens.

This is not all bad. One 2013 study found that first-person actor video games boost decision-making and visual skills.[8] These immersive games force players to make snap decisions based on visual cues, which enhances visuospatial attention skills or the capability to analyze details of your physical environment. Gamers also prove to be superior at detecting contrast in objects in darker environments.

Technology has altered human physiology.

Additionally, complex, strategy-based games like *StarCraft* may improve the brain's 'cognitive flexibility' or the ability to switch between tasks, thus expanding the much-disputed ability to multitask.[9] A kid's hand-eye coordination can also be accelerated as they utilize technology and spend hours toggling between sites on screens. While the content on the screen may be less than educational, the tasks can be positive and developmental.

Generation Z gives new meaning to TGIF (Twitter, Google, Instagram, and Facebook). This new world that futurist Dr. Leonard Sweet speaks of enables today's students to search and find answers, whether those answers are educational or entertaining. Kids may need to memorize less than I did as a student, but they can find more solutions more quickly. They are more savvy than I was on global information, and they are exposed to such information at very young ages.

Journalist Rebecca Hiscott concludes, "Some cognition experts have praised the effects of tech on the brain, lauding its ability to organize our lives and free our minds for deeper thinking."[10]

But, is "deeper thinking" happening in the brains of Gen Z kids today? Unfortunately, not always. In fact, because smart technology has emerged more quickly than our ability to master it, the very technology we just discussed has been a source of hardship in a teenager's brain today. Let me offer a few examples.

## 1. Sleeplessness

It is common for today's students to go to bed and attempt to fall asleep with their tablets, phones, or laptops still displaying a glowing screen. These screens send puzzling internal light cues to their bodies, minds, and sleep-inducing hormones. One of the more memorable comments we received from eighth-grade students in our 2017 focus group was, "My parents have no idea what my life is like... after I go to bed." They meant, of course, that they're not sleeping. They're on a screen, "tubing" (on YouTube), sexting (sending nude selfies), creating Finstas (fake Instagram accounts), and surfing websites.

Neuroscientists now believe the glowing lights on a laptop, smartphone, or tablet confuse our body's internal cues and prevent sleep. Exposure to bright lights can convince the brain that it's still daytime and can affect the body's circadian rhythms (our internal clocks). Our eyes grow blurry, being especially sensitive to screen light, making it more difficult to fall asleep. Doctors are now explicitly concerned about sleep patterns in today's teens.[11]

## 2. Anxiety and Depression

Terms have surfaced in our day to describe the increasing levels of anxiety or depression we feel: FOMO (Fear of Missing Out) and FOBO (Fear of Being Off-line). The *New York Times* defines FOMO as "the blend of anxiety, inadequacy and irritation that can flare up while skimming social media." So, we might conclude: *Then, just get off your phone!* Not so fast. Another shift technology has brought to both teens and adults is FOBO. Millions now grow anxious when away from their phones. Many students we interviewed suffered from withdraw symptoms (like drug addicts) when their phones were taken away. In short, they're often anxious when on their devices but also anxious without them.

The data shows today's teens suffer from greater levels of anxiety than previous generations of adolescents. Students "ages 15-21, reported the worst mental health of any generation included in the *American Psychological Association's* annual 'Stress in America' 2018 report. The data is based on nearly 3,500 interviews with people ages 18 and older, plus 300 interviews with teens, ages 15-17 [...] It appears that stress is mostly to blame, with 91 percent of

Generation Z respondents saying they felt physical or emotional symptoms, such as depression or anxiety, associated with stress."[12] As we entered the 21st century, the APA stated: "The average child today experiences the same level of anxiety as a psychiatric patient did in the 1950s."[13]

### 3. Poorer Memories

When I was a student, learning by rote was a prized skill. A college course consisted of lecture, drill, memorization, and test. The greater your memory, the better the student you were and the higher grades you got. Today, we possess a Google-reflex, where we can ask a device for any scrap of information. It's at our fingertips instantly. We don't bother retaining facts. Who needs to memorize who our ninth U.S. president was when we can just ask Siri or Alexa? This is both good news and bad news.

Our memories remain important ingredients for successful living and to our emotional and social intelligence.

In 2007, one neuroscientist polled three thousand people and found that younger respondents were less likely to remember standard personal information, such as a family member's birthday or even their own phone number.[14] Similarly, studies show that calculators may decrease simple mathematical skills.[15] Some people are unable to navigate their own cities without the help of a GPS. While I applaud today's smart technology, our memories remain important ingredients for successful living and to our emotional and social intelligence.

### 4. Diminished Attention Spans

In the year 2000, the average adolescent attention span was twelve seconds. This meant a teen would pay attention and stay engaged with a person or program for twelve seconds before being distracted by something more engaging. Today, that average attention span has dropped to eight seconds. Once more, the culprit seems to be social media and the Internet. People immersed in digital media find it difficult to read books for long periods of time and often skim articles online rather than read every word.[16] Journalist Rebecca Hiscott summarizes the challenge this way: "This phenomenon can be particularly troubling for youth, whose brains are more malleable and, therefore, may fail to develop concentration skills. [...] Others fear tech has crippled our attention spans and made us uncreative and impatient when it comes to anything analog."[17]

One study reported that young adults between the ages of eighteen and thirty-three interact with their phones an astounding eighty-five times a day, spending several hours doing so. What's interesting is the usage was largely unconscious. Those young adults all thought they spent about half that time.[18] With phones beeping and pinging all day long, focus is becoming a lost art.

## 5. Impulsivity

You don't have to look far to see that people today seem to have a difficult time delaying gratification. Folks are often impulsive: they are regularly spending freely, reacting to social media posts, or quitting relationships. This world is the only one our young have experienced. The 2013 study I cited earlier "found video games like *Halo* can inhibit players' ability to rein in impulsive or aggressive behavior.

Researchers concluded that forcing players to make snap decisions in violent situations inhibited 'proactive executive control' over knee-jerk reactions and impulses, meaning they were more likely to react with immediate, unchecked hostility or aggression in real life."[19] There have been other recent studies that substantiated the link between violent video games (or other violent media) and users becoming aggressive and impulsive.[20]

This list above is certainly not exhaustive, but it's enough to motivate me to ask: How do I equip young people in this world where our portable devices tend to steal our...

- Peace of mind
- Focus
- Memories
- Time

- Sleep
- Moral compass
- Ability to delay gratification
- Drive to succeed

Even a decade ago, I was seeing these realities emerge. Following several societal earthquakes, we were experiencing the aftershock of those tremors in our culture. In my (Tim) book *Generation iY—Our Last Chance to Save Their Future*, I warned how we must not fall behind in addressing what our 21st century realities were doing to our kids, such as creating immature teens, emotionally fragile young adults, and unready employees in the workforce. It was encouraging for me to see many adults respond to these warnings (not just by me but other authors, observers, and culture critics as well). Millions of parents, for instance, paid heed to our admonishment about preparing the path for the child instead of the child for the path. I think those families are better for it.

I talked with a mother recently who attended an event where I was speaking. She smiled as she told me she wanted me to meet her son. Stepping from behind her, a young eighteen-year-old boy reached out to shake my hand. His name was Thad, and his mother considered him a miracle. Thad was failing high school three years earlier and had no ambition except playing video games. After reading *Generation iY*, his mother made a decision she had to lead her son differently. She began speaking words of belief to her son and incentivized him to work a job and finish school. She gave him boundaries on his portable devices and was able to motivate him to pursue a scholarship—which he had just received.

I shook his hand again, congratulating him on the change in his lifestyle. He said thank you but quickly pointed out it was the change in his mother's leadership that had made all the difference in his perspective. It was her action that prompted his action.

This is what I dream of seeing again and again today.

Now that we've moved from leading Generation iY to leading Generation Z, a very similar challenge is before us. If they are going to succeed, we need more leaders, parents, teachers, and coaches who will take action once again. If you are going to do that, however, you must face the nine greatest challenges that are keeping this young and anxious population from reaching their full potential, and that's where we are headed next.

FIVE

# *Facing the Nine Challenges*

*These nine important issues deserve our attention as we lead them.*

Have you ever put together one of those gigantic two thousand-piece puzzles before? It is usually a challenging and time-consuming process. It is even more difficult to complete one of those massive puzzles when you don't have the box top. Why? Because the box top furnishes you with the big picture. Each piece can only make sense as you see it in light of the big picture.

So, before we go any further in this book, we'd like to offer you the box top.

You might have noticed already how this book is different from other books that describe Generation Z. Our goal is actually to complement those books. Most of the others offer information on Gen Z; this book is about application. While you can readily find helpful data on this population of young people who grew up in the twenty-first century, this book aims to interpret that data and provide practical steps on how to lead them into healthy, productive lives. We will examine a handful of the most significant challenges facing kids living in today's culture and furnish solutions for those challenges. In short, you will find this book to be research-based, yet solution biased.

## What This Book Attempts to Accomplish

As you read through the next few chapters in this book, we encourage you to consider the challenges that Generation Z faces, which are unlike the challenges of past generations. Consider how you'll respond to the research. Consider the action steps we offer and what it would look like to lead them from belief and high expectations.

Over the course of the next section of this book, we will outline nine of the most significant challenges facing children, teens, and young adults today. We will primarily focus on the issues facing 21st century students, brought on by:

- Social media
- Parenting styles
- Artificial intelligence
- Student performance cultures
- On-demand lifestyles
- Portable devices
- Significant cultural shifts

Here's the good news that makes this book different. In addition to the data, we will offer researched-based solutions to these challenges, answers you can utilize in your home, your classroom, your athletic field, your youth group, or your workplace.

We want these kids to grow into healthy adults who exhibit: responsibility, resourcefulness, and resilience.

Many of today's realities that young people experience have an upside and a downside to them. Many are issues adults have not had to analyze or address in the past. If we fail to lead them well, they will arrive at adulthood unready and even unhealthy.

Our goal is to furnish the tools for you to offer life-giving leadership.

The Latin root words for "disciplining with authority" connotes giving life to a child's learning. The Hebrew root for "train" was the same word used when a midwife takes a newborn and "clears out the mouth" so it could breathe. Again, it was a term for giving life to the child. Our teaching, parenting, coaching, and training should be life-giving. It has to be about more than mere "rewards, punishments, charts, stickers, stars, threats and bribes," as author Barbara Coloroso puts it.[1]

In the end, we want these kids to grow into healthy adults who exhibit: responsibility, resourcefulness, and resilience.

In order to accomplish this, we must recognize we're not merely raising children, we are raising future adults. We are not merely teaching students; we are preparing future citizens. We are not merely coaching young athletes; we're equipping problem solvers, who possess grit and grace in life. It's up to us to see the big picture.

## THE NINE CHALLENGES

Below are the nine challenges we will address in the coming pages. In addition, we follow each challenge with a chapter covering potential solutions to that challenge. These challenges are so tangible we also chose to create a discussion guide for you and colleagues (or friends) to talk them over. We also created table topics to spark discussion with your students to help you get the most out of this content. Both of these resources are available at www.generationzunfiltered.com. We are hopeful these resources allow your application of this book to become a joint effort between you and Generation Z.

### Challenge #1 | Empowerment Without Wisdom

Kids today are empowered with resources, thanks to smart devices, but may lack the maturity to wisely use that power. Common sense is becoming uncommon in our smart world. The most efficient path from information to wisdom, in any age, is to learn from first-hand experience. We must nudge them to explore a world beyond screens and theories. Maturation comes through application.

**Our Solution:** Leading with First-Hand Experiences

### Challenge #2 | Stimulation Without Ownership

Adults have over-prescribed students' activities but neglected to allow for ownership and self-direction. Kids spend more hours in supervised activity than ever before. Ironically, this has created anxious and unprepared young adults today. We haven't offered control to them. What they need is to practice metacognition in order to own their own growth and learning. Maturation comes through participation.

**Our Solution:** Moving from Prescriptive to Descriptive Leadership

### Challenge #3 | Privileges Without Responsibility

Culture has ambushed kids, giving them a sense of entitlement to so many benefits that people once worked for and earned through responsible actions. They are growing up in a time when our population enjoys more perks than ever. In order to overcome this, we must incentivize them by giving them authentic and expanding responsibilities as they grow older. Maturation comes through production.

Our Solution: Breaking Free from the Shackles of Entitlement

### Challenge #4 | Involvement Without Boundaries

Kids today enjoy options everywhere, but with those options come anxiety. They become overwhelmed by all that is going on and may not have healthy boundaries in life. Adolescents consume as many as ten thousand messages a day amidst multiple activities. They need both boundaries and a set of skills to help them thrive during busy days. Stress does not have to become distress. Maturation comes from prioritization.

Our Solution: Coping with the Anxiety Epidemic

### Challenge #5 | Individualism Without Perspective

Adolescents yearn to be their own persons in a pluralistic and often uncivil world but may have no guide enabling them to find their place in a diverse society. Too often, kids merely react to the shifting world around them, without a clear vision for where they belong. Their days can be filled with reactions rather than actions. They need to see the big picture. Maturation comes through clear direction.

Our Solution: Guiding Them to Find Their Place in a Larger Story

### Challenge #6 | Accessibility Without Accountability

So much is accessible to kids today (ideas, entertainment, people) but with reduced accountability for their ethics and values. They can post on social media or behave poorly with few consequences. Adults often lower expectations of them. Grade inflation prevails.

Cheating is now normal in college. Too often, expediency rules the day. Kids need accountability. Maturation comes from conviction and cooperation.

Our Solution: Preparing Them to Live by Values and Ethics

### Challenge #7 | Fluidity Without Integrity

Kids live in a world of constant updates and upgrades. Nothing stays the same, even their own sense of identity. While change can be good, they often lack congruency. Without a clear, unified sense of identity, they can lack a firm foundation and sense of security. While we must recognize their sense of self does grow and change, a root system is needed as they grow. Maturation comes through identification.

Our Solution: Establishing an Identity with Integrity

### Challenge #8 | Opportunity Without Resilience

With so many options, our young can hop rapidly from one opportunity to another when their current opportunities become difficult. Along the way, they may fail to develop grit. They may experience little adaptability to recover from mistakes. As we watch them move to greener grass, we may have failed to help them see that grass still needs to be mowed. Maturation comes through determination.

Our Solution: Learning to Bounce Back After Hardship

### Challenge #9 | Consumption Without Reflection

Kids can be consumers (of everything) yet remain superficial since adults have not taught them to critically reflect on or apply what they consume. Many have made their way through our educational process without ever learning to think critically or evaluate the worth and meaning of their experiences. We are raising them in a world that is wide but seldom deep. We must enable them to digest what they consume and process what they absorb. Maturation comes through reflection.

Our Solution: Training Them to Be Critical Thinkers

## WE CAN'T AFFORD TO FAIL TO ACT

I recognize these are nine significant challenges kids face today, and we've invited you to be part of the solution for them. It can be daunting. I offer a reminder below that beckons me to act and I hope that it will do the same for you.

We all remember the tragic and awful school shooting that happened in Parkland, Florida. It was Valentine's Day in 2018. In all, seventeen people died on Marjorie Stoneman Douglas High School's campus that day, including students, staff, and faculty. One particular story within this tragedy captured my imagination, and I believe it's one that serves as a cautionary tale for those of us who lead students.

In June of 2019, resource officer Scot Peterson faced charges over what authorities described as "inaction in a mass shooting in Florida." You see, Officer Peterson had been hired to protect people on that campus from such a school shooting. In fact, more and more security staff have been employed across the country since the Columbine High School massacre in 1999.

 He was charged for not doing something he should have done.

According to USA *Today*, "Peterson faces seven counts of neglect of a child, three counts of culpable negligence and one count of perjury. He was at work on campus that day when the shooting started and when he arrived at the freshman building the carnage was still in progress. The arrest warrant claims Peterson stayed outside, moving several feet to a position of 'increased personal safety' before six of the victims were fatally shot. The charge accuses him of 'failing, declining or refusing to confront the shooter.'"[1]

Did you catch that? This man wasn't charged with doing something wrong. He was charged for not doing something he should have done.

### Failing to Act

Fortunately, you and I are not likely in such grave danger as we guide the students in our care. But like Officer Peterson, we are likely to play defense instead of offense when it comes to our job. Guiding Generation Z in a world full of social media, polarization, angry parents, reduced budgets, cyber-bullying, stress, litigation, and school shootings is not easy. In fact, it can be downright intimidating. Millions of kids today live lives that are too saturated, too sedentary, and too solitary.

*It's scary.*

*It's uncertain.*

*It's overwhelming.*

Just like Scot Peterson, we're afraid. It feels too dangerous to act. What if we make a mistake? So, we just hide and wait. I see too many parents doing nothing. I see leaders defaulting to what they've always done. I see teachers merely imitating past pedagogies and coaches just emulating past emotional outbursts. Why? It's too much work to change. We are satisfied with merely surviving.

As you begin this next section of the book, may I suggest four ideas to move us in the right direction?

1. **Initiate action.**

    We can't afford to wait for someone to do our jobs for us. We must take the initiative. We must make changes where we are not succeeding. Even if our solution isn't strategic, taking a first step can lead to the right step.

2. **Include students in the solution.**

    The best way to get buy-in from students is to invite them into the problem-solving process. They will support what they help create. When answers are a joint effort, you and your students can both enjoy ownership of the solutions.

3. **Imagine the best, not the worst.**

    I've noticed when I fail to initiate, it's difficult to imagine life getting better. I see worst-case scenarios inside my mind. Our best leadership will arise when we envision our kids at their best and help them see that vision too.

4. **Inspire them with the big picture**

    Finally, we must always act in light of the bigger picture. Everyone has bad days, including you and your students. I believe we must find ways to keep the "box top" in front of ourselves and our students as we put our "puzzle" together.

Years ago, I heard a funny story of a police academy on its final day of examinations. The officer proctoring the exam described an overwhelming scenario for his class of trainees—complete with a bank robbery, a fire hydrant spraying water everywhere, a person being mugged, a wild car chase, and people screaming as they ran in every direction. Each cadet was to offer what he or she felt would be his or her response to this horrifying situation.

The most honest answer came from the back of the room. One young trainee stood up and replied, "Remove uniform. Mingle with crowd."

This is an option we can't afford. Let's act now and face these challenges head on.

# SIX

# Empowerment Without Wisdom

## Challenge #1

Over the last decade, I've read too many unbelievable stories of people—usually young people under twenty-five (but not always)—who became consumed with their portable devices, to their own demise.

Ours is a crazy world today.

More than once, I've read about young people who drove their vehicles into a lake or river because their GPSs told them to do so. In 2018, "a driver in Vermont steered his car right into Lake Champlain... The driver says he was using the navigation app Waze, which apparently insisted that driving into the lake was the right way to go," according to the *New York Magazine*. That year, "a guy drove into a lake in Massachusetts and blamed his GPS."[1] The fact is people have been doing this regularly since 2012 when Global Positioning Systems became a norm for drivers.

Do you recall the story of the video gamer who played *Frogger* so much that he felt compelled to do it in real life? Yep, you read that correctly. A twenty-three-year-old man loved the game and wanted to actually do it, even if he lost. In the *Frogger* arcade game, players move frogs through traffic on a busy road and through a hazard-filled river. Police Chief Jimmy Dixon said the man stood beside the busy freeway "and yelled 'go' to his friends and darted out into oncoming traffic in a four-lane highway before he was hit by a SUV."[2] Fortunately, he lived, even though he lost the game.

This is reminiscent of PokemonGo. Do you remember the Pokemon craze from 2017? At the end of that year, police reported that hundreds of people were killed or caused car crashes by playing the outdoor avatar game. Researchers from Purdue University even created a document outlining the dangers of it all in "Death by Pokémon GO."[3]

Believe it or not, in 2015 there were eight shark-related deaths, but twelve selfie-related deaths in our world.[4]

By 2018, we had progressed to five shark-related deaths[5]—but twenty-five selfie-related deaths.[6] The gap just keeps getting bigger.

While I recognize these examples seem like crazy extremes, they do offer us a picture.

Despite the overwhelming amount of research and data available on the hazards of smart technology and video games for kids, we still don't seem to get it. Psychologists have published the damaging effects of too many hours on the screen, be it video games or social media, but kids do it anyway because it's just too addictive.[7] It's as if when our technology became smart, many of us stopped using our smarts or thinking for ourselves. As technology became common, too frequently, we lost our common sense. Did I mention ours is a crazy world?

## THE EMPOWERED GENERATION

We are now raising and teaching an empowered generation of students. By this I mean they have access to all kinds of technology, innovation, video content, and information whether or not they are psychologically ready for it. Unlike the movies in your local cinema that are required to display a rating of G, PG, PG13, R, or NC17, most of the content streaming to our kids has no filter or guidance along with it, coaching them on how to interpret it or to determine if they're even prepared for it emotionally. At best, today's video games are rated E (everyone), E10 (everyone ten years old or older), T (teen), M (mature audiences seventeen and older), or A (adults over eighteen). Now that teens are buying video games online, instead of in a store, many of them can even bypass these restrictions.

Because Generation Z now grows up in this *empowering world*, they face scenarios and enjoy possibilities you and I didn't have as kids. Some of them are pretty cool, too. For instance, a young adult today who wants to write and publish a book doesn't need help from publishers to do so. She can write it, format it, and self-publish it on Amazon. No adult required. If kids want to write and record a song, they don't need a record label or radio station like my generation needed to get the word out about the song. They can record it on their device and post it on YouTube or Sound Cloud. Young people can make independent films, without utilizing a motion picture studio. If they don't have the money for such projects, they can launch a *GoFundMe* or Patreon page and raise that cash from their followers. The fact is Generation Z, unlike former generations of youth, can upload creative content all day long. Ten to fifteen years ago, Millennial teens might have *watched* two or three hours of videos on YouTube after school. Today, Generation Z wants to *make* those videos. In our culture, you can be an author without being an authority.

In such an empowered world, one might think that children and adolescents would mature more quickly. After all, they know so much more than we did at their age. Why wouldn't kids naturally mature more rapidly with such resources at their fingertips? The answer, of course, is that maturation is about so much more than cognitive development. One of the challenges of our 21st century culture is that we forgot to equip kids holistically in our schools, choosing to assess development primarily by measuring academic scores. In other words, success was merely about getting good grades. If you're an athletic coach, far too often, success is merely about winning games or matches. If you employ young professionals, success is, too often, only about the bottom line.

In our culture, you can be an author without being an authority.

The consumption habits of teens might be okay if parents and teachers were approving of them, or if they even vetted their decisions beforehand. Unfortunately, that may not be the case. Parental awareness of the age limit is low, with about eight in ten parents whose kids use Instagram or Snapchat unaware of the restrictions.[8] And more than four in ten would allow their child to use social media prior to them reaching the minimum age requirement. So, let's get this straight. Although studies show kids are consuming online time like "junk food"[9] and social media use "harms moral development"[10], we don't seem to care enough to guide our kids. It appears both social media networks and parents are turning a blind eye when it comes to what kids consume.

In the book *Marching Off the Map*, we noted that today's kids are from the first generation that doesn't need adults to get information.

They also don't need adults to produce information. They are growing up in a culture that empowers them with adult tools but doesn't simultaneously ensure they're emotionally or cognitively equipped to leverage them well. I believe sociology professor Dr. Anthony Campolo summarized the challenge of leading Generation Z best when he said, "I don't believe we live in a world full of bad kids. I believe we live a world full of kids who know too much, too soon."

## THE DAWN OF ARTIFICIAL MATURITY

In my book *Artificial Maturity*, I attempt to summarize a reality that snuck up on us today, leaving our young adults unready for adulthood. The problem is two-fold:

### Today's Kids Are:

1. **Over-exposed to information far earlier than they're ready.**
   In 2011, 38 percent of children under two were using a mobile device for media (compared to 10 percent two years before).[11] It's like a built-in babysitter or playmate. The fact is kids today know so much so early in life, having been exposed to information and websites in early childhood. At first, their knowledge looks like maturity. But alas, for most of them, it is virtual. The speed at which the data reaches them has paradoxically slowed down their emotional maturation.

2. **Under-exposed to first-hand experiences far later than they're ready.**
   Because parents are preoccupied with safety and preventing anything from harming kids, many playgrounds, today, have had the jungle gyms removed because parents assume they're dangerous. Sadly, therapists reveal that scaling those jungle gyms builds the motor skills kids need as young adults to navigate scary new situations. We work to prevent kids from fearing, failing, or falling. In short, our kids got too much information with too little application.

The result? Adolescence is expanding on both sides. With so much early exposure, children tend to enter adolescence in elementary school now and often remain in adolescence well into their twenties—unready for adult responsibility. Once again, students today are consuming information they aren't completely ready to handle. Their *minds* take it in and file it away, but their *emotions* and their *will* are unprepared to act on it in a meaningful way.

Intelligence does not equal maturity. Talent does not equal maturity. In fact, there is no correlation between giftedness and maturity.

Last year, I spoke to an H.R. executive at Bank of America, after she finished onboarding recent college graduates as new employees. She told me she was impressed with the intelligence of these young professionals but was completely shocked with how ill-prepared they were to act like adults at a job. She told me they were already openly calling executives by nicknames. Three came in wearing flip-flops, one came in bare-footed (on a warm day in May), and one female came in wearing a crop top! The executive had to explain they were no longer in a dormitory but in a bank office. To top it off, during the orientation, one young employee raised his hand to ask, "When is spring break?"

I cannot tell you the number of dumbfounded executives who've come to me with stories like these, looking for an explanation. What do I tell them? It's quite simple: Experiences should have been introduced during adolescence that never took place.

During adolescence, the brain is pruning itself—going through changes that will allow a young person to move into adult life effectively. "Ineffective or weak brain connections are pruned in much the same way a gardener would prune a tree or bush, giving the plant the desired shape," says Alison Gopnik, child development expert and professor of psychology at the University of California, Berkeley.[12] Young people can have emotional reactions (such as mood swings) as they experience brain changes, at times demonstrating uncooperative and irresponsible attitudes. And teens can't always explain why they feel the way they do. Their brains are changing from children brains to adult ones. Robert S. Boyd writes, "Regions that specialize in language, for example, grow rapidly until about age 13 and then stop. The frontal lobes of the brain which are responsible for high-level reasoning and decision-making, aren't fully mature until adulthood, around the early 20s, according to Deborah Yurgelun-Todd, a neuroscientist at Harvard's Brain Imaging Center."[13]

In short, the portion of their brains that signals the *rewards* for risky behavior develops faster than the prefrontal cortex, which calculates the *consequences* of risky behavior. This means teens can be impulsive and prone to naturally desire risky challenges as they move into adulthood. (It's why a teenage boy might attempt a skateboard jump when peers are watching and offering "bragging rights" for such a feat). Surprisingly, these activities are the key to helping teens mature *through calculated experiential risk.* Did you catch that? The best way adolescents gain wisdom is by *doing*, not just *listening.* When adults don't allow small but appropriate risks as kids grow up, they are more likely to attempt the ridiculous later in life:

- Like a twenty-three-year old man thinking he can play *Frogger* on a busy freeway.
- Like a young man or woman driving into a lake if the GPS says to do so.
- Like kids causing accidents playing PokemonGo, failing to watch out for others.

The only solution to these challenges is first-hand experiences as kids. Not another class. Not watching a video, laughing at a meme, or listening to a podcast. Teens need genuine, high-stakes experiences that challenge and prepare them for adulthood, all surrounded by conversations to help them process those experiences and mature. Without these experiences and conversations, adolescents frequently get stuck.

## Virtual is Close Enough

In February 2019, *The Hidden Brain* podcast episode entitled "Close Enough" relayed an interesting insight. Human satisfaction is shifting. We are more and more content with a virtual experience, instead of a real one.[14] It used to be that if you wanted to feel what it was like to do something or be somewhere, you had to actually do it or go there. If you wanted to gaze up close at the *Mona Lisa*, you had to go to Paris. Today, that's evaporating. There's a popular genre on YouTube where people merely watch others do things and get to skip the hassle of doing those things themselves. In one scenario, a young woman sits on her bed at night before going to sleep, eating chips in front of her laptop and watches another woman do her evening routines—like washing her face, brushing her teeth, cleaning her make up off—and that is her evening routine. It's easier, faster, and cheaper. And emotionally, it's close enough.

A growing number of people are outsourcing their lives to virtual alter egos, apparently satisfied with watching someone perform activities, but not having to go to the trouble themselves. Videos of experts doing something are more fun and faster than actually doing the grunt work of learning to do it first hand. The videos use multiple cameras and are edited well, splicing out all the boring segments in between cooking a meal or a gym workout, and viewers feel the pleasure of the experience. We're losing our lives, living vicariously through others as we watch their lives. It's reality TV on steroids. And while this has always happened—people watching others do what they do well—today, we have more access to videos of others doing things.

Our problem? We are more sedentary than ever before, but we want to feel like our life is an adventure. The solution? Just watch others having the adventure.

In her book *Rethinking Positive Thinking: Inside the New Science of Motivation*, psychologist Gabriele Oettingen talks about the upside and downside of our brain's ability to envision positive outcomes.[15] We all know how powerful it can be for a golfer to imagine a great golf stroke or for a surgeon to envision successfully removing a tumor. The fact is our brains can't tell the difference between a real experience and an imagined one. Both are equally rewarding to our brain. The downside is people who constantly fantasize about reaching a goal can get the sensation that they've already achieved it. Fantasy masquerades as reality. Virtual reality can lull us into feeling as if we completed something and satisfy us enough to stop short of gaining first-hand experience. I often wonder if this is the reason why so many young men lack ambition; they've already satisfied their ambitions playing video games.

## The Stakes are Fake

During the portion of time when the child part of the brain has been pruned but the adult portion is not fully formed, young people are in an in-between stage of development. Unless they step up to real experiences that challenge them, they remain informed but ill-equipped. I call this *artificial maturity*. It's like fool's gold. It looks like the real thing, but it is not. In fact, quite often, we've created an artificial world for our kids, full of facsimiles of what is real:

- They enjoy virtual reality through headsets and screens.
- They explore virtual relationships via social media.
- They achieve virtual progress by winning video games.
- They experience virtual thrills at a theme park.
- They make virtual connections on the Internet.
- They produce virtual results on quizzes and exams.

None of these are wrong or necessarily bad for them. They just aren't the real thing. They are all supervised or micro-managed. The stakes are low or artificial.

I have said many times over the years that we should borrow a page from history's playbook. A century ago, growing up looked different. Some of it was not so good, but a lot of it was very good, building both wisdom and common sense into the young. Formal education levels were lower, but informal, experiential learning was higher. Consider this: In the first two decades of the 20th century:

- Four-year-olds were doing age-appropriate chores around the house.
- Seven-year-olds were performing tasks on the farm.
- Eleven-year-olds were leading those tasks on the farm.
- Fourteen-year-olds were driving cars.
- Seventeen-year-olds were leading armies in World War I.
- Nineteen-year-olds were getting married and having children.

I am not saying we must return to this lifestyle. I am simply saying that past society proved kids are capable of so much more than posting on Instagram or Snapchat. In our fear of giving them authentic jobs to do, society has now settled for "fake stakes." I believe today's kids have just as much, if not more, potential than past generations of kids, but we're afraid to let them prove it. Our devices are smart, but my question is: Are we producing emotionally smart kids? After reviewing the data of adolescents today, I believe millions of them are victims of our culture:

- **Biologically advanced**
  (Their bodies are reaching puberty earlier.)

- **Cognitively advanced**
  (They are knowledgeable about many topics.)

- **Emotionally behind**
  (Their emotional intelligence is underdeveloped.)

- **Socially behind**
  (They're better on a screen than face to face with others.)

## WHAT ADULTS DO WHEN THEY RECOGNIZE THIS REALITY

When parents, teachers, and coaches recognize this strange phenomenon, we get scared. Seeing intelligent kids turn out as unready adults is enough to make any caring adult feel like a failure. So, we slip further into a safety paradigm. This "safetyism," driven by our concerned perspectives, drives so much of our behavior that it accelerates the creation of an eighteen-year old who is emotionally unready for college or a career. And the source of the problem is not the kids.

As we work with schools, we find ourselves meeting with thousands of parents each year. From east coast to west coast, we find moms and dads are experiencing similar struggles. If I were to summarize them, they would be:

1. **Parents are unsure of themselves.**

   Every abduction story, outbreak, allergy, injury, and statistic we read about can lead us to become uncertain as to whether we're doing everything we can to guarantee our child's growth, health, and well-being. This uncertainty ambushes our self-confidence and clarity. We wonder if there is something more we should be doing to ensure our kids won't need a therapist when they're thirty because we failed them as parents.

2. **Parents are competing with each other.**

   Because so many fellow parents are posting all they do for their children—from buying the latest portable device to taking them on the perfect vacation—we often find ourselves in competition with the Jones or the Smiths to provide the best childhood a kid could ever have. We want them happy, so we cave in to every compelling request our children make, or we simply copy what the neighbors do for their kids. This reality rears its ugly head at youth sports games, theatre competitions, recitals, karate practices, and PTA meetings.

### 3. Parents are worried about the future.

A third reality we see in every state is parental worry about what our world will be like in ten years and whether our children will turn out the way we imagine they should. What will the future look like for them? Will they be able to get into the right college? How about earning that scholarship? Will they date the wrong kind of people? Will they marry a loser? Will they get a job they love and make enough money to live well? Will their adult life reflect inadequate parenting skills on our part?

## What's the Data Tell Us?

As a result of these realities, we are more afraid than ever to take our hands off the control switch. In response, kids are taking longer to engage in the pleasures and responsibilities of adulthood. According to research from psychologist Dr. Jean Twenge, teens are not dating as much as they have in the past, at least without their parents.[16] Today, you might call it supervised dating or virtual dating. Their dates include mom and dad, or the kids date via a screen. Teen surveys from 2010-2016 compared to past teens show a trend:

1. Fewer twelfth graders went out on a date in 2015 than eighth graders did in 2009.[17]

2. In 2015, the majority of sixteen-year-olds did not have a driver's license.[18]

3. In 1979, only 22 percent of seniors did not work a job; by the 2010s, it was about half.[19]

4. In 2016, the most common living arrangement for eighteen- to thirty-four-year-olds was with parents.[20]

Certainly, not all of these trends are negative. They communicate, however, that young adolescents are putting off the scenarios that frequently force a person to mature, learn from experience, and grow wiser.

They're spending more time alone and less time in social interaction. Young adults in their early twenties often act like teenagers and teens often act like younger kids. Too often, they're savvy without emotional maturation.

## THE PRICE OF OUR INTERVENTION

In October 2013, a surprising news report came out of Port Washington, New York. Worries about injuries at a Long Island middle school led to a ban during recess. Kids could no longer play with footballs, baseballs, soccer balls, or anything else that might hurt someone on school grounds. In fact, playing tag and doing cartwheels without a coach were banned as well. I assumed this was a joke at first. It wasn't.

School administrators were concerned about injuries among students and replaced the athletic equipment with Nerf balls. Needless to say, most students were not thrilled with the decision. One said, "You go for recess—and it's our one free time to let loose and recharge." Another student said, "That's all we want to do. We're in school all day sitting behind a desk learning." Another one jumped in: "I think we need the soccer balls, footballs and everything so we can have some fun."[21]

But, alas, these students will have no such options anymore. The school's superintendent explained that there had been an excess of injuries that warranted this policy. After all, experts say without helmets and pads, kids can get hurt. Teachers are simply concerned about the children. And, of course, the lawsuits.

When adults intervene like this, we solve short-term problems. I have no doubt, injuries have gone down on the playground in that Long Island middle school and all the other schools who've jumped on board with the same policy.

Unfortunately, this decision may turn out to be a Pyrrhic victory where we lose more than we gain. Our world is more educated, more sophisticated, more modernized, and more industrialized than ever before, but in our race to make progress, we often leave one important quality behind: common sense.

Robert Ingersoll said, "It is a thousand times better to have common sense without education than to have education without common sense."[22] I even heard someone say recently that common sense is so rare today it should be considered a super power.

I invite you to join me as we equip today's emerging generation to be the leaders and entrepreneurs they're capable of becoming—but to also hold fast to good old common sense. Preventing hurt today often leads to more harm tomorrow. As kids mature into young adults, they won't be equipped for adulthood. I predict one of two outcomes will emerge:

1. The first time they are autonomous, they will try terribly risky behaviors, because they've never calculated the negative consequences of stupid conduct.

2. They will fear any risk because it's all so new. They never learned to navigate risk as a child on a playground. And they now hesitate to become autonomous.

Both of these are far more harmful than the hurt of a skinned knee or broken arm as a child. In our effort to prevent hurt, we've accelerated harm. If we don't act now, it may manifest as they become adults. It's time that we start creating the kind of environment that can help our empowered generation gain wisdom.

# SEVEN

# Leading With First Hand Experiences

Swanson Primary School in Auckland, New Zealand is a vivid case study of what adult leaders could do to cultivate wisdom in students today, offering first hand experiences for their students in a very simple way.

Principal Bruce McLachlan was approached by Professor Grant Schofield and his class regarding the playground rules on the school's campus. Grant noticed the teacher to student ratio was high and all the dangerous playground equipment—like swings, skateboards, and monkey bars—had all been removed in the name of safety. The data showed that Swanson Primary School also had both student engagement problems and bullying problems. Schofield believed the safety obsession might be connected to these issues, so he challenged McLachlan to return all the playground equipment and cut the number of teachers who were supervising. Professor Schofield then asked McLachlan to challenge the students to 'look out for each other' since there would be less adult supervision.

Almost everyone was surprised by what happened.

After nearly a day, the students started to figure it out. The older kids began looking out for the younger ones. It was more about relationships than rules. They rose to the challenge, and the playground actually grew safer. In fact, bullying dropped because students were looking out for each other instead of tormenting each other. Student engagement rose in the classroom because the kids got to play hard, tiring themselves enough so they could settle down when it was time to learn. Grant Schofield wrote afterward:

> *Too many rules can have an adverse effect on children. The great*
> *paradox of sheltering is that it's more dangerous in the long run.*
> *Society's obsession with protecting kids ignores the benefits of risk*
> *taking. Children develop the frontal lobe of their brain when*
> *taking risks, meaning they work through consequences. You can't*
> *teach them that. They have to learn risk on their own terms. It*
> *doesn't develop watching TV. They have to take a risk.*[1]

A growing number of schools are introducing risky tools into learning environments on campuses, including adaptive learning software and power tools for building. More are going outside, exposing kids to fire, weather, and sharp edges all with one goal: to foster wisdom in their kids. And it seems to be working.

Kids make smart choices when exposed to higher stakes. We must stop leading our kids with short-term vision and see the long-term impact of our decisions. Hurt is far better than harm. It's common sense.

So, let's talk about how we can lead them to wisdom in today's empowered world.

## FOUR STAGES IN YOUR LEADERSHIP

Part of our problem has been when our students change, we don't adapt along with them.

When they're young, they need a more directional approach than when they've aged and understand concepts and choices in life much better. Below, I've outlined the sequence of four stages my wife and I experienced as our children grew older. I've noticed these stages have applied when I have coached or led students as well.

1. **Micro-manager** (first six years)

   During their early childhood, children need far more direct and clear leadership. They think concretely, not abstractly. Instructions must be simple to understand and clear to follow. Adults observe everything first hand. Both positive and negative reinforcement are helpful to encourage growth. This stage is about *discipline*: What do we do, and how do we act?

2. **Manager** (next six years)

During elementary school, kids need increased autonomy and responsibility. With each year, they should earn a little more freedom as they can be trusted to be dependable with it. Clarity and simplicity are still important, but kids can act on their own. Autonomy increases as responsibility increases. This stage is about *training*: Why do we do what we do?

3. **Supervisor** (next six years)

During their teen years, kids move from concrete to abstract thought. They can understand concepts like: *You can borrow the car if you put gas in the tank.* Again, autonomy grows with responsibility. Life skills can be taught and "equations" work well. There are benefits and consequences for choices. This stage is about *coaching*—collaborating on good decisions.

4. **Consultant** (next six years)

As they finish high school, our role must move from supervisor to consultant. Our leadership is still present, but young adults must experiment. They learn *just in time*, not *just in case*. We can incentivize their growth by offering experiences that force them to do so. This invites them to seek mentors. This stage is about *friendship*: You are both adults who enjoy interaction.

**Question:** Which stage are you in? Are you leading your kids appropriately?

## How to Become a Caring Yet "Free-Range" Parent

A bit of a firestorm was ignited four years ago, when parents Alexander and Danielle Meitiv allowed their two children (ages six and ten) to play in a nearby park without them watching. A by-stander called 911, and police picked up the kids and returned them to their home. Later, the kids were allowed to play at another park (where they had played dozens of times), and they didn't come home at the designated time. Why? They'd been detained by police again. Soon after Alexander and Danielle were visited and interrogated by Child Protection Services to ensure they were fit parents. Eventually, CPS determined they were a decent mom and dad.

All of this caused Danielle to run for local office to change the laws in their Maryland town. In her campaign messages, she described herself as a "free-range mom." Do you remember this term? As I mentioned earlier, it became popular some years ago when Lenore Skenazy let her son ride the New York subway without her supervision. She received lots of flak from other parents but contends allowing kids to be unsupervised at times will help them become more effective adults.

Now, some lawmakers have joined the chorus. In 2018, Utah became the first state to pass legislation for "free-range parenting." It changes the state's definition of neglect to allow children of "sufficient age and maturity" to engage in independent activities like walking to and from school.[2] The bill's sponsor, State Senator Lincoln Fillmore, said he hopes the law will enable kids to grow up, "learning to take responsibility for themselves."

## Becoming a Free-Range Leader

Many of you who read this are teachers, coaches, youth workers, or employers. You are in front of students regularly and want to empower them yet foster wisdom along with the empowerment. I want to help you do just that.

The purpose of this chapter is to understand today's empowered generation of students and offer a prescription for the unintended consequences it creates. Our goal should not necessarily be to lower the empowerment kids enjoy but to make it age appropriate and to add first-hand experiences to the information they consume. Let's face it, technology is not going away. Teens are going to find a way to get information on-line. The goal should be to increase their empowerment as they mature but to also provide an equal amount of wisdom to match their exposure. Empowerment and wisdom must always coincide.

## Why Free-Range Leaders Are Rare Today

When I talk to adults, almost all of them acknowledge they got to do lots of "free-range" things when they were children, such as walk to school, go skateboarding in a park, and play with friends in another neighborhood. Those same adults, however, also admit those are things they don't let their kids do today.

Why is this? Once again, the answer is fear. Adults tend to have a narrative of fear in their minds about the safety of kids today. Free-Range parent Lenore Skenazy says, "We're being hypocrites because we're coming to the erroneous conclusion that any time a child is unsupervised they're automatically in danger and it's not true."[3]

Parents are often the most frequent culprits of this fear mindset. Dr. Gail Saltz, professor of psychology at New York Presbyterian Hospital, says, "Parents' perception of how dangerous the world is has changed over the years. Parental anxiety is inflamed by a global, always-on news cycle, as well as increased connectivity on social media platforms, which recycles 'over and over again' kidnappings, rape and other threatening incidents."[4] In fact, while violent crime has dropped sharply in the U.S. over the past twenty-five years, Americans generally perceive crime rates are continuing to climb, according to a 2016 survey by Pew Research Center.[5] And perception is reality, at least for many parents today.

Empowerment and wisdom must always coincide.

On top of this, I believe parenting has gone from a community thing, where we all look out for each other's kids, to a competition. We are all trying to be the best mom and often judge others for their lack of engagement or provision. In my book *Twelve Huge Mistakes Parents Can Avoid*, I mention a parent survey that was taken among hundreds of moms and dads across the country. The results? The average grade parents gave themselves on their parenting skills was an A or a B. The average grade they gave their neighbor was a D. How do we change the narrative inside of us?

## Steps Leaders Can Take to Be Engaged Yet Empowering

1. **Ask someone to hold you accountable to resist the fear narrative.**

   We all do better when we know someone is going to ask us about the commitments we've made. Ask a respected, trusted friend to weekly ask you if you're rejecting the fear narrative our culture feeds us. Believe the best about the young people you lead, and offer direction to them out of wisdom, not fear.

2. **Take baby steps forward to allow youth to increase their level of risk.**

   If your kids are young, they obviously need to be watched and directed more closely than when they reach adolescence. As they mature, they need more autonomy and responsibility. Let them take slightly bigger risks each month. Increase their exposure to on-line data and social media as they mature. We will discuss how much time is healthy on their phones in the chapter "Coping with the Anxiety Epidemic."

3. **When information empowers youth, compliment it with experiences.**

   Through conversation and observation, note where the young people you lead are expanding their levels of knowledge, and plan an experience that will compliment that information. For example, if they learn about impoverished countries, take them to feed the homeless in your own city. If they bully a marginalized peer, take them to a hospital to meet kids with a chronic disease. If they take money for granted, help them raise some funds for a great cause.

4. **Let them fail.**

   Young people seldom learn from success alone. Failure is a marvelous and memorable teacher. But we must let them fail when they're young, when the stakes are low, and little can harm them permanently. The sooner they learn they can survive failure, the more they'll pursue dreams and goals as adults. And the more wisdom they'll accumulate along the way.

5. **Parents, invite a community of moms and dads to create a village to watch the kids.**

   I believe it truly does "take a village" to raise good kids. Reject the competitive parenting model we see so often and create a community of parents in your neighborhood or town who will help keep watch over your kids' play time. Spend regular times on the phone to discuss your kids' development.

### 6. Talk about trust with them, and teach them to build it over time.

Students must learn that love is given freely by adults but trust is earned. From the beginning, my wife and I talked to our kids about trust. At home, at school, and at work, they got increasing levels of freedom as they proved they could be trusted with it. Let them earn the right to be free-range students by their mature choices or conduct. Discuss how trust is the currency of all good relationships.

### 7. Provide them with equations, not just rules.

Too often, caring adults become afraid or frustrated with this empowered generation and put more rules in place. We offer legislation more than insight as to how to navigate today's realities. Equations are different. They are about cause and effect: If you do this, that is the consequence; if you do that, this is the benefit. This is how life works. Implement equations in your classroom, workplace, and home—then enforce them. Every choice they make should feel to them like a trade-off.

### 8. Combine a leadership style that's both intentional and laissez faire.

Developing mature teens requires adults to be both intentional (meaning we are deliberate in our planning and what we expose them to) while at the same time being laissez faire (meaning we let them learn on their own). When I wanted my kids to begin learning more about potential careers, I helped line up interviews with colleagues I know who could be mentors, but I let my kids determine when and where to meet and what questions to ask them. Help them do it. Don't do it for them.

In short, application turns information into wisdom. When our two children were ages eight and twelve, my wife and I wanted them to learn people skills. They were both good in front of screens, but we knew they needed to develop emotional intelligence. So, I led family dinner discussions on the topic over several weeks. But while Bethany and Jonathan appeared engaged, I could tell my insights were insufficient. Both of my kids felt they were already astute at social skills and didn't see the need for growth—especially from their dad. I realized at that point, they needed experience.

So, Pam and I planned dinner parties and asked our kids to host them. When our adult friends and neighbors came over, my children learned to start conversations, hang coats, serve desserts, and introduce guests—all on their own. We debriefed afterward. They were humbled by what they didn't know. Together, we interpreted how hard it is to start a conversation with someone who's quiet or reserved. We talked about how some folks lack self-awareness and others don't. It was inspiring to watch my kids proceed from knowledgeable to wise.

## WHAT ARE THE ESSENTIAL INGREDIENTS?

When I see caring adult leaders equipping youth in a holistic way, they always include four elements in the process. These are the same four elements that I practiced with my kids as they were maturing and that I practice still today with the high school and college-aged interns I lead at Growing Leaders. It all comes down to this: I believe there is a natural formula for turning artificial maturity into authentic maturity. I call it The Big IDEA.

### The Big IDEA:

#### I—Instruction

Adults provide verbal insights and explanations through conversations with Generation Z. This furnishes them with both knowledge and understanding. This interaction can take place in a classroom, office, car ride, or anywhere else, so long as the goal is to guide their learning process. I suggest you use images and metaphors or offer memorable phrases that summarize concepts for them.

#### D—Demonstration

Adults find a way to offer an example of what the insight looks like in real life. This furnishes Generation Z with confidence and vision. This experience can be as simple as watching someone, in person or on video, practicing the concepts students are learning. It is an important element in their growth because people do what people see.

## E—Experience

Adults turn Generation Z loose to practice the insight on their own, to apply the knowledge. This furnishes them with skills and abilities. I believe learning isn't complete until students actually experience the insight for themselves. This step ensures theory becomes practice. This is what students lack so often today, due to adult preoccupation with safety.

## A—Assessment

Adults take time to debrief and evaluate the learning process with the Gen Z students they lead. This furnishes them with wisdom and perspective. I don't believe experience is the best teacher; I believe that experience plus evaluation is the best teacher. We must take time to assess what happened so they might gain helpful insight from their practices.

**Talk It Over:** How could you implement the big IDEA with your students?

## THE IMPACT FREE-RANGE LEADERS HAVE ON GENERATION Z

I wish you could meet Ronnetta Simpson, principal of East Paulding High School in Georgia. Her desire to translate education into real life for her students drove her to rethink how her school offered CTAE. When she and her team asked students what they felt they lacked as they considered life after graduation, they said they needed help with finances and business. Like most teens, those kids didn't feel equipped to navigate the intimidating world of money. (In fact, many adults I know still feel intimidated by it!) While Ronnetta knew her school offered an accounting class, it wasn't enough. So, what did this leader do?

Believe it or not, Ronnetta decided to open a bank right on her campus.

She identified a teacher to head up the experience, then contacted a local credit union for help. They transformed two classrooms into a learning center for finances. One remained a classroom for instruction on finance. The other was gutted and transformed into a bank, that now employs student tellers, account advisors, marketing specialists (who solicit new customers), graphic designers (who designed the logo), loan officers and managers (who have access to account codes that even faculty don't have). The credit union told Ronnetta: "You round up the students and we will train them." The experiment began with 6 students but has tripled as word got out. These teens designed a savings plan for freshman students to help them save for prom night, lettermen jackets and graduation. The students even created an entertaining performance they do for middle school students called, "It's Scary Being Broke." These amazing student-bankers are teaching financial literacy.

You may be wondering—is this experience for real? I wondered the same thing. But my doubts were put to rest when I discovered three seniors were actually hired by the credit union once they graduated. Principal Ronnetta Simpson even does her banking with these students. You might say—she literally put her money where her mouth is.

I also wish you could meet Jason Williams and Josh Quinn. I met Jason and Josh in 2018. They're engineering teachers at Fall Creek Middle School, in the Lawrenceville Township of Indianapolis. Enrollment is about fourteen hundred students. They started Project Lead the Way in their classes to address the lack of first-hand experiences provided to students in their school. Like most teachers, they found too many students who just wanted teachers to give them answers.

So, they introduced the Paper Tower Project to their students.

The project involves building a tower out of paper and masking tape, which to some students seems impossible. They give kids two pieces of computer paper and ask them to build a tower thirty-eight inches tall and hang a small toy monkey on top. Josh and Jason's sole purpose is to empower students through trial and error and to learn from failure and success. They refuse to give their students the answers. As kids work, the teachers start conversations using our tool *Habitudes*®, which are images that form leadership habits and attitudes. Each image represents a life principle and is designed to ignite a discussion. (We've found that pictures really are worth a thousand words.) After their course, students often send them letters. They're rarely about the project but are rather to say, "Thanks for teaching me to be a thermostat, not a thermometer."

The two instructors let their eight-step learning process take shape organically, observing what happens to students who grow frustrated when solutions don't come quickly. Jason and Josh have seen students crying or curling up in a fetal position because they've never faced a challenge this difficult. But they don't remove the challenge. In the end, students become extraordinary workers. Here's what Jason told me:

- It allows us to teach persistence and grit because an F can't be fixed immediately.
- It reinforces the idea that we must earn what we get, just like the real world. Everyone starts with a zero until they grow out of it, just like jobs and careers.
- There is no worksheet to fill out to get an A; it's a messy process of discovery. The key is to follow the process, and the product takes care of itself.
- Their process allows students to view failure as opportunity and not as a final condition. Lower performing students sit next to others who also struggle; it's a level playing field as they all find it equally difficult.
- Students have adult guides, but they learn self-sufficiency and self-motivation. The next time they face a tough challenge, they no longer fear it.
- Kids gain incredible confidence through hard work and accomplishment. About 90 percent of students still get an A by the end of the project.

Josh Williams got an email one semester from a high performing student, with a 4.4 grade point average. She was especially stunned by the experience when her teacher pointed out that genuine learning was far more important than mere grades:

*Mr. Williams,*

*I was constantly nervous in the seventh grade. For the first nine weeks, I was terrified of everything. I ran to every class so I wouldn't be late. I wrote over the maximum allowed for written answers on tests. I looked at the ground a lot because I was too scared to look people in the eye. I sat by myself at lunch because I couldn't stand the thought of having to talk to new people. When I auditioned for a program and didn't make it, I cried for three hours because I hated myself so much for not getting it. I know that all sounds super dramatic, but it's true. I'm not kidding. The Paper Tower Project literally changed my whole year because it showed me how to fail. I freaked out that I couldn't build it correctly at first. I felt like my whole world fell apart. Up until then, I didn't allow myself to fail. Being good at school was all I had. It's where I put my confidence. Without amazing grades, I wasn't worth anything. Or at least that's what I thought. But you showed me what really matters in life; grades are only the tip of the iceberg. You gave me opportunities to show myself the qualities I possess besides getting 100 percent test scores. I honestly never had failed in class before, and this experience changed me. I want you to know that you've helped me beyond what books can teach.*

*Thank you!*

*Gwen*

This kind of note beckons me to continue working to build empowered students into wise students.

# EIGHT

# Stimulation Without Ownership

*Challenge #2*

I had to chuckle at what I was hearing. Seated with a group of fourteen young teenagers, I asked them what they liked and what they didn't like about their lives. Check out what came from our discussion:

**A summary of what they liked:**
Mom and dad plan everything, from after-school tutoring to piano lessons and recitals to karate classes to program rehearsals to soccer team practices. They take me to school and drive me to all my stuff after school.

**A summary of what they didn't like:**
I feel like I don't have time just to come up with my own plans, like hanging out with my friends or goofing around outside or even coming up with my own school projects. I wish my life wasn't so full of stuff.

Did you catch the essence of their answers?

Of course, they have a love-hate relationship with their lives, as have most teenagers for the last one hundred years. What's different today and quite telling is that what they liked and didn't like were virtually the same things. They loved the fact that they didn't have to lift a finger to ensure they had lots of activities in their week. An adult does it for them. But after the initial pleasure of having someone plan their lives has evaporated, they didn't like the fact that they did not get a chance to do it themselves. This is one of the paradoxes of Generation Z's life in the 21st century.

## WE ASSUME GENERATION Z NEEDS A PRESCRIPTION

Over the past three decades, U.S. child-rearing has taken on a whole new approach. Decades ago, families had so many children that moms simply issued a list of chores for them to do, and once kids finished them, they were on their own to play outside. There were few hovering "helicopter parents"—often because there were too many children to hover over. Today, parents have fewer kids (often just one) and are very directive and prescriptive, making sure they have a healthy diet of activities, which serve to prepare them for the right college. We see helicopter, snowplow and lawnmower parents everywhere preparing the path for the child instead of the child for the path. For millions of American kids, adults have taken over every waking hour. Kids have less unsupervised time (than I did growing up) and more time prescribed by adults. And there is a purpose for it all. After all, we know what's best, don't we?

The same is true for education. Teachers tell me they feel overwhelmed with all they need to cover during a school semester and end up racing to the bottom line, to make sure students are ready for the standardized tests they must take. With big goals and little time, faculty must teach to the test and often merely give students the answers, in hopes they will be memorized. In our focus groups, students revealed they often ask their instructor, "Is this going to be on the test?" or say, "Just tell me the right answer." A thoughtful faculty member once told me "instead of preparing graduates for life, I am merely preparing them for more school." Teachers consistently say how much they want to see kids "own" their education these days, but it would be difficult for students to do so the way we currently manage our classrooms.

Coaches often say the same thing. By the time student-athletes reach their teen years and certainly their college years, the stakes are too high. To keep their job, a coach must win games. In order to do this, they must maintain a "command and control" leadership style, offering clear instruction to their teams instead of empowering them to think for themselves. We prescribe their weight training, sleep time, drills, practices, and nutrition. It's a science. I found myself smiling at a vivid illustration of this reality. It was a picture of a football coach standing in front of his team in the locker room before their first game of the season. The coach shouted, "Guys, this is YOUR team. This is YOUR season. This is YOUR game. Now—go out and do exactly what I told you to do!"

Speaking of high stakes, employers often feel the same way when a young person comes on staff. Since the young team member often brings little or no job experience, employers feel they must script their sales calls and even their conduct in retail. It makes sense. We don't want to leave anything to chance because the bottom line is at stake. Each quarter must show a profit, so the training and preparation feel more like following a specific recipe and more like we're cooking in a microwave than a crockpot. My career path was slow and steady. Today, it's fast, prescribed, and changing for greater efficiency all the time. It's the world we operate in today. Just follow the script.

So, two decades into the 21st century, here's a snapshot of an average kid's life:

- Parents are prescriptive in their leadership, scheduling each day.
- Teachers are prescriptive in their lesson plans, teaching for the test.
- Coaches are prescriptive on their instructions for practices and games.
- YouTube and Netflix are prescriptive, suggesting what videos to watch next.
- Amazon is prescriptive suggesting other products you might like.
- Employers are prescriptive in their formula to reach the numbers they need.
- Social media apps are prescriptive in their format to keep you watching.

Quite frankly, because today's world is overwhelming, kids often welcome prescriptive leadership. As we saw earlier in our focus group's comments, kids likely don't have time or energy to think for themselves. Our prescribed world, however, comes at a price. So, what has this done to our kids today?

## THE STATE OF GENERATION Z

Research by Peter Gray at Boston College reveals that between 1981 and 1997 free time for kids to play plummeted significantly. The "Time-Use Study" confirmed what doctors already suspected. More and more time was being eaten up in prescribed and supervised activity. In the same study, it was discovered that the time spent in school rose 18 percent and time spent on homework rose 145 percent. Adults just got crazy about helping kids live on purpose. Think about what's happened in the last thirty years:

1. Adults consumed more *time*, and childhood became more *supervised*.
2. Kids took less *risk*, and childhood became more *protected*.
3. Technology got *smarter*, and childhood became more *directed*.

Greg Lukianoff and Jonathan Haidt summarize the issue this way:

> *Beginning in preschool and continuing throughout primary school and beyond, children's days are now more rigidly structured. Opportunities for self-direction, social exploration and scientific discovery are increasingly lost to direct instruction in the core curriculum, which is often driven by the school's focus on preparing students to meet state testing requirements.[1]*

Chris Harris served on our Growing Leaders team for several years. I always admired his ability to problem solve and find ways to achieve his goals. He told me he owed a lot of the credit to Scott, his Boy Scout leader. Why? Because Scott saw the big picture and let Chris "own" his scouting experience. Scott let the boys choose their hikes, plan the details of their outings, and experience leadership, even if it meant failing along the way. Chris remembers forgetting to pack food for a weekend. Scott didn't solve his problem for him. Other boys gave him a few snacks, but Chris had to pace his eating with a little borrowed food at each campsite. Chris never forgot this lesson, and rarely forgets anything today. Scott made sure

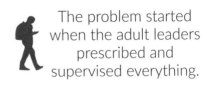

The problem started when the adult leaders prescribed and supervised everything.

his boys didn't harm themselves, but he let his troop figure out how to succeed together.

When Scott retired, however, new leaders took over with a different paradigm. They were prescriptive in their leadership. Wanting to create a perfect experience for the boys, they planned everything themselves. While their plans were executed well, their philosophy was the opposite of Scott's. As a teen, Chris said his scouting experience eventually became disengaging and demotivating.

The problem started when the adult leaders prescribed and supervised everything.

## When Over-Prescription Becomes Theft

Although over-prescriptive adults are well-intentioned, we don't realize what we are stealing from our kids. Generation Z is growing up partially disabled by our theft.

### 1. Brain Development Is Affected

Specific kinds of brain development happen when youth are free to make up their own agenda, to play (create their own games), and to resolve conflict and make choices. In fact, kids need growing levels of risk as they mature into teenagers and young adults. Dr. Peter Gray, a Boston College professor of psychology, says that kids naturally want to dose themselves with "moderate degrees of fear, as if deliberately learning how to deal with both the physical and emotional challenges they generate . . . All such activities are fun to the degree that they are moderately frightening. If too little fear is induced, the activity is boring; if too much is induced, it becomes no longer play but terror. Nobody but the child himself or herself knows the right dose."[2] More about this later in the chapter.

### 2. Problem Solving and Decision-Making Skills Diminish

All kinds of maturation take place in unsupervised times, without established adults around and when kids are in control of the agenda. If there is an adult present in any situation, however, the kids will often defer to the adult and depend on him for choices and solutions. This stands in stark contrast to my young teenage years. For example, I can tell you exactly when and where I learned conflict resolution skills—the art of negotiating and compromising with people. I was twelve years old and after my homework was done, a bunch of boys would gather in a big field beside our neighborhood to play baseball. We would choose teams, determine the batting order, and umpire our own games. It was a prime time to learn conflict resolution. Today, if kids are outside at all, four mothers are out there doing the conflict resolution for them. Their skills atrophy.

## 3. Anxiety and Stress Levels Increase

As I have noted, there is a direct correlation between today's rise in adolescent anxiety and kids feeling out of control of their lives. When adults supervise and determine what will happen, it eventually cultivates an external locus of control and a feeling of angst within the teens. As a child becomes a young adult, he must feel in control of his fate and his future. This outcome is counterintuitive, as we would assume if we control his lives and offer him direction it would lessen his stress levels. Unfortunately, a teen's brain is wired to assume more control as he matures, and when control is not given, he can become unnaturally anxious. This is exactly what's happening. A report issued by the Center for Collegiate Mental Health in 2016 (utilizing data from 139 colleges) found that half of all students that school year attended counseling for mental health problems.[3]

## 4. Motivation Decreases

One of the outcomes we noticed in our 2017-2018 focus groups with eighth and ninth graders across the U.S. was a shift in motivation. While this generation knows they are empowered by technology to learn and do things past generations of teens could not do, a growing number are actually demotivated by their position. This stimuli of smart technology tend to be suggestive rather than inspiring, just like the adults in their lives. This stimuli pushes ideas to the users. It guides their behaviors. Students aren't inspired to change their lives; they're just clicking "play" on the next suggested video.

## 5. Responsibility Levels Shrink

It stands to reason that if adults assume more responsibility for directing children's lives, those kids may experience a decrease in their sense of responsibility. As teens mature into adulthood, the best versions of themselves are revealed as they tackle difficult challenges and own their lives and futures. When we don't give them this opportunity, we see a lesser version. Dr. Peter Gray puts it this way: "Outside of school, children spend more time than ever in settings in which they are directed, protected, catered to, ranked, judged, and rewarded by adults. In all of these settings, adults are in control, not children."[4] Is it any wonder kids look to adults to assume responsibility for them?

What is the bottom line?

"Students are prepared academically, but they're not prepared to deal with day-to-day life, which comes from lack of opportunity to deal with ordinary problems," says Peter Gray.[5] It's an irony. The paradox of our lives today is that some of the things adults and schools do to get kids admitted into college might just make them less able to thrive once they arrive there.

## What's Going on Inside of the Teenage Brain?

Much of what I've described can be explained by what's happening inside kids' brains during adolescence. Two realities occur in a teen's brain as he moves into adulthood:

1. His brain keeps score with dopamine. When the VTA-NAc pathway is stimulated, dopamine is released, sending the message to the prefrontal cortex: *I should do this again!* In an on-demand world, teens tend to repeat pleasure as often as possible. Let's face it—we all want to duplicate gratifying experiences. Teens can especially become addicted to what they believe are rare pleasures in their lives.[6]

2. Teens have a lower baseline of dopamine, so it takes more to "wow" them. But the dopamine releases in response to stimuli are actually higher than normal. This means, it takes more to move them, but when it's released, they feel its impact more

profoundly. That's why emotions rise and fall during these years. They can move from apathy to heightened emotion rapidly.[7]

Given the nature of their brain development and how healthy maturation occurs, adolescents need higher stakes to their decisions to remain engaged and growing. In other words, merely letting them choose the restaurant for dinner is not sufficient to stimulate growth; they need to take on greater responsibility as they transition into adulthood. By mid-teen years, choosing a job, being employed on a job, performing community service that matters, raising money for a great cause, or helping someone in need are all examples of the higher stakes young adults need. As I mentioned, a healthy brain during this period hungers to do something that's very important and almost impossible.

So how is this reality playing out with Generation Z?

## Risk Deprivation Syndrome

Unfortunately, this reality has gotten so severe, that some psychologists now refer to it as risk deprivation syndrome. It is the damage that occurs when kids are unable to navigate risk and learn the lessons life teaches you through scary experiences.

"Alison Gopnik, psychology professor at the University of California Berkeley, found in her research that children in the past 20 years have developed this 'risk deprivation syndrome,' where they are unable to judge risk and face it."[8] Just imagine maturing into adulthood but having no past experience at negotiating risky situations and big decisions with high stakes. Students begin to take a laid back approach with their own lives, letting adults assume all the risks. This is, in fact, what is happening today.

Last year, I spoke to educators who shared stories about students who learned how to work the school system. One example was students who purposely did poorly on their exams at the beginning of the school year. They answered questions almost randomly. By midterms, they put more thought into the tests they took, and by the end of the year, they did their best, knowing they would show improvement.

When asked why they did this, these students revealed what they knew:

- My parents just want to see improvement in my test scores—and I improved.
- My teachers want me to succeed and will do whatever possible to ensure I do.

In both cases, these students were hedging their bets, taking risks because they felt confident the adults would make sure they felt successful in the end. In fact, the adults wanted the students to succeed more than the students did.

## Moral Hazards

This is what economists and psychologists call a moral hazard. In case this is an unfamiliar term, let me remind you of the definition of a moral hazard:

*A moral hazard is the lack of incentive to guard against risk when one is protected from its consequences.*

In the United States today, we see more and more of these moral hazards happening before our very eyes. A financial investor takes more risks with his money when he knows he's insured. This person is more apt to make precarious decisions that benefit him in a payoff because their consequences are placed on the insurance company.

Similarly, an employee who drives a company car may be apt to drive more carelessly because she doesn't have to pay for the repairs of that vehicle. It's a moral hazard. Whenever consequences are diminished for bad choices, people are prone to be less cautious in their conduct.

In other words, people are more prone to make risky decisions when the consequence of those poor decisions is borne primarily by others.

Recently, a miracle treatment was discovered for opioid overdose called Naloxone. It's called the Lazarus Drug, named after Lazarus, the man Jesus brought back to life once he'd died. The drug has been shown to bring unconscious drug abusers back to consciousness within seconds. The testimonials of those who have been revived are amazing. Unfortunately, it's seems to cause opioid users to take more risks.

When researchers studied experimental and control groups, they noticed that deaths by overdose were not going down where this drug was available. In fact, in some parts of the country, deaths by overdose had risen. After examining the evidence, they concluded that the problem was a moral hazard. Because opioid users knew this drug was available, they took more drugs but often did not get the Naloxone quickly enough. When they felt their risk of dying was reduced, they took more risks. This is a natural human inclination we've seen repeatedly throughout history. I remember when we got seatbelts in our cars, we started driving a little faster.

This is also what is happening with our kids today.

## Moral Hazards Among Our Students

Economist Paul Krugman described a moral hazard as "any situation in which one person makes the decision about how much risk to take, while someone else bears the cost if things go badly."[9]

In too many cases, we adults communicate that we have more to gain or lose than our students do when they make decisions—and that's come back to haunt them. We've communicated this by passing more legislation, creating more rules, and developing more safety policies instead of teaching our young to act responsibly and experience the benefits or consequences of their behavior. We own it, not them.

- Students know if they forget their homework, backpack, or permission slip, moms or dads will rush it in, rescue them, and solve their problem.
- Students get harmed or even die from stupid accidents because all of their lives we have passed safety rules instead of teaching them responsibility.
- Students are paralyzed from making decisions because we did it for them all of their lives, too afraid to let them learn and experience tough consequences.

The fact is too many students who've been hovered over by parents, teachers, and coaches are prevented from taking normal risks in adolescence. In the end, those young adults don't even know how to mitigate risk when it is time to face those risks alone. We either did it for them, or we created a foolproof environment.

As they become adults, they require more legislation, more policies, more rules and regulations because they never genuinely owned their lives. Because parents have been so prescriptive in their leadership, doctors are actually prescribing playtime outside and with appropriate risks as children mature.[10] Due to the controlling leadership style adults, in general, have modeled for students, some colleges are now offering classes like Failure 101.[11]

They're all about taking control of your life, refusing to fear failing once in a while and knowing how to learn from it. My personal experience tells me that failures, struggles, hardships, and risky experiences have been my most tangible learning experiences. I've been sent to the hospital four times; I've been in seven auto accidents and survived one plane crash. While I'd never plan any of these again, I would not trade them for the world. Researcher Alison Gopnik says this is even true with children and germs. "Trying to eliminate all such risks from children's lives may be dangerous," Gopnik said. "There may be a psychological analog to the hygiene hypothesis. In the same way, by shielding children from every possible risk, we may lead them to react with exaggerated fear to situations that aren't risky at all and isolate them from the adult skills that they will one day have to master."[12]

A new policy report from the American Academy of Pediatrics suggests that we should allow for big blocks of time devoted to nothing but freedom and autonomy.[13] "Play is not frivolous," the report says. Rather, "research shows that play helps children develop language and executive functioning skills, learn to negotiate with others and manage stress, and figure out how to pursue their goals while ignoring distractions, among other things. The report warns that parents and schools are focusing on academic achievement at the expense of play and recommends that pediatricians attempt to turn the tide by prescribing play during well visits for children."[14]

Artificial Intelligence experts and global CEOs argue that free play encourages kids to develop agency, collaboration, and creativity—the skills that workers will need to maintain an edge over the robots.[15] In other words, good play leads to good work. Who would have thought that in all of the scheduling we do for our kids, we now need to schedule free playtime?

So, let's talk about a game plan.

NINE

# Moving from Prescriptive to Descriptive Leadership

In the last chapter, we discussed the problem of over-prescription in the lives of Generation Z children. Many of today's youth have their entire lives decided for them. The missing piece, I believe, is ownership. Empowering students to own their experiences, their projects, their teams, and their lives. We mean well, but far too often we seize control of their days to ensure everything goes well.

The good news is—there is hope. We can solve this problem. We can equip students for real life. The educational term that describes the antidote for this challenge is:

*Metacognition*

It's a concept that's been around for centuries but has resurfaced today because of where students are developmentally. You might call it an "ancient-future" methodology for learning. By "ancient-future," I mean it's an old technique, but it is the best way to prepare Generation Z for their futures. It's all about turning over the work of discovery and conclusions to the students. It means we serve as a guide, not a god, while we educate our young, and we get out of the way so they can do the heavy lifting.

In the book *Marching Off the Map*, I share how I discovered the power of metacognition accidentally. Twenty-five years ago, I was mentoring a community of college students in leadership. Each week, we would choose a new topic to discuss and an exercise to practice.

One week, a student emailed me, asking who was going to choose the topic for our next discussion. I grabbed my laptop and quickly replied: "I can do that."

Or at least, that's what I thought I had typed. My keypad is probably much like yours, where the letter *I* is positioned next to the letter *U*. In my haste, I accidentally replied, "U can do that."

Little did I know how much that simple response would empower them. At the next week's meeting, we all sat down to begin, but before I could open my mouth to launch the conversation, the student I had corresponded with took over. He started with an engaging game revolving around the topic of their chosen theme. Then, another student led a discussion, and another showed a video clip, which led to more discussion. Yet another led us in our time of application. It was stunning.

It means we serve as a guide, not a god, while we educate our young, and we get out of the way so they can do the heavy lifting.

I never told them it was all an accident.

That day, I learned the power of metacognition. Simply defined, metacognition is the awareness and understanding of one's own thought processes. It is essentially *thinking about thinking*. When students practice metacognition, they quite literally take ownership of their own learning. They direct it. They may not determine what they learn (surprises happen all the time), but they dictate how, when, and why they learn. I believe metacognition is the secret to and the driving motivation behind all effective learning. It means that in our classrooms, our homes, our practice fields, and our workplaces, we prepare our young people to become the drivers of their own learning and stop waiting for adults to do that work for them.

It's how Generation Z learns best. If we want our students to learn as much as possible, then we'll want to maximize the amount of metacognition they're doing. It's a relatively simple equation for students:

*The more they reflect on their learning, the more they learn. The better they engage with the subject and how to communicate it to others, the more they actually own it.*

This is what every instructor dreams about for his students. Our problem is that most classrooms are set up to promote metacognition in the teacher, not the students. Most families are set up to promote metacognition in the parents, not the kids. Most athletic teams are set up where the coach does most of the metacognition, not the players. We are far more engaged than our youngest population. Most Generation Z students have been conditioned to sit back and wait for their teachers to simplify the material and make it easy for them to digest it. Some even want to be "spoon-fed." When we teach this way, we are like a personal trainer in a gym who says, "I'm going to make sure you learn fitness, so stand back and watch as I lift all the weights for you."

We have no one to blame but ourselves. Far too often, we are hoarding all the best learning in our work with Generation Z. Adults are the only ones doing any metacognition.

## Moving from Prescriptive to Descriptive Leadership

I believe untapped ingenuity lies dormant inside Generation Z simply because we don't allow them to think for themselves. We don't foster creativity; we simply tell them what to do and how to do it. It's time we move from prescriptive leadership to descriptive leadership. Let me summarize the difference:

### Prescriptive Leadership:

Sets a goal, then furnishes the precise steps a learner should take in order to reach the goal. The learner doesn't need to think for herself but merely follow the prescribed plan.

### Descriptive Leadership:

Meets with the learner to describe the goal, then allows him or her to come up with his own steps to reach it. This allows for creativity and personal style in order for the learner and the outcome to match.

My friend Janet is a model of descriptive leadership. She's been proving the power of this style in her fifth-grade classroom for years. Janet told me recently she was observing her class as they worked on a project, on their own. One boy raised his hand and bluntly asked her, "Do you get paid to teach us?" When she replied she did, the boy replied, "That's funny. We do all the work!"

And that is as it should be.

## Changing Up the Classroom

I met Uduak Afangideh, PhD, at Faulkner University five years ago. Originally from Nigeria, Dr. Afangideh is the science department chair and professor of biology on campus. She's also a gracious, life-long learner who's in the twenty-fourth year of her career.

This astute professor had made some significant shifts when she heard me speak on the complexions of students from Generation Z. When I sat down to interview her, she explained to me that she knew she needed to let her students create more of the classroom experience. For years, she had controlled that space, ultimately letting them practice very little metacognition. She concluded, "I needed to stop teaching what they could look up on Google."

So, what changes did she make? Let me share with you what she told me.

1. "Desks usually face the professor in a classroom. We had to make a change since I no longer wanted to play the role of the guru." Dr. Afangideh turned the desks to face each other in groups of five. In these learning pods, students began to teach each other. They came up with activities to get to know each other, and they started learning together in a community, sharing their discoveries. In each class period, there was a group leader for each of the pods, and the responsibility rotated between the students. The students not only owned the content but also listened to each other and took notes. It worked like a live Twitter chat or an in-class Wikipedia page creation.

2. "Since students support what they help create, I found ways to let them create our classroom experience." For example, she said, "every year, our syllabus was loaded with information, but I found students still asking questions about what was in it. I got tired of saying, 'Just read the syllabus.' So, I decided to let them create the syllabus. I took my traditional syllabus and whittled it down to the things I can't compromise on due to university regulations (i.e. the final exam must weigh 30 percent of class grade; they must do homework weekly, etc.). The rest would be up to the students." Dr. Afangideh now tells her students, "I want it to be your syllabus, so you must

create it." And they do. She launches into the discussion the first week of class by saying, "I only want to teach what you want to know. What do you want to know about biology?" At this point, students began weighing in. She was surprised to find that "everything they mentioned was what I wanted to teach them." She then asked, "How many tests should we have?' Students differed on this one, but eventually, after debate, they chose the exact number of exams I planned to give."

Students chose the kind of class culture they wanted to have; they chose the topics, the rules, and the way they would interact with the subjects. It was remarkable how often they would forego an easy culture and instead choose a healthy culture, the very one any teacher would want. This time, however, they owned it because they chose it.

As I marveled with Dr. Afangideh about what she had accomplished, she smiled as she said, "I've seen a difference in student performance since making these changes five years ago. They are taking more ownership of their learning. I love it. While it would've been easier for me to continue teaching the way I did, I had to change, and I am so glad I did."

Dr. Afangideh has since written a textbook as a result of all of these discoveries. In her textbook, students have room to both read and to write. That's what I call moving from prescriptive to descriptive leadership.

## Metacognition in the Workplace

The classroom, however, is not the only place metacognition can be the norm.

Perhaps you've read Terrance O'Hanlon's article on the toothpaste company who spent loads of money to solve a problem on the assembly line. It's a great case study for the kind of ingenuity young adults have if we'll just turn them loose to think on their own.

*A toothpaste factory had a problem. They sometimes shipped empty boxes without the tubes inside. Due to the automated production line, a box would make it to the end of the belt from time to time without a tube of toothpaste in it. This created angry customers.*

*The CEO met with the top people in the company, and they decided to hire an outside engineering consultant to solve their empty boxes problem. Six months (and $8 million) later, they had a solution. They solved the problem by using high-tech precision scales that would sound a bell and flash lights whenever a tooth-paste box weighed less than it should. The line would stop and someone would walk over and yank the defective box out of it, pressing another button to restart the line.*

*Weeks later, the CEO noticed that not one empty box was making its way to the end of the line and shipped out. Apparently, the system was getting perfect results. Yet, when the CEO and the foreman looked more closely at the numbers, they noticed that after the first week, not one box was even removed from the line. They had paid a huge sum of money, and now realized there were no empty boxes to identify.*

*What's up with that?*

*It turns out, when the foreman and CEO walked to the part of the line where the scales were positioned, they saw a young employee seated next to an electric fan he'd set up beside the scales. Evidently, this young man got tired of walking over to remove the empty box and turn the system back on when the bell rang— so he purchased a $20 fan to simply blow the empty boxes off the belt.[1]*

Ingenuity comes when it must. In the end, a young team member used his own ingenuity and solved the eight-million-dollar problem with an inexpensive electric fan. Now that's what I call metacognition. It requires descriptive leaders to invite team members into the problem-solving process. Here's how they do it. Descriptive leaders:

1. Constantly cast vision for the big picture to their teams.
2. Communicate problems to their teams as they arise.
3. Share the gritty details of budgets and boundaries that must be managed.

4. Assign people with suitable strengths to solve relevant problems.

5. Stop demanding people take assigned steps and let them create their own steps.

6. Equip people to be resourceful, sharing stories of problems solved cheaply.

7. Reward every effort where someone solves a problem innovatively.

8. Serve as consultants, not controllers. They let people seek them out if they need help.

## "Clean Windows"

One of our *Habitudes®* is called "Clean Windows." Think about the term clean windows. Is the word *clean* a verb or an adjective? Is it an action or a goal? Great leaders target outcomes, not inputs. They are descriptive (using adjectives) not prescriptive (using verbs) in their visions.

Consider this scenario. When you ask someone to wipe down the windows, they will wipe them. The windows may end up with streaks all over them or smudges in certain places, but the person gave you exactly what you asked for—they wiped them.

Instead of telling people what to do, lasting leaders describe the outcomes they hope for and allow people to surprise them with their innovation.

When you ask a team member to make the window crystal clear, they will deliver what you asked for—a beautiful window. The trick is how they clean that window is up to them.

Instead of telling people what to do, lasting leaders describe the outcomes they hope for and allow people to surprise them with their innovation. There are, of course, some young or inexperienced members of Generation Z that need leaders to be prescriptive in their instruction, at least initially. In those cases, leaders must suggest particular steps their young leaders could take and, as they mature, gradually turn more and more of the decision-making process over to them. Most of the time, however, we leaders can become far too controlling, obsessively trying to ensure that Generation Z pursues goals exactly as we would do them ourselves.

Management by objective is my leadership of choice. It occurs when a leader describes an outcome they want to see happen—an objective they desire—and turns a person loose to go after it. The benefits of this style of leadership are many:

- The learners get to use their creativity and gifts.
- The learners begin to own the project themselves.
- The learners likely achieve the goal faster doing it their way.
- The learners spend more energy because they chose the method.

For leaders, the shift must be to:

- Focus on outcomes (ultimate goals) rather than inputs (specific tasks).
- Focus on scoring accomplishments, not merely accomplishing activities.
- Focus on teaching them how to think, not just what to think.
- Focus on describing a goal, not prescribing a role.

"Make sure all the windows in the front of our store are crystal clear at all times," is much better than, "Wipe down the windows with that rag over there when you get a chance." The second statement is plain and simple but does not expect much from the recipient. They are merely following orders. They will likely choose to do the bare minimum just to get by. The first directive above expects excellence and clearly states the desired outcome; it leaves results up to the person the task is given to.

Question: How could you manage more often by objective?

## The Three Elements That Make Metacognition Work

There are at least three elements that make metacognition work effectively with today's emerging generation. I recommend you include these elements as you lead them in your context:

1. **Risk—The element of trying something difficult with no guarantee of success.**

The four cardinal qualities of the adolescent mind are novelty seeking, social engagement, increased emotional intensity, and creative exploration. Dr. Daniel Siegel acknowledges there are upsides and downsides to these. The downside is teens are three times more likely to be injured than adults; their brains push them to try new things, whether they're proven or unproven. The upsides are teens are naturally drawn to what we're discussing here—metacognition. In fact, because today's students live in an empowering world, it's the perfect time to leverage metacognition.

Alex Moore serves as a pastor at New Life Community Church in Kansas City. A few years ago, he wanted to teach this very lesson to the students in his youth group, so he took a group of them out of town on a leadership retreat. After a session, he asked the teens to get into a van, leave their cell phones behind, and ask no questions. He then drove them to a train stop, handed them a manila envelope with some cash in it and drove off. Inside the envelope were instructions to board the MetroLink train in St. Louis and take it to Union Station where he would meet them.

None of these teens had ever been on a train or to a train station. They were forced out of their comfort zone—to sink or swim. And they swam. Alex said he was curious to see how each student would respond when he met them later. He saw both relief and a newfound confidence as they stepped off the train. For some, it was the first time they had risked anything. Their take away? They took a little risk and owned it.

Question: How could you wisely increase the level of risk your students take?

2. **Responsibility—The element of ownership that requires ingenuity.**

Too many students today are *renting* their education rather than *owning* it. One of the advantages of equipping students to practice metacognition is that they begin to own what they're learning and how they learn it. And when you own something instead of renting it, you take much better care of it. When students take responsibility for a problem, creativity comes out, energy surfaces, and ideas flow.

Julian Cantu was just thirteen when his mom was diagnosed with breast cancer. He saw her tumor swell, and it caused his mother to lose both of her breasts before she became cancer-free. At first, Julian felt helpless as a middle school kid. Within a few months, however, he decided he had to do something

 Too many students today are renting their education rather than owning it.

besides hope. He was going to help. Julian found out that, unlike his mother, each year millions of women discover they have breast cancer too late. With the adults in his life—including his mom—encouraging him to own the issue, Julian got to work. Within a couple of years, Julian assembled three friends to form the company *Higia Technologies*, which has developed a wearable device that may be able to detect the early signs of cancer. The prototype, EVA bra, has sensors that can be attached to a normal bra. The sensors identify changes in skin temperature and elasticity, which are among many known signs of the disease. Julian and his invention are getting international attention. Wow. It's amazing what can happen when teenagers decide to own a problem.

**Question:** How could you increase the level of responsibility your students take?

3. **Reward—The element of satisfaction (internal or external) when one achieves.**

The stakes we attach to student's work are seldom discussed but paramount to engaging them and keeping their attention. By the time most kids reach adolescence, they have been given trophies, ribbons, and plaques just for participation and, quite frankly, many find it difficult to conjure up passion for another meaningless reward. We must raise the stakes for what we ask kids to do.

- **The magnitude must increase** (the importance· of the task).

- The difficulty must increase (the fact that few can do this).
- The outcomes must increase (the reward or result in the end).

When our requests fail to include genuinely high stakes—ones that are artificial, not real—they will almost certainly disengage. This is one of the reasons the military is so attractive to young men and women. It involves high stakes and rewards for succeeding.

Two years ago, I heard Coach Mike Krzyzewski, Duke's men's basketball coach, talk about his experience coaching the 2016 U.S. men's Olympic basketball team in Rio de Janeiro. When he first took the job, he was concerned about how to motivate these young men who'd played college ball and now were making millions in the NBA What more could they want? What else could he do to inspire them after all they'd already achieved?

Suddenly, he had an epiphany. He decided to take his team to Arlington Cemetery in Virginia. He planned to walk through the graveyard, reading the epitaphs of those who'd given their lives in service to their country. He hoped some inspiring challenge would come to mind while there that he could relay to his team. While the players began walking through the cemetery, Coach K noticed a young soldier peering down at a grave some distance away. He walked over and greeted the soldier, asking what brought him to Arlington. The young man simply pointed down at a few of the gravestones and said, "I should be there with them."

The soldier then explained how his comrades had given their lives saving him, and now, the least he could do was pay tribute to them. In that moment, Coach K got his inspiration. He asked if the soldier would be willing to take a few minutes to talk to his basketball team about what it means to represent your country.

This experience was exactly what that U.S. basketball team needed. They heard from someone who understood high stakes and who's offered his life for their country. The team played with passion in Rio and came home with gold medals. I'd say they represented their country pretty well.

**Question:** How could you increase the level of reward your students experience?

## Moving from Outside-In to Inside-Out Motivation

To get this right we must make a shift in how we motivate students. We must move from outside-in to inside-out motivation. Let me illustrate. New research confirms what I had suspected for years. Even though students in Generation Z desire to make the world a better place, volunteering is down, not up. Here is a summary of the 2018 findings from the Do Good Institute at the University of Maryland's School of Public Policy:

- Nearly half of incoming college freshmen surveyed wanted to become leaders in their communities and 80 percent indicate a desire to help others. Sadly, volunteerism and charitable giving among high school students has declined since 2005.

- Though eleven states require students to be involved in service-learning projects, there appears to be little correlation between state policy requirements and the rate of volunteerism; in fact, earlier studies suggest high school students who are required to volunteer are less likely to do so.

- Schools may benefit from more intergenerational activities as teens whose parents volunteer were more likely to volunteer as well. Volunteerism among parents, however, has declined.[2]

Carey is a vivid example of these findings. She is a busy rising freshman in college, who told me she wants to major in international business so she can help people who live in developing nations. She also said that her motives were altruistic.

So, does she plan to volunteer this year, helping needy people nearby? Unfortunately, no. Carey performed community service projects in high school, but mostly to pad her application so she could get into a good college. Now that she's made it, she'll be too busy getting good grades and "rushing" a sorority.

Now, don't get me wrong. Carey is a great young lady and a very good student. The problem is her motives for volunteering weren't good enough reasons to keep her involved, once she reached a personal goal. When I dug a little deeper, I saw her motivations for involvement were:

1. She knew it would look good on her resume and college applications.

2. Community service projects were required at her high school.

## Simple Ways to Leverage Metacognition

I believe we'll inspire servant leadership better from within, instead of through a requirement or the fact that it will look good on a resume, which is outside-in motivation. This means moving students be less concerned with how it appears to others and more concerned with what it does for others. Inside-out motivation is about leveraging metacognition with your students through some simple changes:

1. **Try to *expose* rather than *impose*.**
   Instead of making service a requirement they must perform, what if you exposed kids to genuine needs in the community and let them decide what to do about them? Kids learn on a need-to-know basis, and exposing them creates the need to know.

2. **Seek to spot any signs of *interest* or *passion*.**
   As you expose them to various new environments, identify their interests. Ellen Parr once said, "The cure for boredom is curiosity."[3] Fuel the fire of their curiosity. Your part is not to manufacture it but to point it out when you see it.

3. **Try *inspiration* to cultivate *aspiration*.**
   Inspiration is closely linked to aspiration. If you inspire students with stories of leaders who served their communities, they tend to aspire to similar actions. Students will surprise you with their ambition when their imagination is ignited.

4. **Try *descriptive* leadership instead of *prescriptive* leadership.**
   Rather than prescribing the steps students must take in a volunteer program, why not let them describe a goal they came up with, then decide the steps together? Better learning happens when it's just in time rather than just in case.

5. **Try *empathy* instead of *duty* as the motivator.**
   This is inside-out motivation. Empathy develops when students see things from another's perspective and personally experience the need for action, not when they forced to follow a required plan. Empathy transforms motivation from mental gymnastics to heartfelt engagement.

Why is it better to introduce or create an environment where students discover on their own what they must learn? Because when they do, the epiphany itself becomes memorable. The idea may not be polished or perfect; it may be incomplete. But when students walk into a situation where they uncover an insight that will help them grow in a relevant manner, that insight will remain with them for years. Maybe for life. They did the work. They discovered the valuable idea. They initiated the effort.

Students support what they help create.

Remember, students support what they help create. We must let them determine what and how they'll get involved (employing meta-cognition) and turn them loose. Let them explore, stumble, and even fail en route to their solutions. Let them own it.

## Changing the Way We Communicate

For all the reasons we've outlined in this book, we must teach and train Generation Z differently than past generations of students. Because they've been exposed to so much information so early in their lives, mere verbal instruction may not only be *redundant* but *disengaging* to today's 'screenagers.'

Their growth won't happen through a lecture, but through a learning experience. We believe that while Generation Z's brain is migrating from *concrete thinking* to *abstract thinking*, we must begin practicing adult learning (andragogy) more than children's learning (pedagogy) centered around sitting in chairs and listening. Unfortunately, the way most of us learned to "teach" was with pedagogical practices. By the time they reach ten to twelve years old (and beyond) we must begin shifting toward andragogy—"andr," meaning "man" and "agogos," meaning "leading." You can see the value of this transition when you consider the principles of andragogy:

1. Instruction focuses more on process and less on content.
2. It utilizes experiences more than explanations in the learning process.
3. Case studies, role-playing and simulations are most useful.

4. Spaced repetition enables students to retain what they've learned.

5. Instructors adopt a role of facilitator or resource more than commander.

## Your Game Plan: Letting Generation Z PROVE Themselves

Below are five ingredients that set the stage for Generation Z to practice metacognition. I use this as a sort of plan of engagement. It's a checklist to make sure my communication will be effective. They must PROVE themselves:

### P—Problem

Students engage when their work stems from a real-world problem.

### R—Relationships

Students engage when connecting and sparring with others in the learning process.

### O—Ownership

Students engage when they determine the course they should take to reach the goal.

### V—Visuals

Students engage as their imagination is sparked by images, metaphors, and stories.

### E—Experience

Students engage when learning involves experiences and project-based learning.

**Talk It Over:** How can you better practice these ingredients?

## Sensory Stimulation

Generation Z is especially predisposed to engage with sensory stimulation. Their portable devices have induced this bias in them, and they respond well to teachers and leaders who employ it.

This means we would do well to incorporate unique images, to utilize mnemonic devices, and to employ other visual stimuli like colors as a way to help them remember information. After all, the human brain loves colors and visuals, which can help it process and retain information more efficiently.

Part of the reason for the success of the *Habitudes®* curriculum is that they teach students through a unique image that represents a timeless principle. Students can remember them because they think in pictures and they can teach them to others because images allow for their own interpretation of the principle. In addition, because pictures are worth a thousand words, they spark conversation which leads to experiences. And those experiences we've seen can change their lives.

## Making School Come Alive

Paoli High School is one of the schools Growing Leaders has partnered with to help students learn leadership as teenagers. The Paoli High School students regularly discuss what they've learned and have taken application to a whole new level.

Allow me to explain.

Instructor Cory Scott was a bit frustrated over his current role. He was teaching English and Math—but having a difficult time translating those subjects to real life. That is until he got an idea. After talking to his son about a pig he showed at the 4-H Fair, Cory decided to use the pig to not only teach his core subjects but to also teach life and leadership. Yes, it all started with a pig named Ms. Boots.

Cory's students set up a small pen on the property and began learning genetic selection, husbandry, feeding, and even breeding. In fact, Ms. Boots was due to give birth to her baby pigs during Christmas break—and the teens didn't want to miss it. So, some students came to school during their holiday while others were able to see it on a webcam they set up to capture the birth. While the school is located in a small rural town, over fifteen thousand people tuned in. These students were meeting their academic standards via real-life experiences. This, however, was only the beginning.

The next year, they bought two pigs and later several more. Along the way, the learning expanded—from pigs and livestock to horticulture. Believe it or not, the school cafeteria began serving the pork and vegetables from their farm. Because they had proven themselves through this project, the students eventually became a significant part of the campus culture and even leadership decisions.

I believe this is the way school is supposed to be.

As this real-life learning increased, Cory, his colleagues, and the students decided they needed to build a barn. Unfortunately, the district budget didn't have the budget for such an expense. At first, the students were devastated but later decided to meet with key faculty and administration to see if *they* could raise the money to build the barn. And that's exactly what they did. Cory wrote and told us:

> *We began raising money in November 2017, and as of today (a year later), we have raised $212,450.83. The barn is fully paid for with some extra to cover repairs for our greenhouse and make some upgrades to other facilities. The students have given over 100 presentations, including lobbying at the statehouse, which drew visits from our senator and representative to the school. They've taught agriculture to adults and student groups and love telling our story to anyone that will listen.*

This is what happens when we stop prescribing life to Generation Z and start describing the outcomes, we know they are capable of achieving. They can then see themselves as leaders and take ownership of their lives and learning to a higher level.

# TEN

# Privilege Without Responsibility

*Challenge #3*

In February 2019, a twenty-seven-year-old posted a viral video on You-Tube. Wearing a fake beard and sunglasses, Raphael Samuel announced he was suing his parents because he was conceived without his consent. This was not a joke.

Raphael grew up in India and felt he was entitled to receive payments for the rest of his life since he didn't ask for all the hassles life offers, like going to school and finding a job in the first place. After all, he did not give his permission to be born... right?

So, Raphael felt his parents owed him cash. "I want everyone in India and the world to realize one thing: that they are born without their consent. I want them to understand that they do not owe their parents anything," he said. "If we are born without our consent, we should be maintained for life. We should be paid by our parents to live."

Rafael has embraced a life philosophy called anti-natalism, an increasingly popular yet outlandish ideology that believes it is morally wrong for people to procreate and takes a nihilistic approach towards human life.

What's most strange about the story is Raphael actually liked his parents.

"My life has been amazing," he reflected. But he doesn't see why he should have to endure the annoyances of life just because his parents wanted a child. His mother and father, both attorneys, said they admired his temerity, but his mom added: "If Raphael could come up with a rational explanation as to how we could have sought his consent to be born, I will accept my fault."[1]

I think Rafael Samuel takes entitlement to a whole new level. Unfortunately, he illustrates quite well the paradigm of a new generation.

## How Did We Get Here?

As history has evolved, our lives have changed. As human civilization marches forward, we develop new methods and technologies to make life easier, swifter, and more efficient. We call it progress. The unintended consequence of such progress is that as we improve the ease of our lives, we also start to subconsciously adjust our expectations. We expect life to be better, faster, and more efficient. And as expectations increase so does our sense of entitlement. We feel completely entitled to items past generations dreamed about. We feel entitled to...

- Indoor plumbing, heating and air conditioning
- Good customer service
- High-speed Internet and technology
- Perks like money, jobs, and special benefits

The further we climb upward on Abraham Maslow's Hierarchy of Human Need, the more we embrace and expect self-actualization. It's our right. Certainly not all, but many Americans have progressed beyond survival and now have gotten used to luxuries that people in developing nations do not yet enjoy. Call it an entitlement, one that has been progressing with each new wave of technological advancement.

- When the agricultural age became the industrial age, we changed.
- When the industrial age became the information age, we changed even more.
- When the information age morphed into the intelligence age (with smart technology), we changed still more.

## Our SCENE Today

I am not suggesting the changes we're talking about are wrong, but imagine what growing up in this world of assumptions and expectations has done to Generation Z. The results aren't good.

Years ago, we at Growing Leaders created two columns to illustrate the challenge our culture has given to kids growing up in the 21st century. While they may enjoy modern luxuries that make life physically easier, the unintended consequences are emotional hardship. Their emotional muscles have atrophied. Check out the columns below. In short, the columns make it clear how a high-tech lifestyle actually fosters entitlement:

| Our world is full of: | Consequently, kids can assume: |
|---|---|
| S—Speed | Slow is bad. |
| C—Convenience | Hard is bad. |
| E—Entertainment | Boring is bad. |
| N—Nurture | Risk is bad. |
| E—Entitlement | Labor is bad. |

I think we all love the modern-day speed and conveniences we experience, but kids today are growing up in a world that is faster and more efficient than ever, which may foster a wrong assumption in them. For instance, as we said above, our world today is full of entertainment. It now travels with us everywhere on our phones. We can watch streamed videos, programs, social media, sports, you name it. Nothing wrong with that, but we've now become used to the stimuli it offers us. We hate to be bored. It has led many in Generation Z to believe that boring is bad. But that's not true. While I remember hating boredom when I was a kid, today we recognize something I did not understand in my teen years. Neuroscientists today tell us that our brains actually need boredom. It is in times of boredom—when we have margin in our day and quiet time to think—that we develop creativity and empathy.[2]

So, today, we sit more. We consume more. We watch more. We virtually connect more. But this hasn't made things better. Our teens experience higher levels of anxiety and fragility than any generation ever before.

**Talk It Over:** Consider again the SCENE chart. How can we start to become countercultural? How do we cultivate life skills that teach Generation Z these things are good, not bad?

## We May Be a Part of the Problem

A news story broke in 2018 that made its way across the country. At first glance, I couldn't believe it. A Florida teacher was fired for refusing to comply with the school's No Zero policy.[3] The school administration had created a rule that even if a student failed to turn any assignment in, he or she still could not receive a zero for the assignment. They would get a 50 percent grade. In short, they should get half credit for doing nothing.

Wait. Is this really true, you ask?

Yes, it is. In fact, Mrs. Tirado wrote a note on her classroom whiteboard upon her termination that simply shared the facts with her students:

> *Bye kids. Mrs. Tirado loves you and wishes you the best in life. I have been fired for refusing to give you a 50% for not handing anything in.*

What were they thinking? My guess is this school came up with the policy for the same reasons that many similar policies are created: they don't want to face angry parents. I can't see how any administrators could have invented such a hollow rule as this unless parents drove them to do it. The same parents, I am told by administrators across the country, who confront teachers for talking harshly to their children. They advocate for their misbehaving children; they even do homework for their kids. I can't be the only one who's entered a Starbucks and seen parents working on eighth-grade homework. These kinds of actions are sending the wrong message: *You can get something for doing nothing.*

When we create policies like, this students quickly conclude:

- They can literally do no work at all and get some credit.
- The school will acquiesce to parents who bully the educators.
- They can expect the same treatment as an adult—something for nothing.

Let's ponder that final one. Does this grading policy resemble anything remotely like the world they will enter as an adult? Fast forward with me into the future. A recent graduate enters the workforce, with this grading policy as a backdrop. Her supervisor gives her an assignment and a deadline. It's part of a bigger project that several team members are collaborating on. They're depending on her. When the deadline hits, this young professional fails to get anything done. Not only does the entire team fall behind, but they also become resentful and disassociate with her. Gossip spreads about her. She feels bullied and calls mom or dad. Soon, parents are involved with their adult child's workplace, arguing that she can't take this kind of treatment. Only this time, there is no policy like the one she had in school. The company actually gives zeros. In life, it's called getting fired. Suddenly this young female is unemployed and blaming those "mean people" at that company. It's a false narrative, fostered by shortsighted parenting and poor leadership during her childhood and adolescence.

Fast forward into another scenario, painted by this same pitiful school rule. If a student gets a 50 percent grade for doing nothing, do they get 100 percent if they do half the assignment? And if they do the whole assignment, do they get 150 percent? Will they expect special rewards from a supervisor when they only do what is expected?

Mrs. Tirado agrees, "I'm used to kids not handing in their work… and then chasing them until report cards are in to make sure they make it up. But I don't give a grade for nothing." She then concluded, "We're creating monsters out of our children. We give them too much… and people that experience that kind of childhood then that's what you want, you're entitled for the rest of your life."[4]

The bottom line?

Between our rising expectations produced by a high-tech culture and parents who create false expectations about what life is like, children grow into adults who are ill-prepared for life and who carry a sense of entitlement to perks they never earn.

## What Do the Numbers Reveal to Us About Entitlement?

You might be wondering—is this just a handful of stories from an isolated, affluent part of the world? I wish I could say yes. Unfortunately, this sense of entitlement has been increasing in all demographics of our country and many locations across the industrialized world.

Let's examine the issue of teen jobs for a moment. Forty years ago, when I was a teen, I worked a job, starting at age twelve. I rode my bike, delivering newspapers early each morning, and at age sixteen, I flipped hamburgers at a fast-food restaurant. I wasn't alone either. Everyone

one of my friends worked jobs too. It was the only way we'd have any spending money. Today, it's a different story. According to the Bureau of Labor Statistics, today's teens are less likely to be employed than ever before. Almost 60 percent of teens in 1979 had a job, compared to just 34 percent in 2015.[5]

"Fewer teens work during the summer as well: in 1980, 70 percent had a summer job, which sank to 43 percent in the 2010s. The decline in the summer job doesn't seem to be due to the inability to find a job; according to the Bureau of Labor Statistics data, the number of teens who want a summer job but can't find one stayed about the same, but the number who don't want a job has doubled."[6]

It makes one wonder—do these teens get by without any spending money, then? Oh, most seem to find money for clothes, eating out, and portable devices. So, do they get an allowance? Guess again. According to psychologist Jean Twenge, "When teen unemployment began to drop in the 1980s, parents at first responded by giving more teens an allowance. But, after 2000, fewer teens got an allowance and many fewer had money from any job, leaving 20 percent of 17-18-year olds without money of their own to manage."[7]

So, how do they get their money? They just ask mom and dad. "One in five high school seniors asks their parents for what they want instead of managing their own cash flow."[8] For many young adults, they won't experience their first real job until after college.

I realize that millions of high school and college students don't have jobs because of their hectic academic and extra-curricular activity schedules. And while I understand how both of these have expanded, both are facsimiles of real life. They keep a student busy, but that busyness has not translated yet into career readiness. In fact, they often leave a student needing to move back home after graduation. Today 32 percent of eighteen to thirty-four-year-olds live with their parents, compared to 20 percent in 1960.[9]

Did you hear about Michael Rotondo? In May 2018, thirty-year-old Michael was sued by his parents for not moving out of the house when they asked him to. Christina and Mark Rotondo had repeatedly asked their son to move out (He had been there for eight years as an adult.), but he refused. He was paying no rent, and when the judge ruled to evict him, he felt entitled to a six-month notice. The judge, of course, responded that this kind of notice is only applicable to landlords and tenants. Michael's parents felt they'd been gracious, repeatedly asking him to move out and to live on his own, even giving him eleven hundred dollars to find his own apartment. Instead of using it to move out, he spent it on other items. The reports said the parents continued to encourage him to get a job and to take responsibility for his life. In response, he felt it was ridiculous that they'd make such demands of him. How does the saying go? Thirty is the new twenty?

It's just a sad story. While I believe it's a picture of a young man wanting to remain a boy, I also see it as an illustration of parents enabling a sense of entitlement. Something is not right in the parent/child relationship when such realities surface.

- The young adult somehow feels moving out is a punishment.
- The young adult doesn't feel ready for life.
- The established adults must rely on litigation to enforce behavior.

I recognize there are some who actually need to "boomerang." Moving back home after college offers them time to ramp up for life on their own. Tuition debt is larger than ever, and many find it difficult to find jobs that pay enough to cover expenses. In those cases, parents and adult children should strike an agreement and set a mutual deadline for independence. Why? For the health of the young adult who desperately needs to strike out on his own and become the person, he is gifted to be.

I believe this unusual case study can teach us something. Entitlement begins as a lifestyle when children are young. When adults do things for students that they're able to do themselves, adults actually foster an attitude of entitlement and diminish students' sense of empowerment:

- When we tie our five-year-old's shoe when he could do it himself...
- When we rush forgotten gym shorts to school, enabling our kid to forget them again...
- When we negotiate with a high school teacher for an easier assignment...
- When we call an admissions counselor, professor, or coach, to speak on behalf of our child...

These activities sound caring, but they sabotage maturation and leadership development. Often times, these teens become young adults and maintain low self-awareness.

A New York based firm met with a group of recent college graduates to talk about their careers. During the conversation, the potential employer asked the grads this question: *What's the one word HR executives use more than any other to describe the mindset of your generation? It begins with an E. Do you know what that word is?* The young twenty-somethings began thinking out loud. Some said, "entrepreneurial." Others said, "energetic." Still others suggested, "exciting" or "entertaining." Not one of them guessed the correct answer, which was entitled.[10]

**Talk It Over:** What do you do that may increase students' sense of entitlement? What can we do to rightsize their assumptions and entitlement?

## INVERSE RELATIONSHIPS

First, I believe it's important to recognize the inverse relationships that occur when students feel entitled to benefits or perks in life. When certain realities expand, others shrink. Let's take a look at some of these inverse relationships. Once you digest them, consider sparking a conversation with your students about them, admitting that we *all* battle, at least a little bit, an attitude of entitlement.

### The Inverse Relationship Between Entitlement and Resilience

After observing people, both young and old, who possess a deep sense of entitlement, I've noticed they become fragile people over time. When life was tougher, they were correspondingly more robust. As life grew more convenient, they weakened emotionally, physically, and intellectually. In fact, in order to stay physically fit today, most of us have to belong to a fitness center or gym.

Gratitude improves emotional and physical health and can strengthen relationships and communities.

In a more convenient world, staying in shape takes extra intentional effort. It makes sense, doesn't it? It is challenging to repeatedly bounce back and work for something that I assumed should have been mine from the start.

## The Inverse Relationship Between Entitlement and Gratitude

When students feel entitled to perks, they are far less apt to thank anyone for them. Dr. Robert Emmons' team from U.C. Davis found that people who view life as a gift and consciously acquire an attitude of gratitude experience multiple advantages.[11] Gratitude improves emotional and physical health and can strengthen relationships and communities. Some strategies include keeping a gratitude journal, learning prayers of gratitude, and using visual reminders. "Without gratitude, life can be lonely, depressing and impoverished," says Emmons. "Gratitude enriches human life. It elevates, energizes, inspires, and transforms. People are moved, opened, and humbled through expressions of gratitude."

## The Inverse Relationship Between Entitlement and Happiness

It shouldn't shock us that as our sense of entitlement increases, our happiness decreases. In fact, disappointment replaces happiness because we feel we are constantly failing to receive benefits we should be receiving. The more entitled I feel I am to resources, benefits, and opportunities, the more I invite misery into my life, as life frequently will not give us all we feel we deserve. We won't experience all the rights we want, all the privileges we want, or all the friendships we want. We are, in fact, ensuring an outcome of hurt, pain, and disillusionment. It has been said that the happiest people are not the ones who have the most but those who need the least.

**Talk It Over:** Do you recognize any of these inverse relationships in Generation Z?

## SYMPTOMS OF ENTITLEMENT

As I've noted above, possessing a sense of entitlement brings expectations and assumptions with it. Without even thinking, we develop these expectations that naturally lead to problems. We expect more from other people. We assume we deserve more from society and government. We desire more and believe we need more to get by. In fact, we get used to more. I specifically remember as a young kid in the 1960s when my dad first bought a car with air conditioning in it. Up until that point, air conditioning was a luxury. We could ride in that car on a hot, August day and be completely comfortable. We felt like royalty.

Today, we've gotten used to it.

Getting used to more, however, also has its upside. That same car with air conditioning also had seatbelts. We all had to get used to seatbelts and usually needed someone to remind us to wear them. Today, we rarely even think about putting them on. It's natural. We've gotten used to them.

These common additions influence our expectations. Allow me to provide the sequence of how this reality works inside of us.

1. **Happiness in life is pretty much about managing expectations.**
   Managing emotions and managing people often boil down to managing expectations. I am not suggesting we must lower them, just adapt and adjust them. For example, if a student's goal is to have a nice car by the time he or she is sixteen, he may be ambitious. But if he or she feels entitled to that reality, he may be in for a rude awakening.

2. **Conflict occurs when there's a distance between expectations and reality.**
   We've all witnessed this. If you told your spouse you'd meet him or her for dinner at 7:00 pm and arrived at 7:10 pm, it's likely not a big deal. If you showed up at 9:30 pm, you've got a hard conversation awaiting you. It's not that your spouse can't survive without you but that you created an expectation for something different than reality.

3. **Conflict expands when that distance expands.**
   The greater the distance between what a student feels entitled to and what actually happens, the greater the chance that conflict will mount. This is why so many parents and teachers cave, giving in to the wants of students. We want to avoid the conflict even though we know they need to learn to adjust their demands.

Somehow, millions inside this emerging generation have expectations of what life should be like that are not even close to reality. Some become disillusioned with life and begin down a path of cynicism and bitterness. What is most sad is we adults have frequently been unwilling to put in the work to combat this sense of entitlement in our young. It is work, especially when the rest of our culture screams that kids deserve everything to be handed to them. Some of the most common symptoms of entitlement in our students are:

- **Impatience** (I want it now.)
- **Laziness** (I don't want to work for it.)
- **Comparison** (I want it because everyone else has it.)
- **Fragility** (I want someone else to fix my problems.)
- **Irresponsibility** (I don't want to clean up my messes.)
- **Anger** (I am mad that people won't give me what I want.)
- **Disillusionment** (I want someone else to make me happy.)

**Talk It Over:** Do your students battle any of these symptoms?

I wonder how much Raphael Samuel's life might have been different if his parents had led him differently? Could he have seen his life as something to be thankful for, instead of something to be subsidized? If only our students could experience the great joy of being alive, seeing each positive part of their life as a privilege to be thankful for rather than a right that is just as expected.

Consider this truth that my friend David Drury first proposed: *Kids cannot be disillusioned until they are first illusioned.* By this, he meant that we only become miserable and disappointed when we've embraced some fictional expectation or illusion about what life should be like. The sooner we scrap those illusions, the faster kids can get on with the pursuit of what is genuinely satisfying.

Let's examine how we can help this generation embrace a genuinely rewarding life.

# ELEVEN

# Breaking Free from the Shackles of Entitlement

When our two children were in high school, my wife and I determined we would let them choose which college they would like to attend. We were like many parents who wanted our kids to exercise ownership of their education, starting with where they would actually get it. I traveled with them to preview a handful of campuses, and wouldn't you know it, they both chose private universities out of state.

My wife and I saw this as an opportunity to both provide for them and also find ways to let them participate in taking responsibility for their decisions. So, I remember sitting down with my daughter, Bethany, to look over the available scholarships she could apply for and agreeing that she would have to work in between semesters in order to afford her choice. She ended up getting a presidential scholarship *and* followed through on the jobs. My son, Jonathan, chose a college in Los Angeles that was even more expensive. So, I made this offer, "You can attend this school all four years, working jobs in between semesters. Or you can attend a community college and live at home for two years, and we can split the money I save on tuition." It was an obvious choice for Jonathan. He took the money!

Our goal in both cases was for them to experience some level of responsibility. I love how parents and educators are combating a sense of entitlement in students by approaching decisions this way. In preparation for this book, we crowdsourced thousands of caring adults to ask what they did to empower kids to share responsibility for choices.

One mom shared how her young son paid for the karate lessons he took. Extended family members would pay him for tasks he'd do on their property. He built skills to do all kinds of odd jobs and got tips when he did them with excellence. In time, he earned enough money to cover registration for the extra-curricular activity he desired.

Another parent created a layaway plan for all the portable devices and video games his kids wanted but could not afford to purchase. He secured the gadgets to make sure they wouldn't be sold out, but they had to make payments and only got them when they had paid them off in full.

One educator created a classroom experience that resembled the environment her high school students would experience in their careers. They worked in teams; they could earn "bonus bucks" to purchase items they wanted in the dining hall when performing beyond expectations and received monthly reviews of their work.

All of these experiences share something in common. The kids stopped assuming they deserved something and began assuming responsibility. Their assumptions changed.

## WHAT EVERY ENTITLED KID NEEDS

I believe the best way to begin battling a sense of entitlement is with the conversations we mentioned in the previous chapter about the symptoms and causes of entitlement. Once you've hosted these conversations with students, I suggest you work on the following three objectives. Each step enables a student to overcome a false sense of entitlement and to mature in a healthy manner.

### 1. Work That Provides Them with a Big-Picture Perspective

Step back and reflect for a moment. If kids act entitled, it's usually because we adults have allowed them to do so. Someone didn't curb that attitude early on, and now as adolescents, it is in full throttle. But where did it begin?

A sense of entitlement in people tends to happen when two realities collide:

1. When a person doesn't comprehend the big picture.

2. When a person has not experienced life's normal hardships.

According to research from Paul Harvey, associate professor of organizational behavior at the University of New Hampshire, "A lot of what contributes to a sense of entitlement appears to take root very early in life—early childhood experiences in school and with parents... the mentality of 'if something bad happens, it must not be my fault; if something good happens, it must be because of me.'"[1]

Further, "Comprehensive studies of large swaths of different generations... found higher levels of narcissism in the younger generation."[2] One of the reasons we see such a high rates of entitlement among youth today is the rising levels of narcissism among them. Adults of all kinds—parents, teachers, coaches, youth workers, and administrators—have contributed to this mammoth sense of entitlement because we feared being the "bad cop."

Perspective only comes when resources are earned, not merely given to our young. Earning provides both a big-picture perspective on how most of the world lives and exposes kids to real-life challenges that reveal how life really works. While I believe we should resource students with what they need to become adults, the more resources we give them, the less resourceful they tend to become.

"In a series of studies using surveys that measure psychological entitlement and narcissism, University of New Hampshire management professor Paul Harvey found that young adults scored 25% higher than respondents ages 40 to 60 and a whopping 50% higher than those over 61. In addition, youth were twice as likely to rank in the top 20% in their level of entitlement—the "highly entitled range"—as someone between 40 and 60, and four times more likely than" an elder.[3] My conclusion? Without work, kids find it difficult to perceive life correctly. As a group, Harvey says, "They are characterized by a 'very inflated sense of self' that leads to 'unrealistic expectations' and ultimately, 'chronic disappointment.'"[4]

## 2. Gratitude Over What They Already Have

As we discussed earlier, there is an inverse relationship between gratitude and entitlement. Author and researcher Dr. Robert Emmons from U.C. Davis offers some intriguing evidence for what gives life both perspective and meaning.

In a word, it is gratitude.

It is, according to Emmons, a "chosen attitude." We must be willing to recognize and acknowledge that we are the recipients of an unearned benefit.[5] This is especially rare among middle-class high school and college students who've grown up in a world that's revolved around them—one that allows them to build a platform via social media without displaying value, one that repeatedly communicates they are awesome and deserve trophies just for participating. Our world now naturally cultivates a sense of entitlement. And entitlement is virtually the opposite of gratitude. As I feel more entitled, my gratitude shrinks in proportion.

Research indicates that gratitude is not merely a positive emotion. It can improve our health if cultivated. It requires students, however, to give up a victim mentality in order to overcome a sense of entitlement. When someone feels entitled to something, there's little need for gratitude. *I don't need to thank someone; I deserved the gift. In fact, these people are lucky to have me around. I'm amazing.*

When we examine the areas where students struggle today, they are areas in which gratitude would actually aid them in their growth:

- Energy levels and motivation.
- Mental and emotional well-being.
- Academic achievement.
- Healthy, long-term relationships.
- Dealing with tragedy and crisis.

In one study, researchers had participants test a number of different gratitude exercises, such as thinking about a living person for whom they were grateful, writing about someone for whom they were grateful, and writing a letter to deliver to someone whom they were grateful for. Participants in the control condition were asked to describe a room in their house (neutral). Participants who engaged in a gratitude exercise showed increases in positive emotion immediately after the exercise, with this result being strongest for participants who were asked to think about a person whom they were grateful for. What's more, participants who already had grateful personalities showed the greatest benefit from the gratitude exercises. It was discovered that gratitude had less to do with how much a person received or possessed and more to do with an attitude. In other words, it's a state of mind.[6]

Further, cultivating an attitude of gratitude can actually combat other negative emotions in teens such as cynicism, resentment, and anger.

Almost twenty years ago, I led a learning community of high school students as well as a second group of university students in Atlanta. As I noticed a sense of entitlement in many of them, I decided to host some gratitude exercises similar to the examples above. I had those students write down people and experiences they were grateful for and then write out paragraphs explaining why they were thankful. This forced them to think about the specifics of their good fortune. Finally, I asked each student to call a person on their list and actually thank them for these specific reasons.

This became a moving experience.

At first, the conversations were light-hearted and even jovial. The sarcasm in the conversations let me know they were close with the person on the other end of the phone. When the students began to describe in detail why they were so grateful, however, the tone began to change. It became both serious and emotional. Most of the students shed tears, as this was the first time they'd ever reflected on what others had done for them. Their newfound perspective fostered a spirit of humility, generosity, and even deeper gratitude. It was such a moving experience. I never sensed an ounce of entitlement the rest of the year.

## 3. Rights Combined with Responsibility

Today, we live in a unique period of time when we've taught our kids to advocate for their rights (which is a good thing), but we did so without combining it with equal responsibilities. By this I mean, we've often neglected to teach that all rights come with corresponding responsibilities. In 2018, Cheryl, one of our blog readers, replied to an article I posted on this topic. She's noticed that our society feeds the problem.

> *In our community, children can get their own library card. At the age of 13, the library asserts that they have a right to privacy and librarians aren't allowed to tell parents what books their children have checked out. Yet, if the book gets lost or is turned in late, who is responsible for paying the fine? The parents are, of course. Obviously, families can navigate this and other scenarios with their own rules and expectations. It just makes it harder when our culture and public institutions promote the idea that students have a right to their independence and privacy, but parents have a responsibility to continue supporting them financially, no matter what.*

This leads to an imbalanced worldview and sends many of them off to college with a sense of entitlement. For our kids' sake, we must teach them an important truth. Every right has a corresponding responsibility. We must help them succeed without violating how life works. Society is full of equations at work and in life; there are benefits and consequences to our actions. This is why we must find age-appropriate methods to enable them to see how these equations work:

1. A misused library card that penalizes the parent isn't the best method. The child enjoys the right to privacy without the responsibility for that privacy. I believe this is unhealthy for an adolescent whose brain is still developing.

2. A school that prevents teachers from giving poor grades for poor work isn't helpful, like the Florida teacher who was fired for refusing to give a 50 percent grade to teens who turned in no assignment. Rights without responsibilities.

3. A student whose parents purchase them a car and then pays for all expenses (a marvelous right for any teen) without an accompanying responsibility of purchasing gas or insurance is not helpful. Kids gain a wrong preview of life and adulthood.

For some reason, our contemporary culture has gotten this issue confused. Adolescents and young adults actually need responsibilities to mature. This is what produces great citizens. Insisting they take responsibility actually communicates belief in them; we believe they are capable of doing it.

The U.S. Declaration of Independence states we have a right to life, liberty, and the *pursuit* of happiness, not happiness itself. It is that pursuit that often cultivates a sense of responsibility. We should have a guarantee of the freedom to look for work or create work, but no one owes anyone a guarantee of work. We must expand the limited worldview that too many students have adopted. Like so many others, I now wonder if our nation needs both a Bill of Rights and a Bill of Responsibilities.

 We must prepare young adults for a world that has both rights and responsibilities.

My big idea here is not to refuse students mercy or second chances when they make mistakes. Adults can always, and often should, offer such grace in particular situations. What I am saying is we must prepare young adults for a world that has both *rights* and *responsibilities*. I often see high school or college students being fed a diet of rights without any mention of duties. One college instructor told me a student demanded a good grade in his class because his parents paid the tuition. This student could never have arrived at this conclusion unless he was given an unhealthy perspective of how life works.

If you want to develop a balance between rights and responsibilities with Generation Z, consider utilizing some of these suggestions.

1. Whenever you create a new rule, be sure you communicate both the right and the responsibility for that rule.

2. Whenever a younger person demands a right, determine what the accompanying responsibility should be before you give it to him.

3. Teach students that rights are earned through trust. If parents pay for their child's phone, they have a right to look at their social media account. Over time, the child may earn the right to privacy through his trustworthy actions.

4. Consistently communicate how healthy lifestyles operate.

   - When teens turn eighteen, they can enlist to serve in the military, but they also gain the right to vote.

   - When a person only rents an apartment, they're not responsible for the ground's maintenance. When they buy a home, they are. They own it.

   - When a person earns an income, they are responsible to pay taxes on it. Without a job, there's no responsibility to pay income taxes.

Everything is a trade-off. That's how life works. That's how choices work. When we provide a life with only one of the two (rights or responsibilities without the other), we do a disservice to our young adults. Rights and responsibilities are navigated best through a trusting relationship between the student and adult. In the end, this diminishes a sense of entitlement in teens and young adults.

## One Last Personal Reason to Help Them Overcome Entitlement

I wonder if kids' sense of entitlement may be connected to some of their struggles with both sadness and depression. While, there are far deeper reasons for these negative emotions, even chemical reasons, could there be a link?

A recent study on entitlement, a personality trait characterized by exaggerated feelings of deservingness and superiority, connects a sense of entitlement to all sorts of negative emotions. "Entitlement may lead to chronic disappointment," according to researchers from Case Western Reserve University, "and can throw people into a perpetual loop of distress."[7]

One report summarized the data, "The authors [...] found that people who possess high levels of entitlement consistently fall victim to a three-part cycle."[8]

- First, they don't always get everything they think they deserve, leaving them constantly vulnerable to unmet expectations.

- Those unmet expectations are then perceived as injustices, leading to volatile emotions like anger and sadness.

- Finally, to justify those emotions, entitled people reassure themselves of their own specialness. This helps them feel better temporarily but ultimately starts the process all over again.

Julie Exline, PhD, a professor at Case Western Reserve, says, "This research has become increasingly important, as rates of entitlement have risen sharply in the United States in the last 50 years. At the same time, anxiety and depression rates have gone up too. These attitudes are more pervasive in our society, but it's not like they're making us happier."[9]

"Along with perpetual disappointment, the consequences of entitled behavior can also include poor relationships, interpersonal conflicts, and depression," Exline continues. "So much of entitlement is about competition—being better or more deserving than other people," she reported to Health.com. "It really pits you against society, and it can be very isolating."[10]

## What's the Prescription?

There's no easy answer to break free from the shackles of entitlement. It's an attitude fostered by the very culture in which we live. Just watch a commercial on TV and you'll hear that, whatever it is you deserve it. After reviewing the data, however, I found a few steps we (and our students) can take to overcome our sense of entitlement. Talk these over with your students.

1. Since entitlement often involves comparison to others, consider how they are just as special as you are and also deserve some perks. Comparison is a trap.

2. Adopt a service project or take on a job that requires punctuality, discipline, and physical labor. Responsibility usually shrinks a sense of entitlement.

3. Stop and reflect on your own faults and shortcomings. This reminds us of our humanity and the fact that we likely deserve both sunshine and rain.

4. When feeling entitled, reflect on what you're grateful for. In short, think of what you currently have (not what you don't have) and express gratitude.

5. Jot down the areas where you feel entitled. Usually, it isn't every area but certain ones. Then ask yourself, "Why do I feel deserving in this category?"

6. Discuss this research with friends. Invite them to serve as a personal board of directors, holding you accountable to trade entitlement for gratitude.

7. Remember the adage: I cannot be disillusioned unless I am first illusioned. Fight off unrealistic expectations you have of life being easy or comfortable.

The challenge of preparing students for the balance of life between rights and responsibilities will be difficult for many of them. Life is not often easy. It reminds me of a quote from David Brooks in his book *The Road to Character.*

> *No external conflict is as consequential or as dramatic as the inner*
> *campaign against our own deficiencies. This struggle against, say,*
> *selfishness or prejudice or insecurity gives meaning and shape to*
> *life. It is more important than the external journey up the ladder*
> *of success.*[11]

If we can help them focus on bettering themselves, serving others, and pursuing worthwhile goals, we might also get the chance to watch as the disappointment that often comes with entitlement evaporates into gratitude for the often-overlooked good things in life.

I began this chapter by talking about how my children chose their colleges. They had grown up in a nice home in suburban Atlanta and enjoyed the amenities of nice clothes, smart technology, and plenty of good food to eat. In light of this, my wife and I worked to diminish their senses of entitlement, which was visible in many of their friends. One way we did this was to insist they work jobs to pay for extra things they felt they needed. I remember Bethany grumbling about how her friends didn't have to work such jobs; their parents merely gave them everything they wanted. We endured some hard conversations during those high school years as we wrestled with what seemed like a viral sense of entitlement in our area.

It all paid off, however, when Bethany launched into her career.

I'll never forget getting a phone call from her when she worked across the country in the second year of her career. After I greeted her, I asked why she had called me. She paused, and then said, "I guess I just wanted to call and say thanks."

"Well, you're welcome, baby doll. But thanks for what?" I replied.

"Oh, everything," Bethany mused.

When I continued digging for why she'd called in the middle of the day, she finally blurted out, "Well, I see so many colleagues my age who don't have any work ethic. They sit around and complain about their jobs, acting entitled to everything." She paused and continued. "It struck me, you and mom got me ready for this. And, I just wanted to say thanks."

I told Bethany that she had just made my year.

TWELVE

# *Involvement Without Boundaries*

*Challenge #4*

I met two parents while on a family road trip who I believe epitomize a picture of today's culture. Let's call them John and Kerri. They might sound familiar to you. Their three children are the center of their lives. They spend most of their money to resource those children. Both screens and sports occupy the majority of their children's time. Because these parents have some discretionary income, they've built a literal sports complex at their house to enable their kids to excel at the sports of their choice.

Does this sound outlandish to you?

Actually, there is a growing number of affluent parents who "build quasi-professional sports facilities at their homes—in some cases because they believe their children have the potential to become college or professional players and they want to do everything they can to help them get there. While tennis courts and swimming pools have long been *de rigueur* in high-end real estate, more families are building gyms, rinks and courts to help advance their child-athlete's aspirations," reports *The Wall Street Journal*. "Youth sports facilities spending in the U.S. and Canada hit $3.6 billion in 2017, with $320 million of that spent on private facilities in private homes and residential communities, according to WinterGreen Research, a market-research firm in Lexington, Mass."[1]

So many parents are committed to giving their children every possible advantage in life, and they go to huge measures to make it happen.

1. They retain a personal trainer for their children.
2. They build facilities so their kids can play well into the evening.
3. They involve their kids in club sports outside of school.
4. They subscribe to apps and periodicals to provide them with the inside scoop.

So far, so good, right? The problem lies in what message is essentially being communicated to our youth along the way.

The message parents mean to send is simple and clear:

*We believe in you and will spare no expense to develop your talent on behalf of the sport you love most.*

However, the feelings the kids often have are:

*My parents spent a lot to do this for me; I dare not let them down.*
*I can't let my mom and dad know I am burnt out on this activity.*
*I am constantly stressed out to make sure I perform perfectly.*

The truth of the matter is sports are only one part of what's happening to today's kids and adults. Remember, we can binge on anything—and everything—that appears to provide some pleasure to us at the time: sports, portable devices, theatre and dance, video games, social media, Netflix movies, you name it.

We are a generation of extremes. Parents intend to do what's best for the kids, but we frequently don't know how to develop them into emotionally healthy young people. We tend to think: *if a little is good, more is better.* If something makes them happy, then go for it. So, we spend time, money, and emotional energy on a single category, not realizing the possible harm it is doing to our children along the way.

## Overcommitted and Overwhelmed

Today's typical routine involves a mom with her kids after school, racing to practice in the mini-van while eating chicken nuggets she just purchased at a drive-through. Have you seen this? Kids are more active in extra-curricular activities than past generations. "More than 70 percent of parents polled in a 2017 Global News and Ipsos survey say it is important to keep children as busy as possible with structured activities. At the same time, however, more than half of those same parents also said extra-curricular activities can take up too much of their children's schedules."[2]

There is very little margin in the day, almost no quiet time or down-time. The noise and clutter prevent any boredom, but they also prevent any reflective thinking. One seventeen-year-old high school student put it brilliantly, "There are so many activities available today and you sign up for a bunch of them because your friends do too. The trouble us; every one of them demands your soul."

I remember playing little league baseball as a kid. We had one practice a week and a game, whenever it got scheduled, on a Saturday. Recently, a father told me his eight-year-old son (second-grade student) has three practices a week and at least one game every week. When you add that to karate practices and matches, piano lessons and recitals, school play rehearsals and shows, then add school and homework, it's enough to drive any normal student crazy.

My concern is our lack of boundaries.

## GENERATION O.D.

Let's take this a step further. Because kids have unlimited exposure to content and access to activity, it's changing our state of mind. Once students know something is out there being enjoyed by others, they feel they need to enjoy it too. What it has done to their psyche is quite predictable.

### The access has furnished exposure.

Because humankind enjoys unlimited access, they are exposed to ubiquitous content that knows no parameters. Research shows the sheer volume has overwhelmed our children, not to mention the damage some of that content can do to them.

### The exposure has cultivated appetites.

Our appetites can put us on a path with few guardrails. Ultimately, when we act on what we feel we want, it is easy to lose all sense of moderation. Patterns become addictions that migrate from servant to master rapidly.

**The appetites have created assumptions and addictions.**

When you feed an appetite, it becomes stronger. The more we consume, the more we hunger to consume even more. This can create a sense of entitlement to dig further, thanks to the law of diminishing returns. It requires more to satisfy our cravings.

I met with a group of parents before I spoke at an event. Every mom and dad in that group had at least one horror story of their children and mobile phones. One single mom said both her kids had been cyber-bullied to the point that she had to take their phones away and remove one child from the school. Another parent told how his teen daughter had broken up with her boyfriend, and he later sent a filtered photo of her (appearing nude) to hundreds of peers. Still another set of parents shared how their kids met strangers online and later had to take precautions with new social media identities to avoid them. One story that continued to come up was the angst these students endured because they'd been on their phones somewhere between six and eight hours a day.

It's enough to make kids feel overwhelmed and adults who lead them to feel anxious. Are we doing enough for our kids? Are they safe? Are they resourced? In fact, part of the pressure we feel is that we've succumbed to a new "parent report card." Society grades us on whether our kids are happy all the time and whether they experience high self-esteem. Do they not only have everything they need but everything they want? It feels like the unwritten script for how to succeed as a parent.

## Without Boundaries, We All Can Become Addicts

This has produced a population of people who feel entitled to their desires and is full of addictions. We can binge on virtually anything. Millions of young people would say today that they are addicted to something. *I am addicted to…*

- My phone
- Alcohol
- Pornography
- Prescription drugs
- Instagram
- Vaping
- Netflix
- Selfies

Today's kids see this daily and begin believing it's natural. Traditionally, we've used the term OD to stand for overdose. It is most often used in relation to drugs. I believe we're raising Generation OD and the term represents much more.

## WE HAVE UNINTENTIONALLY PRODUCED GENERATION O.D.

1. **They are an over-diagnosed generation**

We have chosen to have our kids diagnosed for every kind of disease, allergy, or psychological condition. Further, our culture has become more educated about medical and mental health terms today. In doing so, people have been able to positively identify and later diagnose anxiety and depression. On the other hand, there have been some negative effects as well. Applying labels to people can create what is called a looping effect. Psychologists use this term to describe the change in a person's behavior who has been labeled, and it becomes a self-fulfilling prophecy for them. Once a symptom has been called to your attention, it is easier and quicker to spot it in the future. Kids frequently know the terminology for medical and psychological conditions and can hide behind them when they simply behave badly. Sometimes a diagnosis prevents them from breaking out of an unhealthy pattern.

2. **They are an on-demand generation**

Today's kids are growing up in an instant world, where entertainment and personal services are automatic and on-demand. We no longer have to wait for a weekly television sitcom if we don't want to; we can be entertained through YouTube and subscribe to Netflix, Hulu, Amazon, and now Apple TV+ and Disney+. You name it; you can stream it. Additionally, we now can request Alexa or Siri to give us information or answers to our questions. Some social scientists quip that we now have a "Google reflex." This actually sounds nice, until we consider how it may influence our students' ability to delay gratification, to wait on some appetite or begin to assume their wants are needs. Patience levels seem to be declining in people of all ages (including me), and our sense of entitlement rises when we are conditioned to expect life to be instant and easy.

### 3. They are an openly-divergent generation

Because they've been exposed to such a variety of inputs and options, kids from Generation Z are transparent about how unlike previous generations they are, especially the Millennials. The term *divergent* means tending to be different or to develop in different directions. And why shouldn't they? They're growing up in a wholly different world than the one adults grew up in. Terror attacks are pinging their phones. They are the first generation that doesn't need adults to get information. As children they saw the first African-American president elected. They feel empowered to experiment with lifestyles and explore online. While I love seeing them find themselves, too many struggle with vacillation and incongruency from managing multiple personas online.

### 4. They are an overly-distracted generation

Growing up in a world of social media, Generation Z is a population with eight-second attention spans, and, according to marketing research firm *Sparks and Honey*, they multi-task on five screens, not two.[3] Comments, posts, memes, text messages, and Snapchat videos are coming at them all the time. They pay attention to so many things but pay little attention to any one item for much time. In addition, they are growing up with parents who don't want them to miss any extra-curricular activity they are interested in (and some they are not interested in). Kids from middle-class Generation Z are growing up involved in multiple teams, club sports, and after school programs. These realities are not evil, but they do leave faculty feeling that students today lack focus, appear superficial, and often, fail to practice critical thinking.

### 5. They are an over-dosed generation

We are raising the most medicated generation of kids in modern history. Diagnosis for anxiety disorders, ADHD, panic attacks, OCD, PTSD, bipolar disorders, eating disorders, psychoses, allergies, and other phobias are now commonplace among the American population. Interestingly, medication has become such a faster and easier option than cognitive behavioral therapy that parents often rush to get their kids on some prescription. In 2016, however, the Center for Disease Control warned parents that Americans may be over-medicating their kids for many diagnoses including ADHD.[5] In 2018, Dr. Nicole Beurkens published an article claiming, "Children with mental health symptoms are overmedicated and under-researched."[6] While I believe many kids do need medication (both of my adult children have taken prescription medications for depression), I believe too many of us have made it a first resort instead of a last one. When this happens, kids often fail to build healthy coping skills.

**Talk It Over:** Do you see any of these OD extremes in the students you lead today?

## Do Your Students Have an Internal or External Locus of Control?

Earlier in this book, we mentioned Dr. Julian Rotter. He developed an assessment that measures our sense of control in the 1950s called *The Internal-External Locus of Control Scale.* "The questionnaire consists of 23 pairs of statements. One statement in each pair represents belief in an *Internal locus of control* (control by the person) and the other represents belief in an *External locus of control* (control by circumstances outside of the person). The person taking the test must decide which statement in each pair is truer. One pair, for example, is the following:

(A) I have found that what is going to happen will happen.

(B) Trusting to fate has never turned out as well for me as making a decision to take a definite course of action.

In this example, choice (A) represents an External locus of control and choice (B) represents an Internal locus of control."[6] People who end up more external are those who somehow believe they are not in control of their lives, that fate or external forces or people are in control and responsible. People with an internal locus are those who believe that their life and success are up to them. They buy into the fact that although there are outside factors, they must pursue and own their future.

By 1963, Rotter and his team concluded that those who score toward the internal end of this scale are measurably more successful in life than those who score toward the external end. They are more likely to get good jobs that they enjoy, take care of their health, and play active roles in their communities. Further, they are less likely to become anxious or depressed. In a research study published a few years ago, "Jean Twenge and her colleagues analyzed the results of several studies that used a scale based on Rotter's work (the *Nowicki-Strickland Scale*) with young people from 1960 through 2002. They found that over this period average scores shifted dramatically (for children aged 9 to 14 as well as for college students) away from the Internal toward the External end of the scale. In fact, the shift was so great that the average young person in 2002 was more External than were 80% of young people in the 1960s. The rise in Externality on Rotter's scale over the 42-year period showed the same linear trend as did the rise in depression and anxiety."[7]

Since 2002, the trend has been even more dramatic. Teen results show an external locus of control more and more over time. Not only do students feel adults (not themselves) are largely in control of their lives and outcomes, but they have a phone with constant pings, rings, and pop-ups, putting them in a reactionary mode. And when people are in a reactionary mode, they tend to develop an external locus of control.

What does this do?

Well, consider your own life for a moment. When things feel out of your control, don't you feel more anxious? In fact, even if teens feel life is in the control of someone they like or trust (like a parent), they feel anxious, as their brains are designed to take more control of their decisions and their lives. In short, by assuming control, some adults are actually fostering anxiety in students' lives.

A 2016 report from the *Center for Collegiate Mental Health* relayed data from 139 colleges and universities. The study found that during the 2015-2016 school year, half of all students surveyed had visited a counselor for mental health concerns.[8]

According to *Live Science*, approximately one in five teens has a serious mental disorder. The problem has become epidemic. One study found that the average high school student in the year 2000 had the same level of anxiety as the average psychiatric patient did in the 1950s, and those rates have only increased in the last decade.[9] Utilizing the Minnesota Multiphasic Personality Inventory (MMPI) to assess psychopathology, Jean Twenge and colleagues found five times as many students in 2007 surpassed clinical cutoffs in one or more mental health categories, compared to those who took the measure several decades ago.[10]

## Survey Says: The Kids Are Not OK

At this point in history, social scientists have collected loads of data on the mental health issues kids face today. In one case study published by *TIME* magazine, Faith-Ann Bishop tells of cutting herself, inflicting wounds on her arms or legs as a response to feeling troubled and overwhelmed. As the report explains, "The pain of the superficial wound was a momentary escape from the anxiety she was fighting constantly, about grades, about her future, about relationships, about everything."[11]

Experts are struggling over how to help the growing number of teens like her.

Anxiety and depression in high school kids have been on the rise since 2012, after several years of plateau.[12] These factors are prevalent across all demographics including urban, suburban, and rural; and even prevalent among both adolescents who are college bound and among those who are not. Teens from different ethnicities and genders are all experiencing the issues associated with angst, although some studies suggest girls are having more trouble with it than boys.[13] Anxiety is now the most common mental-health disorder in the United States, affecting nearly one-third of both adolescents and adults, according to the National Institute of Mental Health.[14]

The Department of Health and Human Services reports that in 2015, some three million teens, ages twelve to seventeen, had at least one *major* depressive episode in the past year. More than two million report experiencing depression that impairs their daily functioning. Sadly, the Child Mind Institute informed us in 2015, that just one in five teens who've had an anxiety disorder get treatment.[15] Most just live with it. Both of my adult children wrestled with depression as they went through adolescence. Both have learned coping skills and needed medication to balance their chemicals. Although they grew up in an emotionally stable home, it was a very real battle. It seems America is just now realizing how serious the issue is.

So, what can we do about it? Let's take a look.

THIRTEEN

# *Coping with the Anxiety Epidemic*

The caring adults I talk with everywhere I travel agree that the number one challenge teens face today is anxiety. We've already discussed common terms like panic attacks, depression, stressed out, obsessions, and anxiety attacks. Many leaders are already working to create ways to counteract these new challenges. One of these leaders is Gary Davison, principal of Lambert High School, who noticed the rise in stress and anxiety levels of his students and decided to think outside of the box. When he asked students why they were so stressed out, many said it was because they had demands on both sides of their school days. They needed as much sleep as possible in the morning (as most teens do) but had several obligations after class with sports, jobs, and other extra-curricular activities. Gary recognized that hundreds of his students couldn't keep up (which was causing their stress), so he decided to schedule a time to catch up for those who couldn't keep up.

Gary told me, "We had seven class periods in our day, but we decided to restructure the day to give an extra hour just to catch up. We shaved a bit of time off the normal schedule to create an eighth period in the middle of the day during lunch, we call Lunch and Learn." During this longer period, the students still eat, but they also have time they can go to the media center and meet with faculty specialists in any discipline to get help and catch up.

If students haven't fallen behind, it's simply a time for them to relax, get homework done, and experience margin in their days. Lambert High School also has therapy dogs that students can pet and play with.

This Lunch and Learn period has done wonders for the students of Lambert High School. Gary told me recently that he's noticed that the stress levels on campus have decreased over the last four years since the school restructured its days. In addition, the social and emotional health of the staff and faculty have improved. The data shows that failure rates have dropped 160 percent! It's been a win for the school, the staff, and the students; and best of all, it didn't cost a nickel to make the change. It just took a leader who was bold enough to think outside of the box.

## Four Ideas to Overcome Anxiety

I think we can make a huge difference if we join Gary on this journey. Below are four big ideas that have been proven as effective responses to student anxiety: margin, mindfulness, moving, and management. These four ideas can be used by any parent, educator, coach, or employer.

### 1. How Do We Help Them Create Margin?

I mention this solution first because it represents the quickest step kids can take to deal with anxiety. The people who maintain a happy life, those who are emotionally healthy, are people who create margin in their calendars. They schedule portions of their days to create space. They remove noise and clutter during those portions of time. They experience solitude. Quiet. Simplicity. They take control of their days instead of remaining at the mercy of all the busyness going on. They are intentional to unplug.

Perhaps nobody saw it coming, but with all the marvelous positive aspects of the smartphone came a subtle and sinister aspect. Too much "stuff" is coming at us each and every day. Between 2008 and 2018, the levels of anxiety in adolescents skyrocketed, measurably. In a relatively short amount of time, the teen experience dramatically shifted.

"What happened that so many more teens, in such a short time, would feel depressed, attempt suicide and commit suicide?" wrote San Diego State University professor Jean Twenge, who authored a study on this issue in a *Washington Post* column. "After scouring several large surveys for clues, I found that all of the possibilities traced back to a major change in teens' lives: the sudden ascendance of the smartphone."

"Teens who spend 5 or more hours online a day were 71 percent more likely than those who spent 1 hour a day to have at least one suicide risk factor," Twenge's research found.[1]

One of our board members told me recently about his high school daughter's report card. Although Rick and his wife both knew she was an intelligent, college-bound teen, her grades were diminishing quickly. After evaluating what was going on in her life, the only controllable they felt might be a reason for this diminishment was the time she was spending on social media. It was about four hours every day. It tended to be all-consuming for her. She was preoccupied. So, what did Rick decide to do? He replaced her smartphone with an inexpensive cell phone he bought from Walmart, which had no capacity for apps. It was simple, yet functional, with only a GPS for tracking where she was and where she needed to go. That's all the teen carried with her, and because she was embarrassed to even take it out of her purse, she rarely was on it.

Rick told me that within forty-eight hours, his daughter's behavior had changed. She was engaged again at home and at school. Her grades began to come back. In fact, it became an inside joke that whenever any member of their family began to slip in meeting their goals, that person would get the "family phone" for a week. Inevitably it helped that individual return to the best version of herself.

Stories like this are all too common today. Students in Generation Z have grown up in a world full of noise and clutter. According to marketing firm Sparks & Honey, kids from Generation Z have average attention spans of about eight seconds, down from twelve seconds for teens in the year 2000.[2] This simply means that after nearly eight seconds, they may get distracted unless they are engaged with something intriguing.  Students in Generation Z have grown up in a world full of noise and clutter. Further, approximately 11 percent of kids from Generation Z have been diagnosed with ADHD.[3] These realities frequently lead students to invite noise and clutter into their lives. They have a difficult time sitting still and being quiet. Unfortunately, this is the very antidote they often need most. Quiet and still.

## Let Them Be Bored

One of the worst travesties kids can imagine today is boredom. As we discussed in "Challenge #3 | Privilege Without Responsibly," they hate to be bored. While I remember hating boredom when I was a teen, we know something today we did not know back then. Our brains actually need boredom to be healthy. The margin we experience when our brains are bored provides us the capacity to become better people. Consider for a moment a typical adolescent's life, filled with noise and pings and activity coming at them all the time. They have little time to care about others. They're simply reacting to everything. To survive the week. That's just it. Many shift into survival mode. Coping becomes the goal.

Leslie Smith and her administrators at Orange Lutheran High School, in Orange, California have recognized the rising levels of anxiety in their students. In response, they've taken numerous steps, including launching R.O.A.M. (Re-vitalize On A Monday). Students get to choose an activity that energizes them, from basketball to ping pong to corn hole to reading, or they can catch up on a subject they've fallen behind in. Most of all, they can just rest and enjoy some margin in their days. It's more than study hall. They actually encourage their college-bound and often stressed-out students to create space in their lives to be healthy humans. They communicated the research and reasoning behind R.O.A.M. and then allowed their students to determine how to revitalize themselves.

Leslie told me their school has made adjustments to the game plan, but students, faculty, and staff are all enjoying a deepened culture of relationships and growth. They mix in real-life activities with discussion and reflection. And the students are winning.

There is measurable growth in the emotional intelligence of everyone, increased focus on the right priorities, authentic conversations among adults and kids, and celebrations of the growth these students enjoy.

## Action Steps to Create Margin

Let me suggest some ideas for steps you can help your students take to increase the margins in their lives and, hence, decrease their levels of anxiety.

1. **First of all, decide to stay current on cultural statistics and trends.**

   Keep up on media outlets and music. This can tip you off when you hear language or terms used by your young people. The statistics can be a sort of translator for you. You can simply Google the most popular sites and apps teens use, and you'll discover lots of information that will help you remain relevant. I watch MTV and VH1 from time to time just so I will know what's being heard and seen by young adults. I find the more I know about what's happening in society, the better I can interpret the patterns of kids.

### 2. Monitor your students' social media accounts.

Apps can help you explore and to monitor your teen's activity on a phone, such as what they are consuming and how many hours they are using it. Keep in mind, the greater the volume of hours on a smartphone, the greater the probability of symptoms of anxiety. There are several apps that are helpful to monitor social media accounts like Norton or TeenSafe.

### 3. Communicate unplugged times and curfews.

Every healthy home I know of has set some boundaries for portable devices, and these boundaries apply to everyone, even the adults. Many families have a basket in their kitchens where all members place their phones during meal times or game times. Some even have a curfew at bedtime just to provide a margin for their brains. Unplugged times can be challenging at first, as kids may view these times as punitive, but after a few days, everyone usually feels liberated from the tether of their phones or tablets. Margins require boundaries. Mental health demands that we separate ourselves from our devices.

### 4. Plan weekly date nights or weekend dates.

These are times where, once again, you enjoy margin in the week, where portable devices are off-limits. These face-to-face times enable kids' brains (and yours too) to refresh themselves over laughter, debriefing the week, or just good conversation. I did this with each of my family members as my kids were growing up. It provided a time of connection where I could listen and earn trust in their lives. The marvelous benefit was the space it created for us to slow down, to breathe, and to reflect. The results found in a study by *Monitoring the Future* found that kids who had more face-to-face time enjoyed better mental health than those who had less and spent their time on portable devices.

## 5. Create a phone contract.

Because the need for margin is almost always associated with over-using our smartphones, I believe it's wise for a parent or teacher to create a phone contract that both the adult and student signs. Yes, you read that correctly. Years ago, I read about a parent who bought a phone for her middle school son but wanted him to use it with the proper perspective. So, she created a simple and clear contract they both signed before she turned it over to him. (By the way, that's the best time to establish boundaries—at the beginning). She reminded him that she bought the phone, so it was her phone. At the same time, she was going to let him use it as long as he stayed within the boundaries of their agreement. She laid out how it should be used during school hours and afternoon hours as well as when it should be turned in at bedtime. While this may sound antiquated, she established a great mindset for him to handle his phone well.

## 6. Delete social media accounts.

My daughter, Bethany, is now a licensed counselor. She's told me the irony of social media use is that it is both self-soothing and a source of anxiety. It makes us feel better and worse. We often resort to it when we don't know what to do with ourselves, yet it frequently becomes a root cause of negative emotions: angst, envy, and the fear of missing out. She often recommends to clients that they simply delete some or all of their social media accounts when their anxiety becomes too much to handle. While it's only one of several solutions, for many, it is a source peace. It diminishes the clutter and noise that lead to anxiety.

## 7. Create boundaries or guidelines on extra-curricular activities.

Some students, for instance, will join three or four extra-curricular activities in the fall or spring and are compelled to make every practice, rehearsal, game, or competition. Every coach, trainer, or instructor seems to demand their "souls" and that they make the activity priority one. Now don't get me wrong, I am a fan of being committed. I just believe we must create sane boundaries for how many commitments we make at one time. My favorite *Habitude*® called Rivers and Floods echoes this truth. People are either rivers or floods. They're either flowing in one direction or expanding in many directions and doing damage. I say this to students all the time, "You can do anything, but you can't do everything. Sooner or later, you must learn the power of saying no if you're going to flow." So, what do rivers have that floods don't? Banks. There is a wall of dirt or rocks that enables a river to flow in a single direction. I am simply asking: What are your banks? What are your student's banks? If you say yes to something, what else are you saying no to in order to create margin in your day or week?

8. **Help them to minimize the possessions they own.**
Minimalism is a fad for many today, but I'm hoping it becomes more than a fad. I believe part of our problem with stress and anxiety is the pressure we feel to own so much. Certainly, there is nothing wrong with owning nice clothes, technology, cars, or luxuries; but too frequently, these things begin to own us. Author Kathi Lipp once said, "Why do teens tend to want so many 'belongings'? Because they 'long to be.'"[4] They can draw their identity from external not internal possessions; our being is derived from stuff rather than an internal sense of belonging—to family, to a community. When we unwittingly put our senses of identity in external items, we're sure to have an up and down experience and will encounter anxiety as life will eventually feel volatile. It's out of our control to keep up. When we feed an appetite, it becomes stronger rather than satisfied. A minimalist believes the richest people are not the ones who have the most but those who need the least. So, talk over these questions with your teens.

- Would it help to clear out the clutter in your life?
- How could we slowly but surely minimize the stuff in our lives?
- What should we give up or give away first?

9. **Host conversations about who's the boss of their time.**
I believe caring adults need to host discussions with students about technology being a wonderful servant but a horrible master. There's nothing inherently wrong with smartphones unless they become the boss of our lives. We all have seen people (of all ages)

become slaves to the pinging of their phones, distracted from relationships and even their own mental health because they feel they
must react to every notification or text message or social media
ping coming at them. When we become the master, not the slave,
of our devices, we can insert margins in our days and maintain
good mental health.

**Question:** How do you help kids practice establishing margins each
week?

## 2. How Can We Help Them Practice Mindfulness?

Mindfulness is a buzzword today. Some folks are wary of it, as it feels
like some ancient Eastern ritual for meditation that won't work today.
Others swear by it. Still, others simply do it because it's fashionable.
Regardless of what you feel when you hear the term, the practice of
being mindful is an assault on poor mental health. It almost works like
medication for millions of people. It calms. It offers perspective, and it
focuses a person on what's most important.

Let's talk about it here.

If you ask people to define mindfulness, you'll likely get a variety of
responses. To define it simply, mindfulness is the basic human ability
to be fully present, aware of where we are and what we're doing and
not overly reactive or overwhelmed by what's going on around us. It
means exchanging all of our multitasking for monotasking. One task or
thought at a time. It includes putting down all the juggling balls for a
bit. It's about embracing the beauty of one thing.

Let's face it. Haven't we all had those moments where we must
admit: *I'm here, but I'm not here?* We are a distracted generation of people, regardless of our ages. There are too many things going on and too
many things being said to be clear and focused. The average American
consumes ten thousand messages a day. Five years ago, I read there were
nine hundred and fifty thousand apps available for our devices. Today,
it is 2.1 million and climbing. There's stuff to consume all the time.
When we practice mindfulness techniques, however, we can overcome
our distractions. According to a new study published in *Psychological
Science*, mindfulness (and clearing or focusing our minds) can control
stress, improve sleep, and even avoid illness.[5] The perks of mindfulness

actually extend further. The American Psychological Association cites it as a hopeful strategy for alleviating depression, anxiety, and pain.

Bestselling author Daniel Goleman reminds us that our bodies are designed to be energetic and active and then recuperate. Frequently, we don't get that recuperation time. Many of us wear our over-stimulation like a badge of honor. We are busy. We are communicating all the time. We are producing. And most of all, multitasking. While our brains can achieve amazing goals, they weren't designed to multitask. And it is adding to our anxiety.

## What to Do About Multitasking

I remember becoming acutely aware of student's multitasking in 2005. I watched my daughter, who was a senior in high school, do her homework while also enjoying four other inputs—music from her iPod, a television show, her laptop, and her phone, which enabled her to continue an ongoing conversation with a friend about a boy.

Today, most of can't imagine doing life without multitasking. Our calendars are so full and our expectations so high, we feel we must accomplish two or more tasks at one time. In 2007, students from Kansas State University surveyed themselves and discovered they cram 27.5 hours of activity into every day—multitasking.[6] I think that number is conservative.

Today, I wonder what multitasking has done to us.

As busy people, most of us would agree that multitasking is helpful. We pick up our child at school while talking with a friend on our mobile device, all the while running errands that enable us to cook dinner that evening. Unfortunately, at the same time, it seems that few people really pay attention to one thing well. We lack clarity.

- We are shallow, not deep.
- We are fuzzy, not focused.
- We are distracted, not aligned.
- We often live with duplicity, not integrity.

## What's Wrong with Multitasking?

Thanks to social media, our students have grown up multitasking. As I suggested earlier, however, I've concluded multitasking is damaging them. Apart from the obvious texting while driving dangers, multitasking plays a role in the anxiety and depression levels our students experience. A squirt of dopamine is released when we accomplish one of the items on our multitasking list. It makes us feel good. We tend to pursue more short-term tasks that give us this dopamine shot, and soon we're caught up in quantity over quality. We actually work harder not smarter. And we don't really focus. Sadly, we trade in health and value for speed and volume.

MIT neuroscientist Earl Miller reveals that our brains are "not wired to multitask well... when people think they're multitasking, they're actually just switching from one task to another very rapidly.[7] And every time they do, there's a cognitive cost."[8]

"A study at the University of London demonstrated that people who multitask while performing cognitive tasks experience measurable IQ drops.[9] Believe it or not, the IQ drops were akin to what you see in those who skip a night of sleep or who smoke marijuana."[10] Wow.

Most of all, doctors tell us that multitasking causes an increase in the production of cortisol, the stress hormone.[11] When our brain consistently shifts gears, it creates stress and tires us out, leaving us feeling mentally fatigued. In addition, the barrage of information is overwhelming. Figuring out what you need to pay attention to and what you don't can be downright exhausting.

## A Game Plan: Monotasking

I have a challenge for you. Why not talk this over with your students and encourage them to look at the data. Then invite them to trade in multitasking for monotasking. You read that correctly. Monotasking is a lost art. It means concentrating on one important task, instead of four or five. It's giving your best effort to one item not your mediocre effort to several. Most importantly, it enables a student to integrate his life. Integration is taken from the same root word as integrity. It means being one person. Clear. Focused. On-mission. It's choosing to shun duplicity and hypocrisy in favor of authenticity. It's really all about mindfulness.

Integration is the smoothest path to overcoming stress and mindfulness is the best path to take toward integration. Mindfulness has become a buzzword in many circles today. In layman's terms, mindfulness is clearing one's mind of the clutter of multitasking and focusing on the here and now. It can go as far as deep breathing and meditation, but it can begin by simply pushing pause on the noise and activity of a stressful day. Neuroscientist Moshe Bar at Harvard Medical School tells us our brains switch back and forth from activity to recovery mode. We need periods of recovery—but often don't get them. Mindfulness, as I said earlier, is about putting down our juggling balls for a while and recovering. The benefits are tangible. The American Psychological Association cites it as a hopeful strategy for alleviating depression, anxiety, and pain.[12] The American Psychological Association tells us that 34 percent of Americans say their stress has shot up in the last year.[13] I believe it's even more so among our youth.

Let's make a trade.

What if we rebelled against the inclination of our culture for noise and clutter? What if we rejected the compulsion to be aware of everything all at once and decided to be mindful? It begins with acknowledging our anxiety then taking the steps to address it. Reject FOMO (fear of missing out), and let's do MONO—as in monotasking.

## Ten Steps to Help Students Be More Mindful

I want to offer some practical steps to become more mindful. Mindfulness doesn't have to be some strange meditative practice. It can be as simple as becoming fully present with the people in front of you or the one task you must finish. So, why not begin by helping students practice mindfulness with these actions.

1. **Balance screen time with face time and alone time.**

   Moderation in all things is wise advice. Talk to kids about balancing time with screens, face-to-face conversations, and alone time. Depending on their personality, it may not be equal, but several daily hours with each is healthy. Reject the binge.

2. **Consume more magnesium.**

   This crucial mineral is depleted when we're under duress. It's a catch twenty-two because when it's low, we feel even more emotionally reactive, according to nutritionist Dana James.[14] Magnesium is in foods like spinach, kale, bananas, cocoa, and almond milk.

### 3. Pause and discuss two questions.

Host conversations in a safe place where you can ask students two important questions:

    a. What are the advantages of our addiction to technology?

    b. What are the disadvantages of our addiction?

### 4. Sit down and do deep breathing.

This may sound weird, but intentional breathing, where you're mindful of your inhaling and exhaling, can do wonders to reduce stress and focus our minds. Have them pause, get quiet, close their eyes, and take long, slow breaths in and out.

### 5. Take a walk in nature.

Anytime we exercise, it can reduce stress and help us center ourselves, but strolling in nature is the best. A Japanese study discovered a link between chemicals released by trees called phytoncides and reduced levels of stress hormones.[15]

### 6. Commit to a regular technology fast.

Everyone I know who's turned off his or her technology says the same thing: At first it was hard, and then it became liberating. Why not choose a weekly period of time and get away from the pinging of the phone? Stress usually drops and peace rises.

### 7. Get eight hours of sleep at night.

It's common knowledge that teens actually need more sleep than their younger or older counterparts but often get less, thanks to 24/7 social media outlets. We need to encourage them to actually turn off their phones and sleep deeply.

### 8. Talk about trade-offs.

Grab some coffee and converse about how successful people make trade-offs in life. They know that while they can do anything, they can't do everything. They learn to make wise decisions and say no to certain options. And they learn to monotask.

9. **Find challenging work that demands your focused attention.**
The research by Hungarian psychologist Mihaly Csikszentmihalyi reveals that we get in a flow when we perform demanding work that forces us to focus our minds on achieving the outcome we desire.[16] We are not distracted but devoted in this period. We are mindful.

10. **Build an integrated personal brand.**
Remind students that everything they say and do is building their personal brands. Our social media posts all play a part in creating this brand—by default or design. Creating an integrated brand is a smart way to align themselves with one persona.

It's vital that the journey out of anxiety begins with students acknowledging anxiety's existence. Solutions come only when we accurately define reality. It is also important for kids to recognize that while emotions are real (and should be acknowledged), they're often fleeting. Self-awareness is vital. There are also some helpful apps like HeadSpace and Calm that can aid in practicing mindfulness.

Question: What could you do to help your students practice mindfulness?

## 3. How Can You Help Them Get Moving?

This might sound cliché but since millions of us in 21st century civilization sit down so much during our typical day and we see a climb in our anxiety rates, there may just be a connection. What if part of our solution was to return to a lifestyle people enjoyed over a century ago that was more active?

Consider for a moment how sedate our lives have become over the last fifty years. As average American families got a television and an air conditioner in their homes, people began to assume a sedate posture more often. Slowly but surely, our economy outsourced blue-collar jobs overseas where active work was cheaper. Parents told their kids they should go to college as they assumed white-collar jobs were preferable. Sadly, most (not all) white-collar jobs involve tasks where an employee sits most of the time. Over time, all of us began to sit more often, as kids traded in outside activities for inside ones.

- We usually sit to play a video game.
- We usually sit to work or play on our laptops.
- We usually sit to use our tablets.
- We usually sit to watch a program.
- We usually sit in a classroom at school.
- We usually sit to do our homework.
- We usually sit at an office at work.
- We usually sit to view or post on our phones.

While there may be no research connecting the sedentary lifestyles we now have with the rise of anxiety and depression, I believe it is no coincidence that the two realities have climbed together. The less active we are the more anxious we become. People who work out on a regular basis tend to benefit both physically and emotionally as well. How?

Physical activity stimulates the release of dopamine, norepinephrine, as well as serotonin. These chemicals play an important part in regulating your mood. Regular exercise also helps equalize your body's level of stress hormones, such as adrenaline. In short, it's a natural way to balance our chemicals well.

## What Do the Tech Guys Know About This?

A few years back, Facebook founder, Mark Zuckerberg, wrote and posted a letter to his newborn daughter. If you read it, you likely found it interesting that he specifically encourages her (and her older sister) to "go outside and play."

Wow. That advice seems to be at odds with the empire Mark has built.

Isn't it interesting that tech icons such as Zuckerberg and Steve Jobs have given the same advice? Upon releasing the Apple iPad, Jobs gave an interview to the *New York Times* and told them he's not giving one of those tablets to his kids.[17] They need to be healthy and play outside. If you follow the technology icons from the Silicon Valley, they all seem to say the same thing: Get out of your indoor prison.

Are you hearing a pattern from these people?

## Technology's Rightful Place

Like most of us, I appreciate new technology. I'm using my MacBook Pro to write this book. I don't want to miss new iterations or products when they're released. But I am reminded of their place today. As I've said, technology should be a servant, not a master and should not force us to stay inside sedate. That's why this sedentary problem needs an active solution.

One inspiring school solved several problems at once with a new activity. Not only do they still provide a recess for the elementary age students, but they also decided to start each day using a Wii. Yep, that's right. When faculty and staff at Conlee Elementary School in Las Cruces, New Mexico, started having students do five minutes of "Just Dance" (an active video game for Nintendo's Wii) at the start of each new day, they noticed a trend. Tardiness went down. Kids began getting to school on time. What's more, they got some exercise every day playing the game. Students loved it. They're now engaged.

Not bad.

Reporter, Nanci Hellmich wrote, "The dance activity is broadcast into classrooms that have TV monitors. The school was inspired to try this idea by researchers at New Mexico State University who are investigating the use of active video games as part of an obesity prevention project."[18] Now, researchers are looking into the use of games in P.E. classes and seeing whether doing an active video game before spelling or math tests improves performance. Kids who once stood along the walls during recess are now involved and getting fit at the same time. I love it.

## Steps We Can Take... Literally

Let me offer a list of suggestions for you and your students to get up and start moving more often and perhaps lower their levels of anxiety.

1. **Join a fitness center and workout each week.**

   Getting one hundred fifty minutes of moderate aerobic activity per week is an important part of staying healthy. If you can't afford a membership to a gym, schedule times to walk or run each week; find a way to get up and moving on a regular basis. Standing is better than sitting, and walking is better than standing.

## 2. Have them review homework shooting hoops/tossing ball.

As I've mentioned, most students do their homework while sitting. But they don't have to. What if you encouraged your students to review their math equations while shooting a basketball or go over the upcoming history test while throwing a baseball with a parent or a friend? For kinesthetic learners, movement during studies will actually help them. For others, it allows them to build healthy habits as they learn.

## 3. Take a family walk after dinner.

If you're a parent, what if you began a custom of taking a family stroll after dinner? Ask everyone to clear the dishes. Then, before doing anything else, you walk a mile or two together. This is also a good habit kids can take with them when they move out one day.

## 4. If your child loves video games, get one that gets them moving.

If your students love video games, remember there are some that ignite physical movement, not just mental activity. Gaming systems like Nintendo's Wii or Xbox 360's Kinect have even been prescribed by some doctors for young people. I will never forget participating with my teenage kids in "Dance, Dance Revolution" years ago, where players actually emulate the dancers on the screen. Is it cheesy? Maybe, but it is tons of fun and, once again, gets students moving.

## 5. Replace passive routines with active ones.

Studies have shown anxiety and stress levels rise when a phone is nearby, even when a student isn't using it.[19] Just sitting on a table within view raises our level of angst, knowing it could ping or ring at any moment. Replacing the phone's "ping" with "ping pong" is a great trade-off. Or, perhaps, the phone's "ring" with a "rink," as in a skating rink. What if Generation Z's past routines that involved hours just scrolling through social media feeds were replaced with routines that involved moving their whole body, not just their fingers and thumbs? Have your students come up with a favorite activity that will consume the time they would have spent sitting and posting.

In short, our young people need quiet times. They need face-to-face interaction, and they need boundaries to fight the rampant anxiety that ails many members of Generation Z. This action step is all about making trade-offs that are healthy.

**Question:** Is there any need to enable your students to become more active?

## 4. How Can We Help Them Manage Their Stress and Anxiety?

Probably the most important solution is the one people talk the least about. Today, everyone must learn to manage their stress and anxiety levels. We all deal with stress, but stress does not need to turn into *distress*. Anxiety is a common part of living in a fast-pace, 21st century culture, but it doesn't have to own our lives. The key to managing anxiety is intentionality. Let me clarify what I am saying.

- The fact that anxiety is normal does not mean we give in and learn to put up with anxiety ruling the day. It doesn't mean we are forced to be slaves to poor mental health and have no recourse at all in managing the damage it does to us.
- The fact that anxiety is normal does mean we must be intentional to take the appropriate steps so that we can make our way through such tumultuous waters with a helm and a rudder. It means we will need to develop skills to lead ourselves well.

### Managing Anxiety in Your Daily Life

Both my daughter and son have had to learn how their minds and bodies react to the stress levels they experience; they have learned to read them and to take steps in response to the symptoms. This is true for any condition we face.

### 1. Develop coping skills and routines.

I've already mentioned new habits students can employ like solitude and quietness, unplugging from the social media apps on our phones, and taking control of our daily calendars. These are all healthy practices that if done daily can make a huge difference for anxiety victims. Let me summarize some fundamental ones below.

a. **Learn your triggers.**

It is paramount for those who suffer from anxiety to learn what contexts trigger them. Do certain people trigger it? How about specific situations? In doing this, be sure you are honest. It is imperative to fight any cognitive distortions. On the one hand, you may have to face a reality that isn't pretty. On the other, you'll want to ask yourself: *Am I jumping to conclusions? Am I exaggerating my situation? Am I personalizing it?*

b. **Name your emotions.**

Once you recognize your triggers, it is helpful to name your emotions. What exactly is it that you are feeling? For some students, this is difficult. If necessary, coach them with helpful descriptive questions like: Are you scared? How about angry? Nervous? Lonely?

c. **Try paced breathing exercises.**

One way to reduce stress and anxiety is to breathe deeply. This is because anxiety attacks usually cause people to hyperventilate, cutting off carbon dioxide levels in their blood and causing light-headedness. This exercise requires them to take long, deep breaths to replace the short, quick breathing that usually accompanies anxiety.

d. **Initiate cognitive behavioral therapy.**

This treats panic attacks by shifting your thought patterns toward anxiety, hence changing the way you react to symptoms and maybe even removing the triggers of those symptoms. The bottom line—changing your cognition can change the entire way you see your situation and help you feel more in control of your life.

e. **Avoid social media notifications.**

As I've mentioned, much of our anxiety directly parallels the input of social media in our lives today. So, what if we put the phones down? Just replacing the noise of a smartphone with the quietness of an hour of solitude may be a game-changer.

Consider this: Neurologists claim that every time you resist acting on your anger, you're actually rewiring your brain to be calmer and more loving.[20] Do you suppose that might work for your anxiety too? The more you are able to resist anxiety by being mindful, practicing quietness, or acting on what is in your control, is it possible to overcome your anxiety this way?

## 2. See a counselor.

Decades ago, a tangible stigma existed regarding seeing a therapist. People thought that if you saw a "shrink" you must be crazy. I am grateful that stigma is evaporating. Counselors represent objective listening ears and empathetic hearts, and they regularly provide wise direction for those suffering from mental health problems. Every person in my family has benefited from a counselor. We each received some perspective we didn't have going into the sessions and often confirmation that we were on the right track as we dealt with our issues.

Sometimes it's difficult for a teen to talk to his parents. The very history you've experienced with your child may be the precise reality that creates a chasm when it comes to opening up about anxiety, depression, or panic attacks. In light of this, counselors are likely the best chance you have of helping your students.

## 3. Find their flow.

One valuable step young people can take to decrease stress and anxiety is finding their flow, where they're able to use their strengths for a greater good. Put another way, kids can stress out when they're doing too many things outside of their gifted area. This is de-energizing to anyone. Finding their flow means they focus their energy on something they believe in and leverage their talent in that area. At Growing Leaders, we are all about empowering kids to solve problems and serve people. When they do this, life often becomes simpler and more purposeful. This may involve helping them take personal assessments on their lives such as:

- StrengthsQuest
- Myers Briggs Type Indicator
- The Enneagram Test
- The DISC Profile

Once a student knows his strengths, it becomes easy to identify activities that will naturally create a flow for him. Focusing on his flow might just be a great step along the way to overcoming anxiety and stress. At Growing Leaders, we offer the IPSAT (Identity Profile Self-Awareness Tool), created by Steve Moore. It enables you to compile the results of your personal assessments and apply them on a team.

## 4. Take medication.

As a last resort, medication may be needed. There's nothing wrong with medicine. I am a type one diabetic and rely on insulin every single day. I simply contend that we should not rely first and only on medicine without fostering healthy habits like the ones on the list above. Once we've taken steps to reduce anxiety in our daily routines, we are in a position to judge (with a doctor's help) whether we need medication, to judge which medication we need and in what doses. Making medication our only source of help is like trying to lose weight by walking each day but never changing from our fast-food diet. After meeting with a counselor, both of my children discovered their situations required balancing the chemicals in their bodies. It wasn't a case of absentee parents or a destructive home life. It was simply that they had too much or too little of a chemical that prevented them from functioning in a healthy, hopeful manner. Just like I lacked insulin because my pancreas didn't function properly, they lacked the right number of chemicals to be themselves.

Taking medication should always be done at the advice or prescription of a licensed therapist or doctor. Because our minds and bodies represent a cocktail of various chemicals and hormones, it is unwise to create a solution without a medical professional involved in the process. Both of my adult children take a prescription today, but arriving at the right medication and the right dosage was a process.

**Question:** What skills have your students developed to manage anxiety?

## THE REWARD OF OVERCOMING ANXIETY

Earlier, I introduced you to my children. My firstborn, Bethany, is now thirty-one years old and flourishing as a productive adult. She doesn't claim to be perfect. She's still learning to manage her budget, to reduce her school debt each month and to handle, all that life throws at her, but she is in a very different place now than she was a dozen years ago.

I now have the privilege of watching her help so many other people. She chose to enter the field of psychology and now serves as a licensed therapist, working with young adults who experience mental health challenges, including schizophrenia, bipolar disorder, delusions, psychosis, narcissistic personality disorder, and even those with anxiety and depression.

She is a deeply wise and empathetic counselor, as you can imagine.

In fact, I now learn from her. We enjoy regular dinner dates to catch up with each other, and I love how I learn and expand my own horizons each time I spend time with this young professional. She's in her element. She's herself again.

She readily admits she is a work in progress—but it's satisfying to see the progress.

FOURTEEN

# Individualism Without Perspective

*Challenge #5*

In 2013, an unbelievable story surfaced in the news. A young man named Ethan Couch got drunk, drove his pickup truck off the road killing four people, and then ran from the accident to avoid the consequences. The story went viral when the world heard his attorney's defense for his conduct in this appalling crime: Affluenza.

What was even more shocking was that the judge bought it.

Affluenza is a term used by some psychologists to describe the inability of an adolescent to know what's appropriate behavior because he or she grew up with the privileges associated with money. In other words, his affluence blinds him from seeing right from wrong. After all, his life up to this point has pretty much been about himself. The judge believed that the affluence Ethan grew up with had clouded his judgment—killing those people wasn't his fault. Due to his Affluenza, Ethan avoided prison time and was put on probation. That is, until late 2015, when the story took a dramatic turn.

Ethan's mother, Tonya, helped him escape his Texas probation and flee to Mexico. His mother felt his light sentence (no prison, just probation) was too much for her boy to handle and wanted to free him from the clutches of the law. In fact, before escaping to Mexico, she actually threw a going away party for him.[1]

While the specifics of Ethan's situation might seem like an extreme case, his story is a clear symptom of an alarming trend that is all too common in our culture. While not every kid suffers from affluenza, every student does now seem to live in a world centered around themselves—thanks to their smartphones. Whereas Ethan's affluenza was brought on by a mother who focused on him and gave him everything he could want, today's kids are often treated the same way by their devices.

Every part of a kid's digital experiences are now customized to their own desires. The search results, the layout, the music, the games are all customized to fit their preferences. Due to self-indulgent behaviors online, every teen today is likely to be experiencing affluenza-like effects in their daily lives. The phenomenon is even causing students to rethink personal responsibility and redefine what it means to be an adult.

An enlightening study was released back in 2015 out of the UK. The research showed that adolescents don't see the transition to adulthood in terms of years but in terms of major life events. Because of this, most don't feel like adulthood really begins until age twenty-nine—the average age of having completed major adult life events like starting a career, getting married, and having your first child.[2] Although our young adults are rich in potential, we don't really expect them to perform responsible acts until a full decade later than we expected kids from a century ago. In most states in the U.S., we give them the rights of adulthood at eighteen or twenty-one, like smoking, drinking, or voting. We do not, however, expect the responsibilities that go along with those rights until years later. Something is wrong.

## NARCISSISM IS ON THE RISE

When Dr. Jean Twenge and Dr. W. Keith Campbell wrote *The Narcissism Epidemic* back in 2009, they identified a number of trends showing the effects of what they called "Narcissistic Culture." Teenagers "are simply more narcissistic than previous generations […] Parents [are more likely to] give their children unique names[, and] Pop songs are more focused on the self[, using] phrases like 'I am special' and 'all about me' more frequently."[3]

Many of these findings, which started with the Millennial generation have continued to trend up as Millennials have given way to the kids of Generation Z. The students we've met in focus groups are more likely to believe that their opinions are unique, that they are savvier than the adults in their lives, and that their greatest achievements come from their longest SnapChat streak, their most-watched YouTube videos, or their highest rankings in Fortnite.

Interestingly, as we discussed in "Challenge #4 | Involvement Without Boundaries," all of this self-interested activity has not led to greater self-esteem.

## Ego-Centralized Teens

When we use the word *individualism* to describe teens today, we are pointing to a reality that you've likely seen. Students whose sense of self is primarily inwardly focused and inwardly rooted. Ever heard the advice to just follow your heart? Whereas previous generations might have answered the question, "Can you tell me about yourself?" by sighting clubs they'd joined, their family history, or their religion, in our focus groups with Generation Z students, we found that they were more likely to talk about personal choices or achievements like their career paths, their hobbies, or their social media profiles. They value personal achievement over supporting the mission or carrying on the virtues of something greater than themselves.

This effect is something we are calling ego-centralization. Your ego is your sense of self-esteem or purpose. Because today's kids are centralizing their egos around personal achievements rather than external ideas or institutions, the naturally-formed result is a self-centered perspective.

Consider some evidence for this change. In every generation, young children are naturally self-centered. Throughout history, a child's self-centeredness was broken up when major decentralizing moments came along and re-oriented their sense of self around more external realities. On farms across the country a century ago, young children would be asked to help with chores, watch younger siblings, and support neighbors. These activities and others like them all left behind a clear message: Your life is not about you.

Chores and responsibilities are what we might call minor decentralizing activities. Young people a century ago were also likely to take on major decentralizing activities early in life—at least what we might call early. While the data is not out yet on Generation Z, if you look back at the three previous generations, you will find that certain major decentralizing activities are being pushed back later and later into life, thereby delaying maturity.

|  | Boomers | Gen X | Millennials |
|---|---|---|---|
| First Job | 16.3[4] | 16.6[4] | 17.2[4] |
| Living with Parents (Age 25-35) | 8%[5] | 11%[5] | 15%[5] |
| First Marriage | 20[6] | 24[6] | 27[6] |
| First Child | 21.4[7] | 23[7] | 26.3[8] |

Think about each of the major life activities represented above. First jobs, moving away from home, getting married, and especially having children are all activities that expand ones view of self to include the other people whose influence shapes ones identity. The more we delay these activities, as each successive generation has, the more likely we are to "lock in" the childish belief that our lives are pretty much about ourselves.

In her book *Screens and Teens: Connecting with Our Kids in a Wireless World*, Dr. Kathy Koch discusses five beliefs in today's world that—at least to us—identify the evidence of Generation Z's centralized ego. Consider how each of these statements is focused on both self-actualization and self-discovery.

1. I am the center of my own universe.

2. I deserve to be happy all the time.

3. I must have choices.

4. I am my own authority.

5. Information is all I need.[9]

It is certainly possible to look at a list like this and wonder: *What's the problem?* Is it really that bad that today's kids derive their sense of self (not to mention self-confidence) from their own preferences? My answer, as you will see in the next chapter, is, unequivocally, yes. But for now, let's take a closer look at another sign of how individualism is shaping the identities of today's generation: incivility.

## The Tribal Switch

In a series of studies throughout the 1960s led by Polish psychologist Henri Tajfel, a remarkable discovery was made about the tribal nature of human beings. Tajfel, a Jew, fought for the French in WWII and was captured in Germany. Tragically, his entire family had been murdered by the Nazi's by the end of the war. Tajfel, trying to make sense of the rise of the Third Reich, desired to understand what leads humans to adhere to morally bankrupt ideologies so long as the majority of people around them are in agreement. In short, he wanted to know what causes groupthink to lead to horrible outcomes.

In Tajfel's study, a series of arbitrary group associations were given to see if test subjects would act to protect or give advantages to those who were in the same arbitrary groups as them. "Tajfel found that no matter how trivial or 'minimal' he made the distinctions between the groups"—including simplistic associations like guessing the number of dots on a page—"people tended to distribute whatever was offered in favor of their in-group members."[10] Tajfel's discoveries, when combined with additional research from neuroscientist David Eagleman leads to a fascinating realization: "When [our] 'tribe switch' is activated, we bind ourselves more tightly to the group, we embrace and defend the group's moral matrix, and we stop thinking for ourselves."[11]

So, what does this tribal switch have to do with individualism? Generation Z kids, as a part of their individualistic nature, create their identities by binding themselves to certain tribes based on common interests (We will dig further into this idea when we discuss the chapter "Challenge #7 | Fluidity Without Integrity"). These petty tribal boundaries make the tribal switch easier and easier to activate. Generation Z students are often activating their tribal switch around issues and topics that, to almost any adult, might seem absurd. Whereas past generations might have flipped their switch to fight for their community, religion, nation, or political party, students today are often guilty of in-group fighting over video games, social media memes, celebrity feuds, and movie preferences. To put it shortly, today's world makes it is easier to identify ourselves by our differences rather than our similarities.

The tragic consequence of the increasing separation between individuals within Generation Z is that their separation breeds indifference and, consequently, incivility. A 2010 *New York Times* article on this very subject pointed the connection between this indifference and a decreasing amount of empathy in today's generation.

> *Over a period of eight years, researchers discovered a 34 percent to 48 percent decline in college students' ability to empathize—making it more essential than ever to teach them how to identify with others and actually demonstrate compassion for them. With a greater access to the needs of others around the world and in our own communities, students appear to be numb to others' needs, and preoccupied with their own. It's a vicious cycle: we feel we have to look out for ourselves since no one else is looking out for us, deepening our self-centered state.[12]*

Another byproduct of the increasing separation and incivility of our culture is the creation of safe spaces. Safe spaces are described as areas in which young people can be confident that they will not be subjected to discrimination, criticism, or harassment. This, of course, is an idea that we are, and should be, fully behind... *on paper*. In actuality, the growing tribalism of Generation Z is often leading students to seek safe spaces over issues that are not actually harming them. The discussion of political ideas and ethical opinions, for instance, are not harmful and have not been harmful in the entire history of the human race. Today, however, students run from those who would cause confrontation over these ideas.

In October 2017, the *New York Times* published an exposé on the startling trend of anxiety and depression among today's high school and college students. One section, discussing this exact issue, caught our eye:

> *[Today's] generation of young people [are] increasingly insistent on safe spaces—and [...] believe their feelings should be protected at all costs. 'Kids are being given some really dangerous messages these days about the fact that they can't handle being triggered,*

*that they shouldn't have to bear witness to anything that makes them uncomfortable and that their external environments should bend to and accommodate their needs.'[13]*

Did you catch that? An entire generation is constantly anxious and in search of safe spaces and the protection of adults. In this example, lies a truth that we must engage with: Generation Z students need to be safe, but they also need to mature into self-sustaining adults. Emotional security is not found in protection from outlandish ideas, but in self-actualization built through personal experience. Ideologies must be engaged, challenged, and debated if empathy and civility are to be recovered.

## Non-Complementary Behavior

Imagine you are at a dinner party with a group of friends, enjoying your time together. Suddenly, the door rattles and then gives way. A burglar bursts in! Not only has this uninvited guest arrived with heinous intentions, but this man is also carrying a gun. Everyone freezes and looks to you. What do you do?

There are plenty of appropriate responses to the situation. Many people, for instance, might respond in kind. They'd run, protect their loved ones, or even attempt to fight off the criminal. In psychology, these responses are termed complementary. They meet the level of the situation. They seem appropriate. This is not, however, what Michael Rabdau did.

As Michael tells the story on the *Invisibilia* podcast episode entitled "Flip the Script," one of his guests decided not to respond in kind to their uninvited guest.[14] Instead, while everyone was frozen, he turned to the burglar and asked, "Would you like to share a glass of wine with us?"[15] To everyone's continued surprise, the thief obliged, diffusing the situation and eventually leading the man to apologize and leave without any trouble.

While we are not suggesting that Generation Z kids invite criminals with guns to have dinner with them, we are asking an important question of our youngest population. Namely, are they mature enough to see life from another's perspective and diffuse a situation, rather than run from it?

In situations of dissension, most people run to a place of physical and emotional safety. Emotionally secure individuals, however, are able to choose not to respond in kind to other people. This is called non-complementary behavior. Even if it's appropriate to respond to violence with violence, it's not what emotionally secure and ego-decentralized young leaders would do. Their perspectives would allow them to choose to respond differently in the face of negative emotions, conflicting opinions, or aggressive actions. It's a choice we can lead them to make. It's a choice they must learn to make.

Reversing the individualistic tendencies of Generation Z is possible. Like Michael's guest, they just need us—their mentors—to help them find perspective.

# FIFTEEN

# Guiding Them to Find Their Place in a Larger Story

On March 25, 1911, a great tragedy struck the New York City garment district. A worker on the eighth floor of a stuffy clothing factory accidentally tossed a cigarette onto a heap of cotton scraps. The scraps caught flame immediately and, because of the abundance of fuel and lack of adequate firefighting practices and systems, quickly spread over the entire floor. The fire may not have been tragic except for two great injustices endemic to the factories of that time period.

First, fearing theft by the workers, the entire building was filled and emptied through just a handful of small chokepoints, meaning that exiting from the building during a fire was slow, crowded, and dangerous. Secondly, because of the fear of losing productivity, managers were instructed to fight fires, instead of allowing their employees to abandon their posts. The factory manager that day, Samuel Bernstein, didn't allow his employees to evacuate until it was too late for many of them.

One young woman, who had been having tea with a friend across the street, heard the commotion and ran outside. She arrived in time to watch as trapped workers on the upper floors of the factory made the horrible decision to jump from the upper windows rather than face the flames. Recalling the scene from her memory the young woman said, "They began to jump. The window was too crowded, and they would jump, and they hit the sidewalk. Every one of them was killed, everybody who jumped was killed. It was a horrifying spectacle."[1]

When the final death toll was tallied, 146 people were lost that day, either from the fire or from jumping to their deaths. What most people saw as an unfortunate tragedy, that young woman on the sidewalk saw from a different perspective. To her, it was a great injustice that needed to be addressed. Her name was Francis Perkins.

Perkins, who was thirty-one at the time, changed the trajectory of her life from that moment on. Through a lifetime of service to the poor and disenfranchised in America, Francis Perkins was able to achieve the goal of lowering the workweek to fifty-four hours. She was also the first woman to serve as New York City's Industrial Commissioner, which is when she met a semi-well-known politician by the name of Franklin D. Roosevelt.

Seeing her potential, Roosevelt asked her to become his Secretary of Labor once he reached the office of President. Along with Roosevelt, Francis Perkins was able to achieve more in the area of labor than perhaps any labor secretary before or after. Perkins saw to the creation of the first minimum wage law, Social Security, the first federal overtime law, sweeping child labor law changes, and also the first unemployment services.

In her writing about her trajectory in life, she always referenced the day of the factory fire as the beginning—the day she was forever changed. Why? Because on that day, she found a purpose greater than herself.

## RESUME VIRTUES AND EULOGY VIRTUES

I (Andrew) was a few years into my first job when I realized I had been pursuing life all wrong. Early in my career, I was working to update my resume, gain experiences that would make me look good, and learning the vernacular that would help me fit in with those in the industry that I admired. These pursuits led to gains but not in the way I thought they would. It's a situation that many young people experience in the 21st century as the rise in personalization and technology has increasingly led hopeful twenty-two-year-olds to their first jobs only to discover frustration and disappointment. Life isn't all regular feedback, clear objectives, and constant affirmation. John Mayer even invented a tongue-in-cheek term for our "condition:" The Quarter-Life Crisis.

The condition of our students today is the result of a lie or series of lies about the kind of life adults told us would satisfy. To put it simply, if I pursue my own self-interest I am rewarded by getting most or all of what I was expecting. Reinhold Niebuhr explained the problem well in his work *Human Nature*, "Man is an individual, but he is not self-sufficing. The law of his nature is love, a harmonious relation of life to life in obedience to the divine center and source of his life. This law is violated when man seeks to make himself the center and source of his own life."[2]

In an essay entitled *The Lonely Man of Faith* (1965), A Rabbi named Joseph Soloveitchik discusses what he determines to be the reality of each of us being two kinds of people at the same time. In his summary of Soloveitchik's work during the opening of *The Road to Character*, David Brooks summarizes these two people into two opposing sets of virtues that we are always drawn to simultaneously: our "resume" self and our "eulogy" self.

The first set of virtues, called resume virtues, are virtues of accomplishment. The kinds of things you would value on a resume: what schools you attended, what commendations you received, what jobs you held, and how much money you made. The second set of virtues, called eulogy virtues, are the kinds of virtues that would be shared during your eulogy: what kind of person you were, what you valued, whom you spent time with, how you loved others. If pressed, every one of us would likely say that the eulogy virtues were the more important ones, and yet, I rarely see Instagram posts highlighting someone's kindness. We much prefer to see pictures of vacations.

In a TED Talk on the subject, Brooks outlined the attitudes of these two selves:[3]

| Resume Virtues | Eulogy Virtues |
| --- | --- |
| • Worldly | • Humble |
| • Ambitious | • Do Good and Be Good |
| • Mastery of External World | • Mastery of Internal Life |
| • Build, Create, Innovate | • Honor Others |
| • Conquer the World | • Hear a Calling from the World |
| • Savor Accomplishment | • Savor Inter-consistency and Strength |
| • Asks How Things Work | • Asks Why We're Here |
| • Motto: Success | • Motto: Love, Redemption, and Return |

It's not that one of these is right and the other is wrong. The problem is that for a healthy life, we should really have virtues in both areas, but alas we do not. From our resume virtues, we should be drawing our drive, creativity, and curiosity, and from our eulogy virtues we should pull our purpose, passion, and goodness. So long as one is missing, we will feel as if we lack.

Young people who have decentralized (dispersed or distributed) their identities are those who are able to see purpose beyond themselves and for something greater than themselves. The most important part of who they are is not found in their favorite movies or television shows, their hobbies, clubs, or even their accomplishments. They set their sights not on what they want to do, but on the kind of person they want to be.

## Four Steps to Helping Generation Z Find Virtues

The trick with eulogy virtues is that they cannot be determined by anyone but you. An overactive mother could finish a science project, negotiate a grade, or even pay her child's way into college. But no loving parent can make her child a good person. Determining your values and virtues is a solo project.

Because today's kids are growing up in an individualistic and self-oriented world, they need practices to actively pursue a source of identity beyond themselves. The greatest leaders in history are those who were able to cut through the temptation to make their lives only about themselves and begin to fight for something outside and enduring.

Luckily, there are ways you can lead Generation Z through this process. Here are four steps that you can follow to get the process started at the dinner table, in the classroom, in the boardroom, or even the locker room.

### Step 1: Write Your Own Eulogy

How's this for a sobering activity? Together with your students, write your ideal eulogies. What words would you use to describe yourself? What stories would you want to be told? What words do you hope are on your gravestone? Use these questions to come up with a list of words that describe the kind of person you hope that you are. These should form phrases of no more than one to three words. You should try to whittle down to three to seven in total. These words are your values.

## Step 2: List Actions That Earn Your Virtues

The words you listed describe the kind of person you want to be, but they may not necessarily describe the kind of person you are. Here is the question: What kinds of things would the person you want to be do? What about their conduct would lead others to describe them in this way? You should create a list of at least twenty habitual actions that are rooted in your virtues. These are not accomplishments. These are regular and repeated acts.

## Step 3: Put Your Actions into Action

For a week or two, go out and put some of your ideas into practice. Be the kind of person you want to be by doing the kind of things that person would do. Throughout the time, ask yourself a series of questions: What did it feel like to do this action? Was it difficult for you? Why or why not? How did others react when you took your actions?

## Step 4: Don't Walk Alone

Ask your children or students if you can continue to hold them accountable to be the person they said they wanted to be. Invite them to hold you accountable as well. Together, put up your values and actions somewhere you will see them. Remind them that becoming the person they want to be is a journey that will take a lifetime.

For Generation Z kids, learning to find purpose outside of themselves is going to be a challenge. There is little in our world that incentivizes them to do so. This is why, if you want them to see the importance of finding purpose, it has to start with us. Dr. Jean Twenge in her book *iGen* said it perfectly, "We adult leaders must live meaningful lives, demonstrating for our young ones what it means to love our work, to love our spouse and friends, to embrace the contribution we make to this world and to love our life (and life station) because we find meaning in it."[4]

## DRAWING A LARGER CIRCLE

In 1959 Dr. Martin Luther King Jr. set out on a trip with his wife to see with their own eyes the power of the Indian movement for freedom. In particular, Dr. King wanted to understand just how the movement, along with its leader, Gandhi, were able to turn a non-violent revolt into the most successful campaign for human rights in history.

"During the trip, he met with Gandhi's son, cousin, grandsons and other relatives and laid a wreath on [Gandhi's] entombed ashes. And he left even more convinced of the power of nonviolent civil disobedience to affect social change."[5]

"It was a marvelous thing to see the amazing results of a nonviolent campaign," King wrote in *Ebony* after his trip. "The aftermath of hatred and bitterness that usually follows a violent campaign was found nowhere in India. Today a mutual friendship based on complete equality exists between the Indian and British people within the commonwealth."[6]

Did you catch that? The movement was characterized by the civility and equality that exists between the formerly oppressed and the former oppressor. This idea so fascinated Dr. King that he spent years processing his trip to India. He realized in the course of his thinking that the success of Gandhi's campaign was not just in its physical non-violence, but in its use of love as an active tool of resistance. "It is possible to resist evil without resorting to violence and to oppose evil itself without opposing the people committing evil [...]. The nonviolent resister not only refuses to shoot his opponent, but he also refuses to hate him."[7]

This perspective is one that is so foreign to us today that you might have read these quotes from Dr. King over and over just to comprehend their meanings. I know I did. Leaders like Dr. King, Gandhi, and Nelson Mandela were so secure in their belief of the justness of their cause and the reasonableness of humanity that they choose to love those who hated them.

Activist Pauli Murray said it this way, "I intend to destroy segregation by positive and embracing methods... When my brothers try to draw a circle to exclude me, I shall draw a larger circle to include them. Where they speak out for the privileges of a puny group, I shall shout for the rights of all mankind."[8]

In our world today, this type of civility feels lost, but it is not lost. The only difference between our world and theirs is the distance between people. Our world is both smaller (It is easier to connect.) and also more separate (It is harder to connect.). This is why Generation Z is losing its grip on civility. Instead of discourse, there are safe (read: separate) spaces. Instead of sit-ins, we write scathing op-eds. Instead of making speeches of unity and love, we write Facebook posts with pessimism and indifference. If these things can be righted for Generation Z, we will have a chance.

Hear us when we say that we do not believe that all of Generation Z is uncivil. They are not. In fact, many of them appear to be just the opposite. Today's generation, though, has grown up in a world that has lost perspective, and the examples that have been set to show them a better way are so few and far between that it's hard for them to know where to look. That is why they need us—to show them the better way and to draw a larger circle.

## Guiding Them From "Us and Them" to "We" Thinking

The idea from Pauli Murry could be best understood visually through a concept that was conceived by missiologist Paul Hiebert. The concept is simple enough to understand. Basically, when you have an opposing viewpoint from another person, there are two ways to view that person in relation to you. "Bounded set" or "us and them" thinking means that you see that person as belonging to a different group from you. I am a part of a group that believes "a" and she is a part of a group that believes "b." A way to visualize this idea is something like this:

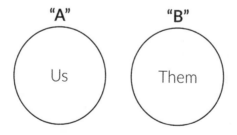

So long as those two sets are bounded in my mind, our differences are clearer to me than our similarities. I am bounded to my ideal and they to theirs. In order to right this perspective, we must follow in the footsteps of the civil rights leaders and draw a larger circle. This might look something like this:

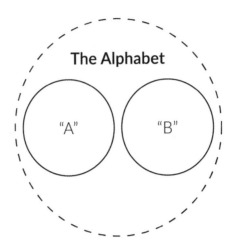

Notice that to draw a larger circle is to focus on what unifies the two groups, rather than what differentiates them. In this case, both "a" and "b" belong to the alphabet. Over time and with a little empathy, those walls begin to come down completely. And we can more readily see our similarities rather than our differences.

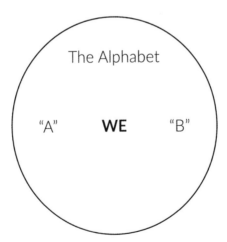

After a period of time, we no longer see us and them. We see we. Heibert called this we thinking "centered set" thinking. When you think this way, the fact that we have differing opinions is no longer a cause of separation between us. This is what was so radical about the efforts of civil rights leaders. They weren't doing this over differing opinions about economic policy. They did this with men and women who believed they were less than human—and it worked. Writing about this very reality, Dr. King talked about the monumental task they were taking on:

> *I do not want to give the impression that nonviolence will work miracles overnight. When the underprivileged demand freedom, the privileged first react with bitterness and resistance. Even when the demands are couched in nonviolent terms, the initial response is the same. So the nonviolent approach does not immediately change the heart of the oppressor. It first does something to the hearts and souls of those committed to it. It gives them new self-respect; it calls up resources of strength and courage that they did not know they had. Finally, it reaches the opponent and so stirs his conscience that reconciliation becomes a reality.*[9]

## EIGHT IDEAS FOR HELPING GENERATION Z KIDS PRACTICE "WE" THINKING

So, how do we help Generation Z kids practice this kind of we thinking? Here are eight ideas for getting started at home, in the classroom, in the car, or in the huddle.

1. **Have them write down their values.**

   The best way to find common ground with others is by shared personal values. Generation Z will need to know their own values first if they are to find shared values with others.

2. **Have them write down areas of personal growth.**

   Us and Them thinking is perpetuated by the belief that I am right and they are wrong. Challenge Generation Z to consider their own weaknesses. Humility always helps.

3. **Have them identify injustices they are passionate about.**

   Just like Francis Perkins, finding outside injustices are a great way to breakdown individualistic thinking.

### 4. Teach them to ask good questions.

When we encounter different perspectives from ours, asking good questions can break down barriers. Instead of why questions (like: why do you believe that?), have them ask how and what questions. (For example: "What experiences have led you to that conclusion?")

### 5. Teach them to use better language.

We get ourselves into trouble when we use attacking language like stupid or ridiculous. Instead, challenge kids to use language like perspective, point of view, or opinion.

### 6. Apply this concept to their lives.

Challenge them to ask: Who is one person that I don't naturally identify with? Brainstorm with them possible shared values that could serve as a middle ground.

### 7. Practice with case studies.

Give your students or kids situations to let them practice seeing things from another's point of view. Help them practice this so that they are more ready to do it in real time.

### 8. Ask them to hold you accountable.

Maybe the best way to get started is to let them call out where they have seen you fail to do this. Consider asking them: "Where have I practiced Us and Them thinking rather than we thinking?

## PEACE REQUIRES SACRIFICE

No generation is naturally selfless. For Generation Z, the challenge before them to see something greater outside of their individual perspective is the same challenge that every adult alive today has had to face. They can learn perspective, selflessness, and civility. They simply need adults who can show them the way and to acknowledge what it will cost them.

Selflessness is, ultimately, self-sacrifice. To walk in peace with others is to give up our desire to satiate our own preferences, anger, resources, and sometimes even our sense of being wronged.

A few years ago, the head football coach at Olivet Middle School in Michigan chose to allow a special needs student named Keith to play on the football team. Keith suffered from a form of autism that left him often unaware of the people around him but in the sweetest way. He is kind to everyone and often seeks a hug from his fellow players who would be far too cool to do such a thing if he wasn't there. The manner in which the coach interacts empathetically with Keith sets an example for the other players on the team. And boy did they take a lead from their coach.

Before the season's end, that team of middle school boys came up with a play to end all plays. One designed to show their teammate Keith just how much they cared for him. Getting as close to the end zone as they could, they called their own special formation, putting Keith at the fullback position. When the ball was snapped, a huge group of players surrounded Keith and pushed him through to the end zone. Keith had scored a touchdown.[10] It may seem like a simple gesture to us, but the adults in the stadium that night knew just how important of a moment this was for their boys. They had finally gotten it. It wasn't about them any longer. There were no longer divisions between teenagers. No one was trying to look cool. It was just a team that decided to do what was right. I'd call that a little perspective.

Selflessness, service, civility, kindness. These things aren't hard to understand, but they don't come naturally either. In our self-centered, technology-driven world, it is far too easy to fall victim to individualism. But, it can be different for your Generation Z students. Leaders and activists like Francis Perkins and Dr. King have shown us the path. It just has to start—as it did with that Olivet Middle School football coach—with an adult who is intentional about modeling the way.

# SIXTEEN

# *Accessibility Without Accountability*

## *Challenge #6*

In May of 2017, I vacationed in London and Paris with my family. My son and daughter had graduated with a bachelor's and master's degree (respectively), so we decided to take a week in Europe to celebrate. One morning, I awoke before everyone else and decided to take a walk to a coffee shop. While waiting for my latte, I happened to overhear two locals debating about a new café that was planned to be opened outside of London. I could tell it was unique as they were enamored with the products and services it offered. I listened intently but was not prepared for what they said next. They described beautiful, female looking robots that would serve the drinks in this boutique café. Apparently, the robots looked like supermodels. I was stunned to hear how customers would soon be able to purchase a drink and a sexual favor from those beautiful robots, anytime between 6:00 am and 11:00 pm

No, I am not kidding.

One of the two men in the discussion argued robots would one day be great for marriages, as men can get their personal needs met through a robot, not bothering their partners. The other saw the issue differently, arguing it would be horrible for marriages if a machine now met the most intimate of human needs. I quickly left the coffee shop, thinking to myself, *I'm not sure we're even ready for this discussion in America.*

This is the world we now live in. Smart technology and artificial intelligence expand each year, making realities available to a world of young people who may or may not be ready to navigate them morally. The gigantic question we all must answer is: If something is possible, is it always beneficial? Is new technology always progress? In his book *The Inevitable*, author Kevin Kelly poses the thought this way: "Our smart technology advances so quickly, it outpaces our ability to civilize it."[1]

In 2015, Hebrew University of Jerusalem professor Yuvai Noah Harari, wrote a book called *Sapiens: A Brief History of Humankind*. In this book, he made the statement:

> *From a biological perspective, nothing is unnatural. Whatever is possible, by definition, is also natural.*[2]

At first glance, this statement makes logical sense. From a purely physiological point of view, it is true. While I have no doubt Professor Harari is brilliant, and I appreciate much of what he says, I believe if we buy into this premise from a macro perspective, we will become a troubled society. I bet you can think of many acts that are possible but not beneficial or natural. I can think of several. In fact, many acts that people are arrested for every year go against our higher nature as humans. One

Kids must learn to experience the perks and the price of accountability.

definition of the word natural is to be in agreement with the character, makeup, or intended design. It is possible to do many things with our minds and bodies that are not aligned or in agreement with the purposes of our minds or bodies. (Placing tin foil in a microwave oven and cooking it is not the microwave's intended purpose and will therefore cause damage.) The fact is, Professor Harari's statement prompts us to view our existence from a merely physical point of view. It separates our judgment of what is natural from the common good.

If our kids have any hope of thriving as adults, we must teach them to interpret their abilities in light of the common good. None of us exist in a vacuum; few of us are hermits. Kids must learn to experience the perks and the price of accountability. This is a distinctive message we must pass on to Generation Z.

## Our Challenge in This New World

Herein lies the challenge of leading and teaching today's students. Kids eventually must mature and join a society, which requires them to function in a certain way, to cooperate with others, and to get along. We all drive on roads, pay bills, attend schools, and live in a community. As kids mature, they have to learn and follow rules, to speak the lexicon and learn to please the teacher and later the boss. They must learn to recode and follow the order of civilization. Hence, we have to teach them how to be accountable for themselves and their actions. If we want to enjoy the benefits of all our society offers us, we must pay a price to do so. We must learn to find our place in the larger world.

On the other hand, we want kids to be themselves, to be unique individuals who find their strengths and leverage them in ways that are satisfying. We don't want them to lose their identities, to copy others or worry about what people think about them. We want them to be true to who they really are. (More on this in chapter nineteen, "Establishing an Identity with Integrity.")

This is a difficult and delicate balancing act.

Yet, if we fail to prepare them ethically to cooperate with society and, more specifically to collaborate with their own community, we will have failed them.

## When Teens Enjoy Accessibility Without Experiencing Accountability

This is new territory for the Western Hemisphere. So much is at a teenager's disposal through technology, but they can hide those often anti-social experiences and realities and not face typical accountability. Let me suggest some outcomes when an adolescent has accessibility without accountability.

### They can act immature or be paranoid due to little experience.

This one is obvious. If I am an adolescent and have unlimited access to any content I wish for, I will be prone to either test boundaries (having a brain that is still undeveloped), or I can be frightened or overwhelmed by it all. In "Challenge #1 | Empowerment without Wisdom," we discussed how information is ubiquitous but first-hand experiences are rare—leaving teens with artificial maturity. One example is the large number of male teens in 2018 informal focus groups I hosted who acknowledged addiction to pornography and assumed girls wanted this kind of encounter in dating relationships. The more you see something, the more it feels common. As increasing numbers of immature peers post outlandish ideas, those ideas move from outlandish to normal.

## They can act without discretion, since privacy allows for it.

Teens are actually enabled to act selfishly with no consequences for their conduct. Generation Z kids, as we have noted, are more private than Millennials and recognize how to remain private and anonymous online. As a result, they are able to remain immature, without guidelines or guardrails for their words or conduct. For example, while Millennials used to post photos of that college party where they got "crunk" (crazy drunk), forgetting they had job interviews on Monday with potential employers who could see their posts, Generation Z will post on Snapchat—still enjoying the pleasure of posting but the video vanishes in seconds.

 They are able to remain immature without guidelines or guardrails for their words or conduct.

## They can drift into amoralism—assuming no ethical boundaries.

Reflect for a moment on this outcome. As teens gain exposure to almost anything—any worldview, any ludicrous idea, any hypothesis, any fake news story—it can lead them to assume anything and everything is acceptable. Our culture conditions them to not judge anyone, so who's to say a strange idea is good or bad, right or wrong? In fact, later in this chapter, we'll see that many college students believe cheating on a test to be wrong only if they get caught. An increasing number of students on university campuses tell me they believe there is no absolute right and wrong. For them, pragmatism trumps principle.

For more than a decade, Roger McNamee served as a mentor to Mark Zuckerberg, the founder of Facebook. He loved the social media platform and for years, remained an investor in it. But of late, Roger has been transparent about the horrific downside of it all. He explains:

> *The massive success of Facebook eventually led to catastrophe. [...] Facebook's algorithms give users what they want, so each person's News Feed becomes a unique reality, a filter bubble that creates an*

*illusion that most people the user knows believe the same things. Showing users only posts they agree with was good for Facebook's bottom line, but research showed it also increased polarization and, as we learned, harmed democracy.*

*To feed its AI and algorithms, Facebook gathered data anywhere it could. Before long, Facebook was spying on everyone, including people who do not use Facebook. [...] From late 2012 to 2017, Facebook perfected a new idea–growth hacking–where it experimented constantly with algorithms, new data types and small changes in design, measuring everything. Growth hacking enabled Facebook to monetize its oceans of data so effectively that growth-hacking metrics blocked out all other considerations[...] Every action a user took gave Facebook a better understanding of that user–and of that user's friends–enabling the company to make tiny "improvements" in the user experience every day, which is to say it got better at manipulating the attention of users. Any advertiser could buy access to that attention.*

*You would think that Facebook's users would be outraged by the way the platform has been used to undermine democracy, human rights, privacy, public health and innovation. Some are, but nearly 1.5 billion people still use Facebook every day.[3]*

As we partner with more than 10,000 schools and organizations globally, we are discovering what I suggested above: students live by pragmatism rather than living by principles. Whatever works, whatever gets you to your goal, go for it.

In fact, our society doesn't value accountability. Deep down, we know we need it. But when others challenge our decisions or unethical actions, we withdraw, or worse, we retaliate. After all, this is a free country, right? Who are they to tell us what to do?

How did this shift take place?

The fact is we didn't see it coming. We got ambushed. While America is, indeed, a free nation, our definition of freedom has shifted. We want our leaders to be held accountable, but we don't want accountability ourselves. One prime example is parents and kids. When I was growing up, my parents knew our neighbors would aid them in raising me to do the right thing. They would scold me or call my mom to let her know if I'd done something wrong. It took a village to raise good kids. Today, parents usually don't welcome the intrusion of another parent pointing out their child's misbehavior. It feels like parenting is a competition. Moms and dads will side with their children in a disagreement at school instead of with the teacher or some other adult.

We have failed to lead them well and teach them ethics, as my parents did for me. We have neglected to be intentional about explaining and exhibiting why timeless values work in any time period. I love how USC men's basketball coach Frank Martin put it: "You know what makes me sick to my stomach? When I hear grown people say that kids have changed. Kids haven't changed. Kids don't know anything about anything. We've changed as adults. We demand less of kids. We expect less of kids. We make their lives easier instead of preparing them for what life is truly about. We're the ones that have changed."

So, let's talk about a game plan.

## THE ETHICAL CHALLENGE OF A NEW GENERATION WITH SMART TECHNOLOGY

Ethics and morality have been controversial subjects in schools for more than fifty years. As America becomes more pluralistic and as science and technology introduce us to opportunities that spark expanding ethical gray areas, the idea of imposing one's values on another feels, well, antiquated. Old fashioned. Like something our grandparents' generation would do.

Over time, however, educators recognized that kids needed to be taught values and ethics. As more homes became two-income households, parents felt they had little time to impart family values. Further, as parents became more educated, they often felt they should not impose specific values on their kids. Their children should make up their own minds.

In any case, the practice of values such as honesty, discipline, respect, work ethic, and empathy have dwindled over the decades. An essay by Tahir Hamid says, "Our basic ability to feel and empathize for the suffering of the poor and the unfortunate seems to be waning." In their place, our culture tends to value "the self, materialism and desire." Hamid continues by reminding us that in the U.S., "one woman is sexually assaulted every 107 seconds… and there are roughly 750,000 teen pregnancies in the U.S. each year…" In one survey from *USA Today*, 94 percent of women in Hollywood say they've experienced some level of sexual harassment on the job. Research from the University of Notre Dame professor Christian Smith relays, "75 percent of university students admit to cheating in order to get through college"[4] and "approximately two in every three young adults, ages 18-24, no longer believe there is an absolute right and wrong."[5]

The reality? Less black and white and many of shades of gray.

## Imagine This Scenario...

In recognition that ethics were waning, schools began leading classroom discussions on values clarification when I was a kid. Teachers would ask students to imagine:

- You can only save one swimmer in an ocean riptide, but three are out there. Which of the swimmers do you save?

- You are hiding from Nazi's in World War II, and your baby is about to cry. Do you smother your baby or allow everyone to be captured?

- A woman is lying on a bridge railroad track with her leg trapped. Freeing her will derail the oncoming train, killing many on board. What do you do?

Each of these scenarios invited students to come up with a value system for deciding what to do. Ethics instructor Deborah Teasley defines the issue this way: "A moral decision is a choice made based on a person's ethics, manners, character and what they believe is proper behavior. These decisions tend to not only affect your wellbeing, but also the wellbeing of others."[6]

My concern is innovation and technology are being introduced so rapidly today our young will intuitively understand it more quickly than older adults. Further, if they don't possess a moral compass inside of them, our culture may simply adopt any and all new technologies without civilizing them. Those of us who want progress will need to quickly find ways to instill timeless ethics and values into our young. Otherwise, we could become a train without a track. Lots of motion but potentially reckless.

## A Case Study: Where Are Our Ethics and Values Heading?

I'd like to dig deeper into the issue of values within a technology-filled culture like the U.S. Our current culture includes a plurality of ethnic groups, worldviews, value systems, and spiritual beliefs. Our country is more diverse than ever before. Often, Americans find it difficult to enjoy civil discourse or make any compromises. We feel strongly about many things and often see those who disagree with us as enemies. Yet, today, most of us do agree on one thing: Something is really wrong.

According to the Barna Research Group, "A majority of American adults across age group, ethnicity, gender, socioeconomic status and political ideology expresses concern about the nation's moral condition—8 in 10 overall (80 percent). The proportion is almost 9 in 10 among Elders (89 percent) and Boomers (87 percent), while about three-quarters of Gen-Xers (75 percent) and Millennials (74 percent) report concern."[7]

What we don't always agree upon is morality itself. We can't find consensus. What is it based upon? Where do we get it? How can someone know what to do when making moral decisions? "According to a majority of American adults (57 percent), knowing what is right or wrong is a matter of personal experience. This view is much more prevalent among younger generations than among older adults. Three-quarters of Millennials (74 percent) agree strongly or somewhat with the statement: 'Whatever is right for your life or works best for you is the only truth you can know,' compared to only 38 percent of Elders."[8]

For a majority of Generation Z kids, ethics are subjective. There's no standard. Expediency is their ethic.

In 2018, The Barna Research Group published a study on Generation Z, surveying 1,490 American teens and their parents. The results were telling. Teens are three times more likely than the previous three generations to say that morals and ethics change over time. Two in three believe lying is not wrong. They are the first generation on record to not list family or faith as the top element that defines them. It's about their own personal success.[9]

In 2014, our organization, Growing Leaders, had the privilege of surveying seventeen thousand public high school students from the state of Georgia. We surveyed students from urban, rural, and suburban areas across the state. The results were surprising, especially for kids living in the South. Regarding values and ethics, we discovered the students saw no correlation between a successful life and an ethical life. Once again, pragmatism trumps principle. A person should do whatever they feel they must do to get what they want. It was a sobering discovery for us.

For a majority of Generation Z kids, ethics are subjective. There's no standard. Expediency is their ethic.

## Today's Trend: Elastic Morality

As I review statistics on today's students, I'm encouraged to see there are signs of improvement in their conduct. I've written about the downward trends in cigarette smoking, drinking while driving, television viewing, and even teen sex. Additionally, youth are drinking more water and fewer soft drinks. This is all good news. However, one escalating reality deserves both our attention and our appropriate response.

My friends Chris Tompkins and John McAuley co-authored a book with Don Postereski that puts a finger on the pulse of what's happening. Their research reveals that young adults today experience elastic morality. Because our culture cherishes qualities such as pluralism and tolerance (which are very helpful in themselves), many of our youth have lost the ability to think critically or make moral judgments (which is unhelpful). As we create space for diversity—which is positive—one unintended consequence is we often fail to prepare them to discern right from wrong. As the old saying goes, "We are so open-minded our brains have fallen out." Our culture is marked by:

- resistance to judgment
- uncensored acceptance
- exchanging certainty for ambiguity
- embracing plurality
- stretching the boundaries of belief and behavior.

Consequently, what is right can expand or bend. Their interviews with college-age students unveil a "dominant view that the 'right choice' is all relative to personal experience, personal convictions and personal opinion."[10]

## Five Sources of Morality

Dr. Christian Smith is the professor of sociology at the University of Notre Dame, a lead researcher, and the author of *Lost in Transition*.[11] His work details the dark side of emerging adulthood today and how ethics are fading as American kids become adults. Smith and his team outline five patterns in their study of college students. These students' patterns demonstrate an evolution in the source of their morality.

1. **Ethics are determined by results or consequences.**

   A growing percentage of students possess very fuzzy morals, and when pressed to explain them, the morals developed purely from the results they produce. In other words, it is right to do something if it got you where you wanted to go. The end justifies the means. If you don't get caught, it's OK. It's why 75 percent of college students cheat on tests to get the grades they want; yet when caught, they generally agree it was wrong.[12] It was right if they got away with it. It's situational morality.

2. **Ethics are determined by pleasure or happiness.**

   Approximately 40 percent of students developed a morality based upon how it made others feel around them.[13] Something is judged as right or wrong if your boyfriend agreed with it or your BFFs felt good about it. In short, it's right if the people around you believe its right at the time. This might be expressed in words like, "If it makes everyone happy, then it must be right." Happiness is the gauge. This, too, is situational morality—just consider how much feelings fluctuate among teens. What's more, there are times when standing for what's right is hard not pleasurable.

3. **Ethics are determined by appearance or reputation.**

   The majority of emerging adults professed to believe in right and wrong morals but have no objective source with which to reference them. Instead, morality is defined by what other people would think of them if they behaved in a certain manner. How would it look if I stole something? How would it appear if I hooked up with her? It's the Facebook Rule, where appearances and reputation govern what we do. This, quite frankly, is a slippery slope, where morality fluctuates with public opinion.

4. **Ethics are determined by context or environment.**

A third of students (34 percent) reported they do believe in specific moral truths but realize they do so because they were raised in a particular culture that teaches right and wrong.[14] They could not project their ethics on all human beings. While I applaud their cultural sensitivity, when we view life this way, we cannot expect terrorists to do anything but continue their mass killings on other nations, nor can we judge them for it, as they developed different values than the rest of the world.

5. **Ethics are determined by effect or influence.**

More than 53 percent of students say they can determine if something is moral if it doesn't hurt someone else.[15] I've heard this before: "Yes, I had sex with someone even though he's engaged, but it didn't hurt anyone." Or: "Yes, I took some petty cash from the organization, but they're rich. They'll never miss it." It's a subjective compass that allows for immorality solely based on how it affects or doesn't affect others.

Sociologist Lisa Wade illustrates this slippery slope as she describes the latest hookup culture among American university students. She suspects that casual sex may not be about love or lust today. Wade believes the increasingly pervasive hookup culture on campuses today is different from the one faced by previous generations. A common scenario takes place at a nightclub. Females may go clubbing together as friends. Perhaps they become a bit intoxicated and some head out onto the dance floor. The music is loud; dancers are very close, even cozy. Soon, a male comes up behind a female and begins dancing very close to her. Instead of looking backward to find out who it is, the young lady looks over to her friends for cues. The signal they give her determines whether she proceeds to hookup with him or not. In other words, it's not about getting to know the person, it's about what your friends think.[16] Ultimately, this behavior is an expression of what happens on social media each and every day.

Once again, this is, at best, a slippery slope. We need students who have an internal sense of values and ethics that serve them better than the changing opinions of their friends online. Let's take a look at what we can do to instill this sense to Generation Z.

# SEVENTEEN

# *Preparing Them to Live by Values and Ethics*

A mother recently told me her fourteen-year old daughter returned home from school one day a bit befuddled. Her civics class had created a debate. One of her friends had declared that peace was the most important virtue in the world while another said justice was, even if we have to fight for it. This was quite a conversation for these young teens. As you can imagine, the debate got emotional and political. This girl wondered who was really right?

Albert Schweitzer said, "The first step in the evolution of ethics is a sense of solidarity with other human beings."[1]

## THE DIFFERENCE BETWEEN RELATIVE AND ABSOLUTE VALUES

The truth is as culture is filled with new realities—including technology, innovation, and alternative lifestyles—it becomes difficult for adolescents to distinguish between what's a current cultural reality and what's timeless. It has always been "in style" for young adults to be progressive, but today, teens and twenty-somethings are often unable to judge anything as absolutely right and wrong. As we discussed in the last chapter, there is a moral relativism residing in millions of them.

Let me be clear—some values or morals are relative. Social norms around things like acceptable clothing styles and public displays of affection have changed many times. They change from culture to culture, from person to person, and era to era. But in our desire to be progressive, I'm concerned we've discarded some timeless truths and have begun to act against our very nature.

Let me explain.

According to researchers at Yale University's Infant Cognition Center, also known as The Baby Lab, babies can actually tell good from evil and right from wrong even as young as three months old. To the skeptics who find it hard to believe an infant can really discern these differences, let me add—I did too at first. It certainly runs counter to our assumption that children are born as blank slates and learn right from wrong entirely from us.

But the research paints a different picture. Puppets are used to demonstrate good and bad behavior. In one case, a puppet is struggling to open a box. Another one, the good puppet, helps it open the box, while another, the bad puppet, slams the box shut. More than 80 percent of the times that experiment is conducted, babies will select the good puppet when presented with both puppets and given the chance to choose either one.

"Humans are born with a hard-wired morality, a sense of good and evil is bred in the bone," says Paul Bloom, Yale Brooks, and Suzanne Ragen professor of psychology.[2]

## Two Kinds of Morality

Ethics instructor Deborah Teasley has written about two types of morality we must understand in order to navigate this subject with students.[3] I paraphrase her thoughts below and encourage you to spark a conversation about these two types of morality.

People base moral decisions on a variety of references, including religious beliefs, personal values, and logical reasoning. From this reasoning comes two different types of morality: absolute morality and relative morality.

**Absolute morality**, strictly defined, is a more rigid belief structure that's based on the idea that there is a right choice for every moral dilemma, which holds true for all situations. A good example of this would be the Judeo-Christian commandment, "Thou shalt not kill." A person who embraces absolute morality would believe this to be true in all situations, even in the case of war. His or her conscience would find it difficult to enlist in the military.

**Relative morality** recognizes that different situations may call for different actions, which might not always adhere to a person's

original values. Let's use the same example: "Thou shalt not kill."
A person who has relative morality would stick with this belief but
might have a different opinion when it comes to military action
or abortion, depending on the situation. Each context provides a
different application.

I find myself somewhere in the middle. I do believe there are absolute
values that are timeless, yet at the same time, there are many that are
relative, depending on the situation.

**Talk It Over:** If you are honest with yourself, which of these two do you
embrace?

## The Rider and the Elephant

Our problem is as we grow up, we begin to form values based on conve-
nience rather than objectivity. Our innate sense of ethics changes.

Jonathan Haidt, professor of leadership ethics at New York University, discussed this in his book *The Righteous Mind*.[4] In it, he compares
human moral development to a metaphor he calls the rider and the
elephant. Haidt contends that inside each one of us is a rider, which is
our rational mind. It is our sense of logic and reasoning. The elephant, in
contrast, represents our human intuition, our gut. He explains that each
one of us assumes we make moral decisions based on careful reasoning
(the rider), but in reality, the rider serves and follows the elephant (our
gut). We tend to digest information or logic that backs our gut feeling
about what is right; in fact, we often look for facts that confirm what we
already felt was right. The elephant is much bigger and stronger than the
rider and will carry us wherever it wants to go.

**Talk It Over:** How have you seen students make and rationalize moral
judgments?

## THE DANGERS OF LIVING IN THE INTELLIGENCE AGE

Pause for a moment and reflect on some of the dangers we face living in
a "smart" world, where our opportunity and capacity may overtake our
moral boundaries. Any person serving in a leadership role or, for that
matter, any gifted person can be at risk of compromising their ethics,

not so much because they are evil or poor decision makers but because their opportunities can take them places they're not ready for morally. Inspired by author Andy Stanley, I've created a list of dangers that leaders must recognize. Consider the following statements:

1. Our talent has the potential to carry us further than our character can sustain us.

2. Trouble brews when our integrity doesn't keep pace with the momentum created by our appetites, our giftedness, or our technology.

3. There is no correlation between giftedness and maturity.

4. A strong intellect enables us to rationalize any decision and make it feel ethical.

5. Our commitment to integrity can be easily eroded by our love of progress.

As we consider how to host conversations about morals, values, and ethics with students, I'd like to suggest two levels of discussion. The first one is the discussion we must have at the organizational level. The second is a discussion with students at the personal or individual level. Let's begin by talking about organizational morals and how we make decisions on progress without losing our ethics and values.

How do we move forward without drifting?

## Five Frameworks for Morality

Over the years, philosophers have recognized five different frameworks for approaching moral issues. These approaches developed over many years, ranging from Ancient Greek times to the 19th century. Each of them is designed to deliver the most virtuous and just resolution to a moral dilemma. The five approaches are:

1. **The Utilitarian Approach** (What's most beneficial to the largest number of people.)

2. **The Rights Approach** (Humans have rights to choose and shouldn't be manipulated.)

3. **The Fairness Approach** (Doing justice and being fair determine what's moral for all.)

4. **The Common Good Approach** (Weighing what is best for the community's future.)

5. **The Virtue Approach** (What represents virtuous behavior, taking the high road.)

If nothing else, we can at least probably agree that the issue of morality is not as simple as it appears on the surface. People living in different ages have made moral decisions based on when and where they lived. While there is a universal sense of "do unto others as you would have them do unto you" written in the conscience of most people around the world, details may vary. Some people have very sensitive consciences while others, who still claim to live with integrity, are less sensitive. For some, speeding while driving is a moral challenge, while others don't think of it this way at all. For some, finding some money on the sidewalk represents a challenge to find the right owner, while to others, it's just their lucky day.

If we're going to be prepared to lead the way into the future, we must know and act on a set of values and ethics.

My conclusion? The greatest way we can develop ethics and, in essence, a moral compass in young people is to create environments where they can work things out themselves practically. Our most effective mentoring tools are modeling ethics for them and helping them reflect on their own experiences

This will be especially true as we race into the future with so many options for smart technology.

So, what's the best way to equip students to make moral decisions today?

## Report Cards and Filters: How to Choose What Is Moral

If we're going to be prepared to lead the way into the future, we must know and act on a set of values and ethics. More than ever, we'll need a moral compass. It may be that the majority of our population will simply drift with the times, missing the moral implications of our smart world. Leaders will be necessary to guide others, serving as the moral conscience of a group or population. I believe the need will be more pronounced than ever.

The bottom line? Individuals need a "report card" or some gauge that enables them to evaluate what is moral for the group. This report card is made up of filters, which enable them to make good judgments. Depending on the context, faith, family, values, and/or community can all play a central role in such decisions. Within the public space, leaders must agree on moral boundaries that serve the cause of "liberty and justice for all." Below are some guidelines to discuss. Perhaps the Generation Z students you lead may feel one of them is unnecessary or that you should add to this list. In either case, I am hopeful it ignites critical thinking. I offer it as a launching pad for your conversation.

Leaders who make moral decisions must choose based upon filters. Here are six filters to consider:

### Filter #1: Keep others in mind not just me.
It prioritizes the best interest of the community not merely my own interests.

### Filter #2: Keep the future in mind not just today.
It benefits the future of our civilization not just my needs today.

### Filter #3: Keep truth in mind not just expediency.
It values honesty among all parties, where we're transparent and forthright.

### Filter #4: Keep respect in mind not just results.
It communicates respect for others not just my special interests.

### Filter #5: Keep justice in mind not just pleasure.
It is based on what is equitable for all parties, where people sense it is fair.

### Filter #6: Keep honor in mind not just gain.
It fosters trust among all parties not suspicion. It represents the high road.

**Talk It Over:** Do you face any decisions today for which any of these could be a guide?

## Building A Moral Rudder

This list of statements on our moral report card encourages us (as leaders and future leaders) to pursue four goals. A moral rudder enables us to achieve goals:

1. **See the Big Picture.** (Try to perceive all viewpoints.)
2. **Take the High Road.** (Work to believe the best about others.)
3. **Think Long Term.** (Ponder the future implications of our words and actions.)
4. **Choose Win/Win.** (Act based upon the best interest of the future for everyone.)

In 2003, I founded Growing Leaders, a non-profit organization created to transform everyday students into growing leaders. Immediately, I began work on the first book in a series called, *Habitudes®: Images That Form Leadership Habits and Attitudes*. I knew that today's student is usually a visual learner and that pictures are worth a thousand words. I believed if I could anchor a timeless principle with an image, conversations, and experiences I could cultivate a new generation of ethical leaders. Book one focuses on the "Art of Self-Leadership." Our character is the foundation for all lasting leadership. If we can lead ourselves well, we will earn the right to be followed by others. I once heard Dee Hock, the founder of VISA International, say that executives should spend half their time investing in their own self-leadership. I couldn't agree more.

## One More Important Reality

I would be remiss if I failed to remind you of the most important factor in passing on a solid moral compass to students. We must embody a compass ourselves. Ethics are more caught than taught. In fact, if we talk about this issue, but fail to model it, our message becomes hollow and hypocritical. People do what people see.

When our daughter, Bethany, was five years old, my wife Pam took her to the supermarket to buy some groceries. Upon returning to the car with bags of food, Pam noticed they'd gotten out of the store with an extra can of green beans. It was an accident, but it was obvious to her she hadn't paid for it. Promptly, Pam picked Bethany up, grabbed the green beans, and returned to the checkout counter. When she explained she was returning the item because she hadn't paid for it, the clerk was stunned. Who does that? After thanking her, the clerk added, "Most customers wouldn't have bothered to return the product. It's not a big deal."

My wife smiled as she replied, "It is if your child is watching."

May I state the obvious? Students represent our future. Ready or not, they'll be leading our nation and our world in the next twenty years. I say, let's get them ready.

## Assignment

Why not meet with your students and talk over the ideas in this chapter. Even look at the data on how morals and values are shifting. Then, talk about the need for ethics.

Next, ask each one to create a list of words that describe his core values. What are the terms that he want to live by as an adult? What terms or phrases does he want others who observe him to use as they describe him? Some kids may take hours or even days to create this list. The list should be limited to four to six words or phrases.

Then, discuss the values together. Why did each student include them? Ask for the reasons these terms are top-of-mind for your students.

Finally, challenge each student to find at least one person to hold them accountable to live by their core values. Ideally, Accountability Partners are folks you TRUST.

### T—Transparent
(They will be honest and genuine in conversation.)

### R—Respected
(You both respect each other and won't lie to one another.)

### U—Understanding
(You believe they understand you and your values.)

### S—Safe
(You are certain they will keep discussions confidential.)

### T—Trustworthy
(You trust them as a close, mature friend.)

# EIGHTEEN

# *Fluidity Without Integrity*

*Challenge #7*

Several years ago, I speaking to a group of students and I met a girl in her early teens. Let's call her Rachel. Rachel and I spoke for a few minutes before I stepped on stage. When I speak to a group of students, I try to get to know a few of them to get context for my audience before my talk. Rachel and I had the privilege of a conversation by virtue of the fact that she sat on the front row.

As I was trying to get to know Rachel, I asked all of the questions that you might ask a young person.

- How old are you?
- What grade are you in?
- What's your favorite subject in school?
- What are some of your after-school hobbies?

After a while, Rachel could see what I was doing, but in her opinion, I was doing it all wrong.

"If you really want to get to know me," she interrupted, "you should really check out my Myspace profile." (Did I mention this was several years ago?)

Even then, I could see the beginning of a strange trend. Young people who are unable to describe themselves, prefer instead for others to view the curated—and increasingly disintegrated—digital version of who they are and who they want to be. The best term I have found for this strange new world is fluidity.

## AN IDENTITY-FLUID WORLD

Inside of each of us, at our very core, we find something deeper than the outside or visible definitions of who we are. It is who we say we are. We call this identity.

We live in an identity-fluid world. How we define ourselves is changing and changing faster than ever. Our world is in a constant state of flux: updates, breaking news, influencers, clickbait, streams, and screens. This constantly-changing exterior world is affecting our interior lives, and it's happening most drastically to Generation Z.

Today's teens belong to a complex ecosystem of belonging. They are constantly reinventing themselves to stay relevant and noticed in the ever-changing digital environment. Typical teens are likely to belong to multiple social media platforms, each with a different purpose. On each of these platforms, they are under the pressures of social expectations to perform for their followers to the tune of multiple posts per day. Each of these platforms require a different part of your personality and interests to shine. Some are to show off intelligence. Others are designed to establish your personal brand. Others are for connecting with friends. Still, others are designed to showcase your creativity, and then there is Facebook, which, of course, is to let your grandmother know you're still alive. Keeping up with all of this pressure is exhausting.

In order to relieve the stress of maintaining the *right* image on platforms like Instagram, teens will create multiple "finstas" (fake-Instagram accounts). Each of their accounts will be built around a distinct aspect of their identity: one for posting about their favorite artists, one for silly pictures, one for posting their art, one for posting their original songs, and the list goes on. This is just one platform of many. And if it seems like this new world of social expectations would cause more stress and anxiety and provide less of a return of happiness for Generation Z—you would be correct.

In an article in *The Atlantic*, Dr. Jean Twenge describes the effect of digital life on teens:

> *The Monitoring the Future survey, funded by the National Institute on Drug Abuse and designed to be nationally representative, has asked 12th-graders more than 1,000 questions every year since 1975 and queried eighth and 10th-graders since 1991. The survey asks teens how happy they are and also how much of*

*their leisure time they spend on various activities [...] The results could not be clearer: Teens who spend more time than average on screen activities are more likely to be unhappy, and those who spend more time than average on non-screen activities are more likely to be happy.[1]*

To a budding adolescent brain, it's hard to understand what's happening. It's even harder to tell when something so benign as uploading a selfie to Instagram is shaping that brain into a confused, stressed-out, and (ultimately) disintegrated human being.

But that is exactly what is happening.

## Fluid: A Metaphor

Imagine pouring a bottle filled with water into a vase and then back into the bottle. It's an image you've seen thousands of times, so you don't even notice the remarkable un-forming and reforming that is taking place. The structure of the fluid allows it to take the shape of any container into which it is poured. It's remarkable.

There are, however, drawbacks to the shape of water. The first is just that it has no shape. Because it is only ever shaped like the container into which it is poured, it cannot be said to have a shape. Its shape has no name, no identity of its own.

Water is also ever-changing. If the container is at rest, then the water rests, but if the container moves, water must move along with it. The water in the glass has no volition.

Water is, lastly, always losing some of itself. In each transfer from one container to the next, a little bit of water is lost. The more times it is moved—violently—from one container to the next, the less and less of it will be left.

By now, you realize my analogy. The adolescent identities of the kids from Generation Z resemble this fluid in many ways.

As they move from social media to video games to school to religious gathering to sport to family to friends, each of these environments require them to change their shape, the way they present themselves.

Their identity is also constantly changing to reflect the values of each world they belong to. They are creative (YouTube), then poised (Instagram), then silly (SnapChat). This constant change invokes a sense of confusion and anxiety to an adolescent brain, one that is built to follow patterns and habits. No wonder so many kids feel no control over their lives.

Finally, each adjustment of their identity takes a little bit out of them. Until they eventually feel like they have nothing left. Generation Z is feeling the after-effects of an identity-fluid lifestyle.

## THREE ERAS OF IDENTITY FORMATION

In the last chapter of our book *Marching off the Map*, Tim and I discuss the three eras of identity formation as we see them down through history. Because of space and the focus of the book, we only allowed ourselves a few paragraphs to explain the phenomena. I would like to dig a little deeper now in order to understand why the identity formation of kids today has changed so drastically in just the last few years.

### The First Era: Tribalism

Young people in ancient cultures formulated their identities in community. In fact, it would be fair to say that ancient adolescents had no concept of self outside of their communities. Tribal cultures were circular in nature, groups of people all facing inward, toward the others in their community. Everyone slightly different, but equally committed to preserving an agreed-upon way of life. The tribe was everything, and everyone outside was *other*. There are examples even today of remote tribal cultures that are content in complete isolation from the outside world. How could they survive this way? Why would they want to be isolated? It's simple. They've been raised to care only for their own culture and their own people.

There is good reason for such a dogmatic perspective. Even the most self-focused individuals within a society would have realized that if their society declined, so would they. Though not entirely tribal, even ancient kings, understanding the power of socio-cultural structures, developed weapons of warfare that specifically targeted the cultures of their enemies. The Babylonians, for instance, stole away all of the most promising young people of a conquered culture and infused in them Babylonian customs and values. The even more ancient Assyrians were known to kill the entire ruling class of a conquered society and then strip the monarch naked and ride him on an animal in front of commoners, demoralizing his social structure. These culture-decimating tactics show just how valuable cultural identity was to ancient city-states. It is reasonable to assume that any member of a tribal culture would fight tooth and nail to preserve the culture's way of life. After all, loss of culture necessarily meant loss of self.

As a child growing up in an ancient culture, your identity was formed based on the norms of your culture, the circle of people who talked, dressed, believed, and acted the same as you. It's hard to imagine this because of how individualistic our social structures have become, but people of this time would, with very few exceptions, not have believed that it was possible to think or act differently from your culture. If you did, difference of opinion was often a death sentence. After all, how could a tribal culture suffer a threat against its way of life?

The toll all of this took on identity should now seem obvious. An individual's purpose and identity are uniquely tied to the values of the whole culture. There is almost no individual sense of identity. I is we.

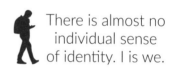

One of the best pictures of this reality I have heard comes from a 1969 experiment in Papua New Guinea by now legendary anthropologist Edmund Carpenter. Carpenter, along with his future wife Adelaide de Menil, went into the jungles of Papua New Guinea with a desire see how modern media would affect completely isolated tribal cultures. "I wanted to observe, for example," he wrote in his 1972 book, *Oh, What a Blow That Phantom Gave Me!* "what happens when a person—for the first time—sees himself in a mirror, in a photograph, on films, hears his voice; sees his name." In other words, he was to introduce individual identity to a society that had up to that point only had a tribal identity.

The results were startling.

For his first experiment, Carpenter took a Polaroid of a villager and showed it to him. The villager, of course, didn't understand he was looking at a picture of himself; He'd never seen himself before. After some interpretation work, the ball dropped. "The impact would be startling to them," Carpenter said in a 2003 interview. "Once they understood that they could see their soul, their image, their identity outside of themselves... they would turn away."[2] Upon later reflection, Carpenter developed a term for this moment of self-realization, instant alienation.

The photo made the self come alive for the first time. "After a while, everyone started walking around with their images of themselves on their foreheads... I don't think there [could be] any return to their initial innocence."[3]

Did you get that? Isolated tribal cultures were so caught up in a cultural identity that they literally didn't have a concept of self without the context of the group. That is, at least, until a single invention started a cultural revolution that changed everything.

## Summary of the Tribalism Era

**Identity** in a tribal culture comes from the community, there is no vision of the self separate from the group.

**Purpose** in a tribal culture comes from storytelling, keeping tradition alive, and connection to the community.

## The Second Era: Gatekeepers

Tribal cultures eventually became diverse civilizations. It wasn't until the invention of the printing press that adolescent identities really started drastically changing.

When Johann Gutenberg invented the printing press, he brought on an age of cultural elite who are known in certain circles as gatekeepers. Before the press, the only way to share an idea that could spread across cultures was to write down that idea and have it copied by hand over and over. The time-consuming nature of writing meant that most civilizations were illiterate, oral cultures. It was simply more efficient that way. Even around the year 1440, when the printing press was invented, very little would have changed overnight. Identities would still have been mostly shaped by local customs. Slowly but surely, that began to change. As people learned to read and as new inventions made dissemination of information faster and more efficient, people became shaped more and more by key voices and ideas that came from a small group of influential people.

In his book *To Change the World*, James Davidson Hunter introduces a concept he calls gatekeepers as those elite people with their hands "on the press" so to speak. They are the people whose power is best described by the word, choice. They choose whose voices get amplified and whose voices are stifled. Sometimes gatekeepers are public figures, those whose voices get amplified. Other times, they are happy to maintain their power in secret. From the printing press to the radio, from the radio to the television, each method of public media became faster and more powerful.

It is in this modern age, adolescent identities began aligning to ideas rather than communities. Young people formed and shaped their idea of self-based on which cultural voices, personalities, and ideas were brought to us by the owners of media outlets and the operators of institutions. The gatekeeper era made possible institutionalized religion, rationalism, science, and even civil rights. Each of these movements were built on a simple idea our entire culture agreed upon: When a great idea is presented from a respected source, that idea should spread to rational humans everywhere. As we leave this era behind in the wake of the internet, denominations, movements, leaders, and ideas may never be as powerful as they were.

Each individual in society during this time was less dependent on their own local cultural identity because they were provided a number of ways to achieve belonging without the approval of their parents or their community. Let's take a look at this "gatekeeper era through two prominent examples: one exemplary and the other horrifying.

## The Civil Rights Movement

The civil rights movement of the 1960s was organized, purposeful, and directional. Without the power of radio and television, it would not have been possible for African American civil rights leaders to push toward equality in such big leaps and bounds. The genius of this movement was that its leaders understood how ideas spread in a society owned by media elite. They made sure they made the news. In newspapers across the country, the people of the world were confronted by sit-ins, police brutality, and horrified atrocities to rally around. With the attention of media institutions, the movement was empowered and propelled toward achieving many of its goals. In their history of television news *Unsilent Revolution*, journalists Robert Donovan and Ray Scherer immortalized the movement this way, "The civil-rights revolution in the South began when a man and the eye of the television film camera came together, giving the camera a focal point for events breaking from state to state, and the man, Martin Luther King Jr., high exposure on television sets from coast to coast."[4]

## Fascism

Communism and—it's evil cousin—fascism are the ultimate experiment of the modern gatekeeper identity. After all, the ultimate form of a gatekeeper is one who gets an entire society to form their identity around a single individual. In the early 20th century, people were well accustomed to a life of people on radio and in print telling them what to buy and how to think. They were used to the best ideas coming from the top. Historically speaking, it didn't take long for the world to realize how horrible fascism was. But the fact that an idea like this could spread led not only to most of the western world's commitment to annihilating communist ideals but also to a growing mistrust in ideas that come from the top in general. Fascism and Communism exposed the danger behind the friendly face on the evening news and led entire generations to fear the rise of powerful voices, even the seemingly benign ones.

The power of gatekeepers caused some of the greatest atrocities in human history and some of the most beautiful movements of justice. It would have been the most complicated era of identity formation if not for the internet. When the first people logged on to interconnected computers, a shift began that has stripped power from the gatekeeper elite and handed it to anyone with a smartphone and a Twitter login.

## Summary of the Gatekeeper Era

**Identity** in the gatekeeper era comes from the worldview that you subscribe to and is not bound to your community or family experience.

**Purpose** in the gatekeeper era comes from following the directives and suggestions of popular ideas, movements, and people.

## The Third Era: Neo-Tribalism

When the printing press was thirty years old, there were probably only a few books in circulation, and the population of the world was probably still 95 percent illiterate. Gutenberg knew he had invented something significant, but the implications of the invention didn't even start to play out for at least another one hundred years. This is why I like to say the Internet is just getting started.

In terms of sociological impact, the Internet is such a young development that there is just absolutely no way that we could know exactly what this technology might make of the world—or us.

Internet saturation today has progressed far faster than reading rates in the 1400s. Estimates say that upwards of 40 percent of the world has access to the Internet today.[5] And just as Gutenberg only got a few books out in the first years, our intelligent use of this new technology is hilariously short-sighted. The Internet of apps has developed very little beyond expanding upon already familiar ideas. Consider, for instance, that the top three apps by daily use in the world in the fall of 2019 are WhatsApp, Facebook Messenger, and Facebook (all three of which are owned by Facebook).[6] Each of these applications does little more than improve and widen our scope of communication, give us access to on-demand (and personalized content), and help us spy on our friends and family.

The Internet is such a young development that there is just absolutely no way that we could know exactly what this technology might make of the world—or us.

Even despite this small level of development, in terms of how Generation Z is figuring out who they are, the world is a completely different place. Each kid is now handed a connection to the world and its information (and often misinformation). Once they log in, they are asked to decide their interests and then prompted to find people who share them.

Fascinatingly, each new group of similar people they join becomes to them like a little tribe. In this new world, there are fewer and fewer singular voices or ideas that are shared by large numbers of people. Instead, today's world mimics the original tribal identities of our forefathers. Though rather than belonging to one tribe, today's kids belong to many at the same time. They are constantly updating, expanding, and changing the groups they are a part of; and, consequently, they are also updating, expanding, and changing themselves too.

Perhaps the greatest picture of the Internet and how it functions is the website Reddit. I don't get on Reddit too often because it is just too overwhelming. Reddit prides itself on being the front page of the Internet, and it does that by shaping itself into a vessel for any tribal subculture. Like most social sites, Reddit creates absolutely zero content. Its power lies in providing spaces—subreddits—where anyone can create an interest group. It then creates a front page by pulling the most viral posts from those millions of little subreddits.

A subreddit is a forum where people go to talk about a specific subject. There are subreddits for certain video games, television shows, sports teams, hobbies, and much darker stuff too. Reddit prides itself on being a place where anyone can discuss and share anything. And it's the perfect picture of how our neo-tribalist culture functions. There are little pockets all over the Internet where people who are interested in very specific things can find one another and discuss that interest. In your little group, you build an identity around this shared interest. If you are into "Fathism" a religion started by a schizophrenic dentist in the 19th century, there's a subreddit for that. Or if you are interested in skating, rubber ducks, miniature painting, or just about anything else, you can find it there too.

What's most interesting about this is what happens to an adolescent who is a part of dozens or even hundreds of these little communities. The youth of today create their identity out of the groups of things that they love most. To today's youth, there are no longer simplistic dualities like N'Sync or Backstreet Boys, republicans or democrats, and even religious people or atheists. Generation Z kids' identities are a mixture of the things that make them popular, what they like to watch, the beliefs that make the most sense to them, and the little interests that they share with their friends. To them, there are no singular voices of influence. No religious, political, or philosophical leaders whom everyone can look up to. Just a thousand little voices that continually reshape their worlds.

## Summary of the Neo-Tribalism Era

**Identity** in the neo-tribalism era comes from the groups of interests, beliefs, and hobbies you choose and the groups of people with whom you share them.

**Purpose** in the neo-tribalism era comes from the approval, acceptance, and appreciation of your contributions by the tribal groups to which you belong.

## Disintegrated, Decentralized, and Integrated

The neo-tribal identities of Generation Z are causing increasingly disintegrated structures of identity. This is one cause, we believe, for the rise of stress and anxiety in today's kids. In a fully integrated identity, a person has a singular sense of self that connects with and, therefore, shapes all of their areas of interest. Meaning that whether they are online, spending time with friends, or at school, they act and feel very similar.

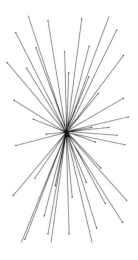

In a decentralized identity, the framework of understanding who you are is spread from the center. This is the typical adolescent who acts a little different when he is with friends than he might while at home. He might change his appearance, use different language, and even have different hobbies in these spaces. Typically, there is still some association of values between all of these different aspects of who he is. In a decentralized identity, though he may act a little differently, he is still fundamentally the same person.

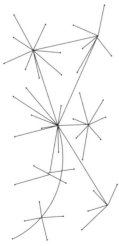

What's happening today is something entirely different. Huge numbers of Generation Z kids are starting to show signs of what we are calling disintegrated identities. Their interests and hobbies are so varied that the various parts of who they are don't come together in any obvious way. This is the ninth grader I met who has five "finsta" accounts and is constantly logging in and out of her various personalities. This is the college freshman I spoke to who told me it's sometimes confusing to talk to friends "in person [...] because they seem so happy on Instagram but they aren't [in real life]."

If the effect of the Internet on our social selves were to be explained with a metaphor, it would have to be an earthquake. The Internet is the great quake with a thousand aftershocks. The aftershocks you know very well. Kids today are 'always on their phones.' They are more stressed and anxious. They don't spend time with their friends in person. It's also a big part of the reason we feel so disconnected from them. They are often only showing us a small piece of who they really are.

If we really want to solve their fluid problem and help them form a rooted sense of identity, we are going to have to look back and recover one of the oldest methods of initiation in human history. That's where we're headed in the next chapter.

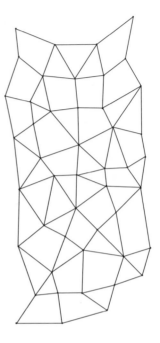

# NINETEEN

# *Establishing an Identity with Integrity*

In 1896, the country of Japan was hit by a devastating tsunami, which left many towns and villages completely destroyed. Across the country, the people began the long process of rebuilding, hoping better-designed buildings would provide a solution for future storms. They were wrong.

A few decades later, in 1930, the exact same coast was hit again. Because many towns had been rebuilt in the exact same place, they were once again completely destroyed. This time, many elders across Japan who had experienced both disasters wisely decided to make a change. Towns all across the country, like the small town of Aneyoshi, decided to rebuild at a much higher elevation so that their town would not be under threat again. On top of that, they made, perhaps, an even wiser choice.

To commemorate the move and to remind future unborn generations to follow in their footsteps, they built stones of remembrance called tsunami stones. These stones of various sizes can be spotted all over the country now, leaving behind wisdom and warning for future generations. The one in the small town of Aneyoshi reads, "Do not build any homes below this point. High dwellings are the peace and harmony of our descendants. Remember the calamity of the great tsunamis."[1]

It feels today like this kind of wisdom, passed down from one generation to another within a given culture, is a lost practice. Kids today are growing up in a world where wisdom is sought more often from peers and artificial intelligence than from elders, if it comes at all. Something in the way we raise our children drastically changed between the 1930s and today, and if we are going to help our kids reintegrate themselves in this ever-changing world, we had better figure out what practices have been lost.

## Learning Integration from the Ancient World

In his seminal work on the power of rites of passage in the religious context, *Adam's Return*, Richard Rohr speaks of what happens when adults fail to provide an initiation process for their youth. We need training, Rohr says, "in both detachment and attachment, Detachment from the passing so we can attach to the substantial. But if you do not acquire good training in detachment, you may attach to all the wrong things, especially your own self-image and its desire for security."[2]

Doesn't this sound like our culture today?

Today's generation reminds us of the tribe members in Papua New Guinea. They are so often presented with perfected images of themselves and not often enough presented with their own frailties and faults. They attach to an idea of themselves grounded in nonsense like TV shows and video games. If we want to help them succeed, we are going to have to take them through an ancient process, a ritual designed to remind them of their faults, their need for community, and that true purpose lies in what we do for others, not ourselves.

In the same way that Generation Z kids disintegrated themselves in order to fit into the digital world, they must now integrate their identities if they are going to survive and thrive in our technology-filled world. In all forms, the Latin root *integ* means wholeness or completeness. Each of these *integ* words, integrity, integrated, and dis-integrated, are meant to be understood as either black or white. A person either has everything needed for wholeness, or they are not whole. In the case of our kids today, far too often, the latter is true.

It's worth noting here that I am not saying our technology is bad. What I am saying is that our technology—and in particular our devices—are tools for adults, not kids—tools that should only be given once a child has been initiated into adulthood.

In ancient tribal cultures, the goal of the maturation process was to integrate young persons into the tribe to which they sought to belong. Interestingly, tribal cultures did not consider their children to be a part of the whole society until this initiation process was complete. After hundreds of years of studying these ancient tribal cultures, social scientists gave these initiation practices a name: rites of passage.

For the next few pages, we are going to explore this idea of rites of passage because we believe it is the secret to solving the problem of Generation Z's identity crisis. As we walk through the elements of each phase, consider how you could create a rite of passage experience for the Generation Z students you lead.

## Rites of Passage

The word rite comes from the Latin *ritus* and is synonymous with custom, ceremony, habit, and even liturgy. Rites are repeated ceremonial processes designed to elevate a person to a certain status or orient them to a new frame of mind. In the ancient world, rites were commonly physically taxing, which was a way of both testing the initiate and extracting something from them, replacing the old identity with a new self-orientation.

Arnold Van Gennep was not the first social scientist to write about rites of passage, but he is commonly thought of as the father of our modern understanding of rites of passage because of his book *The Rites of Passage*, which was written originally in 1909. In his work, Gennep collects and categorizes rite of passage customs from all over the world, and most helpfully, finds a pattern that unites all rites of passage.

What Gennep discovered are the three stages of a rite of passage. They are pre-liminal rites, liminal rites, and post-liminal rites.[3] According to Gennep, in this three-stage process "the basic procedure is always the same…[initiates] must stop, wait, go through a transitional period, enter, be incorporated."[4]

### Step 1: Pre-Liminal Rites

The first of these rites are the pre-liminal rites. These are also known as the rites of separation, and this stage is often compared with a sort of death. This stage is a ceremony or process in which the initiate must cut away the old parts of his life, childhood, immaturity, and dependency on parents. "The intention of all that is done at this ceremony," says Gennep, "is to make a momentous change in the boy's life; the past is to be cut off from him by a gulf which he can never re-pass."[5] Of course, we have pre-liminal rites in our world today. When a new soldier has his head shaved, a freshman is dropped off at college, or a newly married person changes their name, it symbolizes the transition from one state to another. There cannot be a reidentification without first relinquishing the old identity.

## Step 2: Liminal Rites

The middle rites, known as the liminal rites, are the most ambiguous and also the most purposeful. These rites are known as the rites of transition. Whereas the pre- and post-liminal stages are typically short periods or single events. This stage is a process. This process can happen over the course of a few weeks, a few months, or even (in rare cases) a few years. The word liminal literally means transition. The intention of this period is that the initiate goes through a series of experiences that test and prepare him for a new identity. In the words of Arnold Van Gennep, initiates "take off their usual habits and put on others."[6]

Three things to note on the liminal stage. Firstly, initiates should take on habits and challenges that are designed to simulate the new stage of life they are entering into. Secondly, habit formation should be both positive and negative. Positive rights are habits that you would pick up, and negative rights (which Gennep calls "taboos"[7]) are old habits you would discontinue. Lastly, in the liminal stage, it is deeply important that initiates spend time with initiated adults of the same gender. This could be a father or mother, relatives, or friends; but if there are no obvious candidates, it is important that a replacement is found.

## Step 3: Post-Liminal Rites

The third stage and final stage are the post-liminal rites. These are also called the rites of incorporation, as this is the emergence from the "wilderness" and the incorporation back into society. According to Gennep, "The final act is a religious ceremony [wherein...] a special mutilation [takes place] which varies with the tribe[...] and which makes the novice forever identical with the adult members."[8] Once the liminal experiences are over, the post-liminal ceremony transitions the initiate into their new identity in front of the whole community.

Post-liminal ceremonies are still quite common in our world today: graduations, bar mitzvas, and bat mitzvas, quinceañeras, weddings, military promotions, and even driver's licenses are all examples of post-liminal ceremonies. Interestingly, our culture has maintained these post-liminal ceremonies often without any preceding pre-liminal or liminal rites. Meaning we give our kids the rights of adulthood without asking them to pass through the rites of adulthood. No wonder our kids feel so entitled today.

As we have studied rites of passage, as well as human development, we have become increasingly convinced of the need for initiations to help ground Generation Z kids in solidified identities that can sustain the onslaught of information begging for their time and attention each day. Only initiated adults are able to say no to good things in order to pursue better things, and we desperately need Generation Z kids to become adults who can make these kinds of decisions.

## A Simple Process to Initiate Generation Z

We believe that initiating Generation Z can be simpler than we might be tempted to make it. To initiate a young person, you just have to follow a few simple steps. To provide examples of these steps, I will speak specifically to parenting, but these same steps could apply to any other type of leadership with Generation Z—from coaching to teaching to mentoring.

### 1. Outline the Goal of the Process

You can't start the process of initiation with your child without knowing where you are headed. The best way to understand this concept is in this simple statement: "Rites earn rights."

For every right your child wants, whether autonomy, information, privacy, or an iPhone, they need to go through a rite that teaches them both the value and the potential dangers of that right. We should never hand out rights to our children without accompanying conversations and experiences that teach them to value the power of their newfound freedoms. Instead, we should ask two questions:

1. At the end of this process, what rights will they receive?
2. What skills and knowledge will they need to handle these rights wisely?

Let's talk about an example of this. Imagine you were about to host a yearlong initiation process, and at the end of that process, your children were going to get a few rights. In this case, you're planning to give them iPhones, let them start accounts on Instagram and Snapchat, grant them the right to stay home without a babysitter, and the freedom to go out on their own with their friends. Now, what life skills will they need in order to act wisely with these new rights? Here's a good start. We believe a child would need to possess character, responsibility, self-control, the ability to stand up to their friends, honesty, and emotional stability, just to name a few.

## 2. Have a Conversation

Once your child starts desiring some of the freedoms of adulthood and you know the skills you are going to help them form, it is time for a conversation. I find that one of the most significant mistakes adults often make, especially with electronic devices, is to allow those devices to be seen as an entitlement and not a reward. In other words, "I get an iPhone because I turned twelve." Instead, our children should say, "I get an iPhone because I proved to my parents that I can handle it."

Have a conversation to help your child understand that electronic devices are tools for adults that come along with responsibility. You can only responsibly possess these things if you are an adult. In other words, you cannot have adult rights without also taking on adult responsibilities. This relationship is a normal part of adulthood. If I buy a car, I have to assume the responsibility of paying for it.

Once they understand the cost, they will better understand what they are really asking for when they want an iPhone. Adulthood is so much more than Instagram.

## 3. Plan the Process

After you know the life skills they will need and have spoken to them about the cost of becoming an adult, you can build an initiation process around the skills you know they will need.

In the *pre-liminal process*, you should help your child put off the habits, environments, and attitudes of childhood. Just as a military recruit cuts his hair at the beginning of Boot Camp, or a newly married couple moves out of their parent's house, our children must symbolize the act of separation from childhood.

Here are some ideas for how to do this with your kids. Paint and redecorate their rooms to a more adult look. Buy new clothes and change their hairstyle. Have them get rid of old toys and stuffed animals. Get rid of childlike habits like reading a bedtime story with mom, or consider no longer watching kids' movies and TV shows. It may seem to them like there isn't a connection between getting rid of childhood toys and signing up for Instagram, but it is vital that they understand that they can't live in both worlds. They must understand that they are becoming a different person.

In the *liminal process*, whether it lasts a couple of months or more than a year, you should plan a series of experiences and conversations that are designed to build the life skills you want them to develop. Choosing when to do this could be difficult since boys and girls develop biologically at very different rates and times. If you are unsure when to start this process, consider beginning around the twelfth year and into the thirteenth, as it is a natural transition in western culture. During this liminal period, you should begin introducing new habits (like chores or helping plan family vacations), which will continue even after the liminal process is over. Now, here are some ideas for experiences and conversations you could create to develop life skills.

- *Character*: Watch a documentary together about the moral failures of a politician or athlete. Afterward, discuss how the person ended up making his or her poor decisions. Discuss what that person should do to avoid these kinds of situations.

- *Responsibility*: If your child has never driven before, take him to an empty parking lot and let him get behind the wheel. Teach him about the rules of the road. Afterwards, talk about the feeling of getting behind the wheel and the responsibility that comes with it. Now compare that situation to life. We have to take responsibility (the wheel) of our lives if we want to succeed.

- *Self-Control*: Pick an item that your child wants really badly and tell him that you will pay for only half of it; he has to save up the rest. See if he can resist spending money needlessly on treats, going out with friends, or small items to save up for something he ultimately wants more. Check on him from time to time to see how it's going. After he has done it, talk about the value of setting goals and delaying gratification in life.

One great way to get the most out of the liminal process is to do it along with other adults and their children. When Tim went through this process with both of his children, he asked his son's and daughter's friends and their parents if they wanted to go through the process together. Pooling their resources, they were able to take trips and create even more powerful experiences for their kids.

Finally, in the *post-liminal stage*, there must be a celebration. Consider hosting a special event or planning around an already approaching event like a birthday. In front of your child's friends and family, you should formally praise him for "passing the test" and earning the skills needed to succeed as an adult. Consider even having him share what he has learned in front of his friends. Recognize him as entering adulthood and give him some of the rights that come with it.

As a last note, remember that this is a transition for you too. Just as you hold your child to new standards associated with adulthood, you must also challenge yourself not to fall back into the habit of treating him as you once did. He is now moving from childhood, through adolescence, and into adulthood. Treat him accordingly.

## #1000BlackGirlBooks

Marley Dias is a perfect example of integration in action. As a sixth grader from New Jersey, Marley had a problem. She loved to read but kept finding that the characters in the books that she was reading in school were not like her. In her own words, the books she was assigned were mostly about "white boys and dogs." She knew something had to change, and because she had been raised well, she knew she could make that change.

Using the power of social media to tell her story, Marley challenged the people of the world to send her books that were about black girls.

Her goal was to find one thousand unique books about black girls and then to give those books away. It was an additional plus if she could find books that were written by black female authors. She even created a hashtag to go along with the campaign, #1000BlackGirlBooks.

It shouldn't surprise you to hear that Marley has already surpassed her goal. In fact, since she started the campaign, she's received over nine thousand books total, and over fifteen hundred unique books.[9] Once she reached her goal, she gave away those one thousand books at an orphanage in Jamaica. That's quite an accomplishment for a twelve-year-old.

If you were to talk to Marley, I think you would find that she is a lot like the other members of her generation. She doesn't have supernatural intelligence or some special advantage. Marley's secret is that she has been integrated. Her parents, immigrants from Jamaica, helped to raise her into the kind of young woman who understands the value of hard work, representation, and kindness. She is a living testimony of a truth we at Growing Leaders have been saying for years: When we challenge our students using the language of belief, they will rise to the occasion. All they need are adults who know how to push.

## Integrated Communities

In 2011, the now much larger village of Aneyoshi, Japan was once again hit by another tsunami—or at least it would have been. While the rest of the country was devastated, the wise people of this village sat comfortably above the waterline. For nearly a century after the disaster in 1930, generation after generation heeded the warning of their ancestors and refused to build homes and businesses below the tsunami stones.[10]

It's pretty remarkable what can happen when one generation finds a way to pass on wisdom to the next. The story Generation Z kids will embody in this world is entirely dependent on whether or not we raise them into an integrated adulthood. Will they get everything they ask from us, leading them to a fluid understanding of themselves and the world, or will we raise them with integrity?

TWENTY

## *Opportunity Without Resilience*

*Challenge #8*

As I strolled out of the lobby of a metro-Atlanta area high school, I bumped into a friend of mine. She's the mother of a teen who attends that school. When I asked her why she was there, she timidly stated that her son had forgotten his science project, his lunch, and a permission slip he needed that day. She was there to drop off all the things he had forgotten.

When she asked me why I was there, I hesitated.

I had just finished speaking to the faculty about over-functioning parents. I told her about my meeting with staff and teachers, which led to an interesting conversation between the two of us. I discovered that this mom—like millions of others—feels the need to rescue her children from mistakes they make and to cover for them as they prepare for college. This has led her to not only rush forgotten items to a school campus but to perform other tasks as well:

- She will finish homework for her teens.
- She still lays out their clothes before each day begins.
- She will spy on her kids with binoculars on occasion to ensure they're safe.
- She serves them a Starbucks as she picks them up from school.
- She won't allow them to attend a college that's more than an hour away.
- She won't allow her kids to go for more than two hours without checking in.

She gave me permission to share this story with you, as long as I did not share her name. This kind of leadership has become quite common (as I mentioned in earlier chapters), but I'd like to examine why educated adults (parents, teachers, coaches, and others) continue to do such things, and how these efforts lead to negative consequences.

When I asked her about her reasoning, it was predictable. She sees how anxious her kids are (ages eleven, fourteen, and sixteen). They seem stressed out over the many activities in their lives, and she feels they won't be able to keep up without her help. A nurturing mother, seeing a struggling adolescent, almost immediately jumps to help. It seems natural. And those adults who do this actually do help.

At least for now.

What's tragic about these scenarios is we have cultivated a large population of young adults who have become helpless because we've helped them too much. They are not resourceful because we've resourced them so much. I am not suggesting that helping teens is wrong, simply that the way we've chosen to help them may be wrong. We have failed to think about the ultimate consequences since we're consumed with the immediate need. Too often, we think only of short-term fixes instead of long-term solutions. I've observed the miserable outcomes of our over-functioning practices on thousands of high school and college campuses across the country. In my book, *Twelve Huge Mistakes Parents Can Avoid*, I suggest:

1. **We risk too little.** (We won't let them take risks or get hurt.)

2. **We rescue too quickly.** (We won't let them fail or fall or forget.)

3. **We rave too easily.** (We exaggerate our praise for expected performance.)

4. **We reward too frequently.** (We offer prizes for mere participation.)

Each of these decisions is logical, but they are not preparing students for the future. These decisions leave students ill-equipped for a professor or employer or spouse who will interact with them very differently than we have. My friend Tim Tassopoulos taught me something years ago that I've applied to both my profession and my parenting: *The further you can see into the future, the better decision you'll make today.*

What we must recognize is there must be a weaning process if we hope to build resilient kids. Over time, we must balance what we do as their leaders and what we invite them to take on as emerging adults. Research states that kids are actually anti-fragile by nature. Greg Lukianoff and Jonathan Haidt relay this in their groundbreaking book *The Coddling of the American Mind.* As kids mature, they naturally grow stronger when deeper challenges are introduced into their days. In fact, it's these challenges that foster maturity.

The further you can see into the future, the better decision you'll make today.

Kids need new opportunities to master a skill, to solve a problem; to encounter new people, and to take on a challenge. Just like a fitness center only helps you get stronger if you lift heavy weights, so kids must experience stretching to grow stronger.

So, how much is too much?

It is only when they cross a certain line that they learn helplessness and give up. In the next chapter, we'll discuss helping kids draw this line for themselves. Unfortunately, in today's society, we have drawn that line for them and have failed to empower them to stretch. We draw the line too closely to safety and too far from stretching.

Far too often, we've actually robbed them of resilience.

## THE INVERSE RELATIONSHIP BETWEEN OPPORTUNITY AND GRIT

In previous chapters, I argued that life has never been easier or more convenient, offering swifter service and solutions delivered to our doors or on our screens. Collectively, Generation Z has more opportunity than any previous generation in history. What we are finding now is that all that opportunity is causing a grit problem.

University of Pennsylvania researcher and psychologist Angela Duckworth, authored the most extensive study on grit, defining it as "perseverance and passion for long-term goals." Dr. Duckworth created a test called the Grit Scale, assessing students on a series of eight to twelve issues, which reveal their perspective and aptitude in the areas of resilience and perseverance. Duckworth's team has found that a person's grit score is highly predictive of achievement in challenging situations.[1] In fact, Dr. Duckworth and her team have found that grit is a greater predictor of success in life than grades.

I saw this in action in 2018 during my visit to the U. S. Military Academy at West Point. I discovered a cadet's grit score was the best predictor of success in the rigorous summer training program known as Beast Barracks. Grit mattered more than intelligence, talent, leadership ability, or physical fitness. In fact, the cadets most likely to succeed actually had less than average talent, perhaps intuitively knowing that what they lacked in talent they could make up for in tenacity.

Duckworth herself found that at the Scripps National Spelling Bee, it was the grittiest contestants, not necessarily the smartest ones with the highest IQs, who were most likely to advance to the finals, in part due to the fact they would study longer and with greater focus.[2]

This, of course, is where the rubber meets the road.

I believe adults have actually diminished the development of grit in American kids. We've conditioned kids to avoid pain or hurt at any costs, which has diminished the cultivation of resilience in them. We work to make life simpler and easier than in past generations. We have a safety-first policy on everything, placing helmets and pads on kids and protectors on every device. Parents do so because we believe a lie that if our kids get hurt, it damages them in the long run. Educators do so because we want to avoid litigation. While this safety-first policy makes sense in the moment, it leaves teens miserably unready for adulthood, where they'll spend most of their lives.

> We've conditioned kids to avoid pain or hurt at any costs, which has diminished the cultivation of resilience in them.

May I offer another example of the dangers of our meddling?

Recent studies have found that some of the new allergies kids have developed since the 1990s may be due to the over-protective styles we've assumed as adults. In 2015 a LEAP (Learning Early About Peanut Allergies) study was unveiled. The hypothesis was that if children were introduced to peanut-based products during their mother's pregnancy, it would elicit a stronger immune system and a resistance to allergies. The results were stunning. Those who were protected from peanuts were five times more prone to become allergic than those who were exposed to peanuts. Seventeen percent of the protected kids got allergies, compared to only 3 percent of the unprotected kids. Authors of the study concluded that our protection was harmful and the earlier advice we'd all heard was incorrect.[3]

It's merely an illustration, but the human body is amazing. Immune systems actually require exposure to a range of foods, bacteria, and even parasites early on to develop their adaptive response to overcoming hardships. Our muscles need stressors to become strong and be able to lift weights. No pain, no gain. And so it is with life. Alison Gopnik, from U.C. Berkeley, states the issue succinctly:

> *Thanks to hygiene, antibiotics, and too little outdoor play, children don't get exposed to microbes as they once did. This may lead them to develop immune systems that overreact to substances that aren't actually threatening—causing allergies. In the same way, by shielding children from every possible risk, we may lead them to react with exaggerated fear to situations that aren't risky at all and isolate them from the adult skills that they will one day have to master.[4]*

I share Dr. Gopnik's concern. In 2010, I began warning that kindergarten through twelfth-grade students may head off to college unready for the rigors of higher education and diverse ideas. And that's exactly what's happened. Too many students feel they needed someone else to keep them emotionally safe on university campuses. They want administrators to prevent controversial speeches that might spark emotion. They want trigger warnings for microaggressions. This is not a healthy preparation for the world that awaits them. When it comes to equipping our kids for the future, the answer is rarely to remove a hardship. Professor Dieter Wolke, the professor of developmental psychology at the University of Warwick has done interdisciplinary research, tracking children's development from experiences in the womb right through adulthood.

He has shown that trying to remove the trials and obstacle from a child's path in her formative years merely stores up trouble for later. Dr. Warwick states, "We have objective data from Nullfield Foundation Studies, tracking what is changing over time, and it shows that on nearly every indicator, life has become objectively better for children.

They have, on average, more pocket money, they have to work less, they do better in school and have much less homework. But we find that young people are less happy. We call this the 'wealth paradox.' As life becomes seemingly easier for them, well-being is reduced."[5]

Statistician Nassim Nicholas Taleb is the professor of risk engineering at New York University. He wrote a book called, *Antifragile*, which defines fragile as the opposite of resilient. He opens the book with a metaphor that summarizes this issue:

*The wind extinguishes a candle but energizes a brushfire.*[6]

My goal is for those who lead this younger generation to cultivate strong brushfires, not delicate candles, that can't be blown out by small breezes. Unfortunately, today's realities have unintentionally produced the opposite. Instead, the last twenty-five years of parents have been unsure about how to lead their kids and unwittingly helped to create the nickname snowflake generation.

## THE SNOWFLAKE GENERATION

For years, we've heard journalists, educators, and employers tell us that our youngest generation in America could be called a snowflake generation. Why? Because so many of these kids have been raised in a delicate, soft environment, protected from life's harsh realities and responsibilities. Some even wrote that we've coddled them, protecting them with "bubble wrap."

Initially, the term snowflake generation was mere slang, but it didn't stay that way for long. In 2016, the *Financial Times* included the term *snowflake* in their annual Year in a Word list, defining it as "A derogatory term for someone deemed too emotionally vulnerable to cope with views that challenge their own, particularly in universities and other forums once known for robust debate."[7]

So, how and why did these snowflakes appear? Let's explore some of the cultural factors that have led to the rise of the snowflake generation.

### Helicopter parents

More than thirty years ago, parenting styles began to shift. Moms and dads became preoccupied with the safety and self-esteem of their kids. In the name of helping our kids, parents would do their child's homework, hover over them at soccer practice, and join their graduates at their first job interviews.

### Participation ribbons and trophies

Eventually, youth sport leagues felt it was important to celebrate participation more than winning. A few years ago, I visited a friend's home and saw his child's room literally filled with trophies and ribbons he'd been given. He had never won any championships. This has fostered an expectation of rewards just for showing up.

### Grade inflation

Student's grades have been on the rise for over forty years. In the 1960s, the average grade given was a C. Why? Because C means average. Today, the average grade is an A. I spoke in one school district where faculty told me they were not allowed to use red ink when grading papers because it was too harsh. Others told me they were not permitted to use the word no because it was too negative.

### Virtual realities and prescribed activity

Instead of making teens work jobs, we got them involved with recitals, practices, and games, all supervised and prescribed by adults. While piano, ballet, and sports can begin to cultivate discipline, these activities are still virtual realities, only facsimiles of the real world. When teens say they want to do something that actually matters but an adult places them in a supervised program that only emulates the real world, it often fosters dependency and reduces ownership.

### Technology and the media

Kids today are exposed to tens of thousands of images each day, often causing them to feel jealous over what friends are doing (having seen their Instagram posts) and believing they deserve the latest smart device, the coolest jeans, the latest video game console, the latest Nike shoes, and a subscription to Netflix. Entitlement and materialism usually walk hand in hand.

### Safe places in college

As students enter college, they begin to clamor for safe places, free from opposition or harsh feedback. This came to light in a confrontation between Yale University students and faculty head of college, Nicholas Christakis. The confrontation arose after Christakis' wife, Erika, a university lecturer, suggested students should "relax a bit rather than labeling fancy dress Halloween costumes as culturally insensitive."[8] This sparked a "screaming, almost hysterical mob of students." Even if their views were right, the answer isn't always to remove opposition. It's to know how to handle students in these situations.

## BUILDING SNOWMEN (AND WOMEN) FROM A SNOWFLAKE GENERATION

In the end, far too often, these snowflakes are products of our making. Not seeing what was happening soon enough, parents, teachers, and other adults forgot that raising children was not primarily about protecting. It was about preparing. If we want to turn this trend around and give our students a firm grounding in reality, we are going to have to build a generation of snowflakes into snowmen (and women).

### 1. Grit and Gravity

Zero gravity environments cause muscles to atrophy. We learned this from NASA over fifty years ago. Astronauts in space had to perform exercises to prevent them from becoming weak in a space capsule that had no push or pull from gravity.

Metaphorically speaking, this principle is applicable on earth as well. When adults remove the "gravity" (the push or pull that stretches people) our young will be unable to do tasks that past generations of young adults were able to do. Strength comes with stretching. Grit grows with gravity. As their leaders, we must introduce (or allow) gravity to take effect, knowing it's a positive and essential element of their growth. Learning to pay bills, assuming responsibility for tasks, negotiating projects with both teachers and employers cannot be learned on a screen or with a lecture. Projects require action. Growing up works like riding a bike. You must do it yourself. Sure, kids begin with a tricycle and then move to a bike with training wheels. But eventually, the training wheels must come off or embarrassment will prevail. Like teaching a child to ride a bike, our leadership must offer a balance between support and letting go.

Today, our young will only cultivate grit when they are forced to be resourceful. Grit comes, psychologist Angela Duckworth says, when students must reach down inside themselves and find a way to achieve something on their own. The more resources we give them, the less resourceful they tend to become. Further, research tells us we must encourage them to stick with a commitment for at least two years to see lasting results.[9] So, when you hear a young person complain about how tough something is just ask yourself, *Is my response or solution going to increase or decrease their grit?*

## 2. Control and Hope

In experiments with adolescent rats, psychologists discovered what they later called learned helplessness. It happens when participants pursue a goal and when nothing happens for a period of time. They conclude the goal is out of their control. And they stop trying. As we will discuss in the next chapter, studies reveal that when the activities in their days are controlled by adults (and hence, not in their control) both their angst and hopelessness rise. The more we govern and prescribe the agenda, the less they feel hopeful and the more they feel helpless.

Further, learned helplessness promotes irresponsibility. Kids feel little responsibility to work because it's not up to them. I believe most middle-class students assume that if they make a mistake, some adult will swoop in and rescue them. While this may feel good, it hinders development. Feeling that outcomes are in their control gives them a greater sense of hope and ownership.

Established generations must slowly encourage and even insist on giving them control of the agenda. This is the only way to build ownership, engagement, and responsibility. It requires trust and flexibility since young people may not perform to our standards. Ask yourself what you want most from them: *perfection* or *growth*?

### 3. Belief and Reality

What message do you suppose is received by a student when the adults in his life continue to swoop in and save him whenever something goes wrong? While it may feel good at first, it communicates, "We don't think you have it in you to solve this problem. You need an adult to help you." Consequently, these young people don't feel like adults themselves until somewhere between ages twenty-six and twenty-nine. They can remain on their parents' insurance policy until age twenty-six. In one survey, young adults reported they believe adult-life begins with "having their first child."[10] Today, this doesn't happen until long after eighteen years old. So, while we give them the right to vote, they may have no concept of reality. Rights without responsibilities create virtual adults and, often, spoiled brats.

As I mentioned earlier, adults have filled our kids' lives with artificial experiences. They're like the real thing, but we've not trusted them to take on something genuinely important, which has high stakes. And they've gotten the message loud and clear: You are just a child. You don't know better. You need help. You're not an adult.

When an adult is both supportive and demanding, it accomplishes something amazing. A young teen begins to believe in herself because her leader believed in her first. And that belief is displayed by offering real-life experiences to the young person, which communicates, "I believe in you and your ability to handle this opportunity." It may be an overseas trip, or a job, or even raising funds for a significant cause. But it's all about great expectations. One experiment found that a specific type of feedback given to young teens increased the students' efforts between 40 and 300 percent. What was the feedback? It was simply: "I am giving you these comments because I have high expectations of you and I know you can reach them."[11] So, the next time you owe some feedback to a young person, ask yourself: *Are the remarks I am about to make communicating belief in him?*

A Chinese student from Hong Kong vividly illustrates this point. Tsang Tsz Kwan finished high school several years ago, which was a feat in itself since she was severely hearing impaired, completely blind, and had limited feeling in her fingers. Most disabled students would be happy to just graduate high school. This girl, however, wanted to attend college. Due to her disablement, she was not required to take the normal entrance exams—but she wanted no special favors.[12]

Tsang's parents taught her that achievement would be harder for her than others, but they encouraged her, teaching her that every problem had a possibility inside of it. So, she taught herself to read braille with her lips. That's right, Tsang read through entire books touching her lips to the raised letters on the page. She took the exam, scoring in the top 5 percent of her class and gained two scholarships from the Chinese University of Hong Kong. She then won a scholarship for a master's degree from a top U.K. school. This only happens when opportunity meets up with resilience.

So, how do we develop mental toughness in our young? In the next chapter, we will discuss steps we can take to help Generation Z learn to bounce back from hardship.

TWENTY-ONE

# *Learning to Bounce Back After Hardship*

Back during my years working with Dr. John C. Maxwell, I recall him sharing a story with me from his boyhood. He remembers wrestling his older brother, Larry, in the living room. Larry was bigger and more experienced, which meant he beat John every single time, pinning him on his back. Over time, the defeats came more quickly and quickly, as John became conditioned to losing. One day, his dad was watching and challenged John to a match. As they wrestled, dad put up a fight, but as John exerted effort, his father allowed John to pin him and win. Young John smiled from ear to ear. As an adult, he remembers this key moment. He also recalls his brother Larry never pinning him again.

John's dad knew that once he tasted victory from his effort, he could associate that effort with winning and would keep on trying. He also knew that if his youngest son never won, eventually he would experience something we call: learned helplessness.

Let's take a closer look at the science behind this strategy to increase resilience in our students.

## What Are the Effects of Learned Helplessness?

Learned helplessness was a term coined by Psychologist Martin Seligman when he initiated research in 1967 at the University of Pennsylvania as an extension of his interest in depression.[1] In experiments with both dogs and rats, Dr. Seligman and his team discovered that once an individual sees no results after repeated effort, he or she begins to believe that outcomes are out of his or her control, and he or she then stops trying. He learns to be helpless when he feels his work is hopeless.

For students who compete at a high level (academics or athletics), the early stages of practice and drills can foster this same result. Young adults need to see their effort produces some kind of positive outcome, or they reduce or even stop putting out any effort. Let's face it. We've all confronted a tough problem, and after a few moments of trying to solve it, our minds automatically ask the questions: Is this really worth the effort? How badly do I want this anyway? Every coach has witnessed athletes who quit after a few two-a-days or when the drills become too grueling. Every teacher has seen this during a tough math equation.

If a goal feels out of reach, people experience:

- **Stress and anxiety.** (Angst rises when anything feels out of our control.)
- **Hopelessness.** (Despondency increases when we have no vision of progress.)
- **Demotivation.** (We lose inspiration and energy without signs of improvement.)

Believe it or not, stress and grit are inversely related.

## How to Foster an Environment that Encourages Learned Industriousness

The good news is, adult leaders can cultivate an opposite effect in their students. It's called learned industriousness. This term describes a behavioral theory from Robert Eisenberger to explain how people exert more effort when they see even the slightest results. Individuals with a history of positive reinforcement for their efforts usually transfer this effort to other endeavors. Lab rats that pull a lever twenty times to get food are prone to try harder and longer with another challenge later. They have been conditioned to sustain effort, believing it will produce results. Endorphins are released from both the feeling of hope and from the positive outcome.

I watched this work for my son, Jonathan, when he was seven years old. One morning, he tried to open a peanut butter jar. The lid was tight, and after several attempts, he was beginning to question how much he wanted that peanut butter. After a while, he gave up and walked away. When he walked out of the kitchen, I unscrewed the lid of that jar, then screwed it back on just tight enough that it would require effort but would be possible for my young son to accomplish his goal. I called him back in the kitchen and asked him to try to open the jar one more time. When he assured me he could not, I told him to work at it for ten full seconds. When he did, he opened the jar. He smiled in triumph and from that point on, my son was positively challenged to open any and all jars—pickles, mustard, relish, you name it.

It's learned industriousness. He applied to other areas the belief he developed with one jar: I can accomplish difficult tasks with extra effort.

Psychologist Donna Jackson Nakazawa reminds us, "In 1995, physicians Vincent Felitti and Robert Anda launched a large-scale epidemiological study that probed the child and adolescent histories of 17,000 subjects, comparing their childhood experiences to their later adult health records. The results were shocking. Nearly two-thirds of individuals had encountered one or more Adverse Childhood Experiences (ACEs)—a term Felitti and Anda coined to encompass the chronic, unpredictable, and stress-inducing events some children face."[2] Chronic stressors include divorce, neglect or abuse, and parents with addictions or mental illnesses.

This research, plus a study done at Yale University more recently, reveals conclusions that should inform how we lead and mentor students today.

1. For the most part, youth exposed to adversity while growing up actually become stronger for having experienced it. Their "emotional muscles" grow stronger. Without these stressors or when adults rescue kids from such stressors, they begin to give up more quickly, believing they need adults around to save them from hardship. Youth are naturally anti-fragile, and it is adults who make them fragile over time.

2. It is only when the stressors become toxic and chronic (continue for years) that children begin to surrender their will and stop trying. "When we're thrust over and over again into stress-inducing situations during childhood or adolescence, our physiological stress response shifts into overdrive, and we lose the ability to respond appropriately and effectively to future stressors—10, 20, even 30 years later."[3]

The difference between the two outcomes is clear. Kids who give up have endured chronic stressors with no adult who offers them hope often feel they are alone and that there's no hope or help available. Kids who grow stronger, however, experience periodical stressors yet have adults who encourage them to continue. They learn they can change their reality.

## FOUR SIMPLE STRATEGIES TO HELP KIDS DEVELOP LEARNED INDUSTRIOUSNESS

Ultimately, students must author their own development of grit and resilience. We cannot do it for them. We can, however, create an environment where grit can grow.

Let me suggest four simple strategies for coaches, teachers, parents, and leaders to induce learned industriousness. Consider these fundamentals.

### 1. Talk about a growth mindset.

Stanford psychologist, Carol Dweck, has become a hero of mine. From her research at Columbia University, she spotted the power of two mindsets that kids (and adults) develop, usually unwittingly, over time:

- **Fixed Mindset:** assumes that realities are fixed and don't change. This mindset causes kids to assume *I'm either good at math or I'm not. And I'm not.*

- **Growth Mindset:** believes our brains are like muscles and can grow. Realities can improve. Kids may say *I am not good at math… yet.*[4]

I've visited Singapore numerous times and have dear friends there. Singapore approaches math class differently than America does. Not only do math instructors make the subject concrete, not merely abstract equations, but they also embed discussions into the curriculum on positive attitudes, perseverance, and resilience. In other words, becoming good at math requires both hard skills and soft skills. In one experiment, Singaporean students were given a difficult math problem and told they could work on it as long as they wanted to before finishing or giving up. The average time students worked on the problem was one hour. Several achieved the correct answer. When the same experiment was performed in America, the average student lasted less than a minute before giving up.[5] It was stunning. I don't believe U.S. students are that less intelligent. Grit and resilience are not yet a part of their vocabulary and lifestyle.

## 2. Provide them with hope.

Napoleon Bonaparte said it most succinctly: "Leaders are dealers of hope." Adults can provide experiences that allow students to feel the progress of a strong effort. Carol Dweck told me a few years ago that her favorite word was yet. What she meant was regardless of how kids perform today, adding that simple three-letter word to a declaration changes the narrative in their heads. "I am not good at math—yet." For example, coaches must find ways to give student-athletes enough of a workout to challenge them but just enough that they can also conquer it and cultivate hope that they're growing. In the beginning, coaches may even want to rig the practice so first-year athletes are given this sense of improvement. Set up initial drills and practices to ensure they require effort but also allow players to see results. Hope is vital for effort.

Teachers may want to slowly increase the time and effort necessary to achieve an assignment and talk about students' progress along the way. Even if it's small, identifying the improvement will keep hope alive. Parents may teach their children how to ride a bike or drive a car, working on milestones steadily, calling attention to progress along the way. Hope is revived when improvement is celebrated. The opposite is true as well. John Maxwell taught me: "when there's no hope in the future, there's no power in the present."[6] As students see progress, they build a growth mindset. Without it, they unwittingly build a fixed mindset, believing they can't affect any change.

## 3. Furnish them with a visual aid.

We are leading a very visual generation, so we must be intentional about what this generation is observing each day. I learned this forty years ago when Head Coach Hayden Frye took over the Iowa Hawkeye football team. Coach Frye was determined to turn the team's losing ways around. One of the many changes he made was the uniforms. Frye decided the Iowa uniforms should look exactly like the Pittsburgh Steelers, who dominated the NFL at the time. He wanted his players to look at their teammates on game day and see champions. It worked. By 1982, Iowa was playing in the Rose Bowl. He led the Hawkeyes to fourteen bowl games and three Big Ten titles. Remember, people do what people see.

Leaders must find ways to provide visual reinforcement that students' efforts are paying off.

**Educators,** what if you changed the way you teach? It is interesting to note that communication is not what we think it is. John Medina, a University of Washington biologist, has published broad research into persuasion and how the brain processes information. His counsel is to get rid of most of your PowerPoint slide decks and start over with fewer words and more pictures. According to his book *Brain Rules*, Medina says, "We're incredible at remembering pictures. Hear a piece of information, and three days later you'll remember 10 percent of it. Add a picture and you'll remember 65 percent."[7] This is why we created an entire curriculum that teaches life skills using visuals—*Habitudes®: Images That Form Leadership Habits and Attitudes*.

**Parents,** what if you posted photos of kids at their best in your home? Introduce them to successful people in your community who do what they dream of doing. As a parent, if you pay your kids for doing chores, why not pay them for reading biographies of people who overcame obstacles?

## 4. Give them control.

The more ownership a student has over her learning, the more she learns. Metacognition is a crucial element to learning. The more she thinks about her thinking, the more she processes what she must do to reach a goal (not merely receive a mandate from a coach) and the more she will engage and own what's happening. I remember ten years ago when Coach Mack Brown gave ownership of part of the Texas Longhorn practices to Colt McCoy and his teammates. Mack asked his student-athletes how they felt they should prepare for the next Saturday's game. Suddenly, those young players took responsibility for every result they achieved. Why? It was up to the players to reach their goals. The result? A trip to the national championship. When people feel they are in control, it actually reduces stress and liberates them to grow and improve. Learned industriousness is a game changer.

**Talk It Over:** What do you see more of in your students, helplessness or industriousness?

## BUILDING CONFIDENCE IN STUDENTS

When Brandon told me, he wanted to start a YouTube channel that helped people who share the same vision get together and collaborate, I smiled and asked him, "What's stopping you?"

"I don't have the confidence," he acknowledged.

Over the next several minutes, Brandon and four of his friends joined me in a conversation about why teens may lack the confidence to try things they really want to do in their lives. By the way, it's true. So many feel both empowered yet fearful. When Growing Leaders surveyed students from three of our partner countries (India, Singapore, and Mexico), it found that the number one reason these students don't think they can lead is they lack confidence. By the way, this response came before both funding and strategy. We find that too many suffer from FOMU: Fear of Messing Up.

More often than the Millennial generation before them, Generation Z experiences less confidence in trying new activities or taking risks. According to Sparks & Honey's research, 72 percent of high school students today want to be entrepreneurs and create their own startups.[8] Sadly, those students are part of the most risk-averse generation we've ever measured. The two just don't go together.

The irony is many parents today work hard to instill confidence in their kids. For over twenty years, parents have praised their children, given them ribbons and trophies just for participating on the soccer team, negotiated with their teachers for a certain grade, and told them they were smart just for taking a hard test. Parents were determined to boost their self-esteem by bolstering their confidence.

So, why hasn't it worked so well?

### Two Kinds of Confidence

Boyd Varty, author of *Cathedral of the Wild*, suggests that there are different kinds of confidence in people, and we see it vividly in today's students. Boyd was raised in Africa by parents who started a nature preserve for wild animals. In his book, Boyd reflects that his parents always cared for their children but never overprotected them. They felt good decision-making skills came from a little freedom. He suggests there are two kinds of confidence:

1. The kind that comes from never being burned, never falling down, or seldom experiencing a negative incident as a kid.

2. The kind that comes from having been in situations where it all went wrong and kids learned to be resourceful and to problem solve.

Boyd writes, "Our parents never set out to put us in danger, of course; they would have defended us from anything and died before they'd let us be harmed. But they would not shelter us. To shelter us, where we grew up, would have failed to prepare us."[9]

What Boyd is talking about here is a reality that we see all over the country. Kids who have confidence, but that confidence seems to be unstable. Their confidence is often a veneer that doesn't go deep and often cracks at the first sign of hardship. I'd like to talk about our developing the wrong kind of confidence in kids.

Every parent, teacher, and coach wants confident youth to emerge while under their care. But with more attention given to this subject than at any time since I've been alive, we seem to be failing miserably. Why? I believe it's because we've unwittingly tried to build the wrong kind of confidence. Far too often, the confidence we build is a false confidence that comes from not trying anything but only watching videos about people who did. It's a false confidence from hearing they are "awesome" without doing anything even close to excellent. It's a false confidence that stems from always being resourced with money and never having had to earn it themselves. Can you see the problem?

We somehow feel that preventing bad stuff from happening will cultivate confidence. While it might work for the short term, in the end, it may just backfire. As I mentioned earlier, when we rescue our students from the consequences of forgetting their permission slips, their gym shorts, or some other responsibility, one of two things happen. First, they may develop a false sense of confidence, only to be eaten alive when they enter the real world where their professors or employers won't rescue them. Second, they begin to suspect they really don't have what it takes because they've not tested their skills, often leading them to shrink away from risks.

So, the kind of confidence that's easy to build doesn't work very well. It's built off of our mere words and sentiments. The kind that's tougher to build lasts longer.

| Wrong Kind of Confidence | Right Kind of Confidence |
|---|---|
| 1. It's Fragile | 1. It's Robust |
| 2. It Fades | 2. It Remains |
| 3. It Is Fake | 3. It Is Real |

I have a challenge for you. This school year, let's commit to building the right kind of confidence in students, the kind that believes they have what it takes and demonstrates this by letting them try new risky projects even if they falter, fall, or fail. We might be amazed at what students can really do. Eventually, they'll begin to take their places as responsible, confident leaders. Boyd Varty remembers living in Africa, saying, "I saw an eight-year-old Masai boy shepherding his cattle with no adult around for miles. Everyone contributed by age four; we all had to do our part."

I sure would like to say that in America.

## THE FOUR PHASES OF RESILIENCE

If our young have any hope of building resilience and grit, their leaders must foster a four-phase process on a week-to-week basis. My guess is these four phases are the steps you experienced when you began to cultivate resilience in yourself.

### Try

For some kids, trying something new is a huge step. I believe millions of kids from Generation Z have been conditioned by social media to refuse trying anything new for fear someone will capture it on video and post it. No one enjoys committing an epic fail only to find it on YouTube a day later for all to comment on. So, step one is equipping your students to believe it is OK to try and fail, to attempt new endeavors with friends around who have turned their phones off and are present to cheer on the risk-taker. This is when learned industriousness can begin to take effect.

### Learn

Whether the attempt is a success or a failure, we must be intentional about pausing to help our students reflect on what can be learned from the experience. I'm certain I learned far more from failing than succeeding as a teen. Fortunately, I lived in a day when making mistakes was not a catastrophe. The vital element, however, was a coach or teacher who helped me stop and discover what I learned from it all. Experience is not the best teacher. Experience with assessment is the best teacher. I have seen too many students have bad experiences and draw the wrong conclusions.

### Adapt

Phase three is enabling students to adapt their efforts based on what they learned from failing. There is a close relationship between adaptability and resilience. When a person or an object is resilient, it means it can bend with the stressors and not break. It is flexible, not brittle. When I was a kid, I played little league baseball. For two years, our team was the absolute worst in the league. We lost every single game, some by large margins. I recall, however, our coach never became exasperated by this reality. We would always take several minutes to discuss what we'd learned from our strikeouts and errors and take steps to improve the next week.

### Recover

This final phase is essential. Merely adapting may or may not get those kids to their goals. They must adapt and bend to their stressors, then return to their original shape to become strong again. Recovery is about bouncing back to become even more industrious afterward. This is what makes employees or athletes valuable to their teams. They not only endure, but they comeback. Just like a rubber band isn't useful until it is stretched so it is with people on a team. Survival is not the goal; success is. The most resilient and gritty people demonstrate this in the grind of daily life.

I have known Dave Dravecky for more than thirty years. Dave was an incredible major league pitcher for the San Diego Padres and later the San Francisco Giants. He became famous nationwide in 1988 when cancer was discovered in his pitching arm. It was devastating for him, for his family, and for his team, since he played such a vital role on the Giants. What makes his story great is that Dave walked through the four phases above. When the doctors spotted the cancer, their prognosis was that Dave would never pitch again. Dave smiled, prayed, worked, and bounced back. In 1989, Dravecky was on the mound again, pitching to cheering fans who could barely believe their eyes. The man who had cancer in his pitching arm was now pitching again, throwing eight innings against the Cincinnati Reds and winning the game. He wrote a book called *Comeback*, which is about what grit can do for people.

Then, he was dealt another blow.

In the next game, Dave threw the "pitch heard round the world." As he propelled the ball toward home plate, viewers could see his arm literally break. His body fell to the ground, this time never to pitch again. Dave lost his arm two years later. Resilience, however, is about so much more than physical ability.

Dave spiraled into clinical depression. "The loss of an arm, the loss of a career. What am I going to do with the next part of my life?" He wondered. "When I went through clinical depression… I mean, we were in counseling for 30 months. The first 18 months of our counseling was just dealing with this whole identity crisis."[10]

Dravecky had to cope with the loss of everything he worked so hard to achieve. Formerly a lefty, he had to learn how to live his life doing everything right-handed. Formerly a major league pitcher, he now had to find an identity in something beyond baseball, placing it in something that could not be taken away. And while he once drew his confidence from his athletic talent, he now had to build competencies around new gifts inside of him. Dave tried, learned, adapted, and recovered. He had to find a new version of himself. And he did.

Dave began to define resilience more broadly than merely bouncing back and doing what he once did. He wrote a book entitled *When You Can't Comeback*. It's all about being resilient when your circumstances prevent you from doing what you'd like to do, but you still must go on. Dave is a husband, father, philanthropist, author, and speaker. He's continued to work with the Giants and adds value to that organization off of the pitcher's mound. He is a living example of try, learn, adapt, and recover. Dave does with one arm what most people have a tough time doing with two. What he lacks in a left arm, he makes up for in resilience.

TWENTY-TWO

# Consumption Without Reflection

*Challenge #9*

I will never forget a conversation I had with a college student a few years ago. She was a sophomore, majoring in psychology. In our brief exchange, she was buzzing about a news story she'd just recently read and was eager to pass on to her friends. Evidently, a cat and a dog had mated and given birth to a hybrid cat/dog. I'm not sure if they called it a kitten or puppy. Maybe it was a "putten" or a "kippy."

Whatever the case, this young lady simply had no idea the story was fake news. Biologically speaking, it is impossible for these two species to give birth to a hybrid. It turns out this fake story has cycled through cyberspace for years, complete with a Photoshopped picture of the animal. It was all made up. This student, however, was so ecstatic she got to share the news, she didn't take the time to check out the facts. In her passion to get the story out, she didn't ensure she got the story straight.

It's common. It's human. We are often emotional more than we are rational.

The truth is, critical thinking is a skillset that university faculty are begging to see developed in students today. For that matter, so are employers. Simply defined, critical thinking is the objective analysis and evaluation of an issue in order to form a judgment.

## Why Is This a Vital Issue Today?

In January 2016, the *World Economic Forum* issued a report entitled "The Future of Jobs." It states: "The Fourth Industrial Revolution, which

includes developments in previously disjointed fields such as artificial intelligence and machine-learning, robotics, nanotechnology, 3-D
printing, and genetics and biotechnology, will cause widespread disrup-
tion not only to business models but also to labor markets over the next
five years, with enormous change predicted in the skill sets needed to
thrive in the new landscape."[1] In fact, in 2015, critical thinking was
listed as the number four skill graduates need in the workplace. By 2020,
it will be number two, right behind complex problem-solving skills.[2] In
the upcoming "smart world," we all need to think critically. It is rated as
the number one skill of increasing importance over the next five years.

Sadly, studies of higher education demonstrate three disturbing
facts.

1. Most college faculty at all levels lack a substantive concept of
   critical thinking.

2. Most college faculty don't realize they lack this skill, assuming
   they sufficiently understand it and that they're already
   teaching it to students.

3. Lecture, rote memorization, and short-term study habits are
   still the norm in college instruction and learning today.[3]

With this in mind, we still face formidable gaps between today's classroom and career-ready graduates who demonstrate critical thinking
skills.

This may sound elementary to you, but you'd be surprised if you
knew how many people just stop thinking once they land a job or reach
a goal. It's like they turn their brains off and stop practicing critical
thinking. Evidently, it's too much work. So, they let commercials, magazines, websites, and social media do their thinking for them. Life seems
so complicated they don't trust their own judgment. They don't do any
research, and they fear being wrong.

Rich Milgram, CEO of the career network "Beyond," said: "The
most sought-after skill-sets for recruiters are becoming less and less
about proficiency in tasks and more about how you think systems
through and work within the context of the team. Learning technology
is the easy part. Having the mindset to apply it, having the logic to process it, being thorough and detail-oriented while doing so, these are the
critical skills."[4] Based on Milgram's research at "Beyond," the top three
most sought-after skill sets were listed in nine out of ten jobs.

1. **Critical Thinking.** (Using logic and reasoning to identify the strengths and weaknesses of alternative solutions, conclusions, or approaches to problems.)

2. **Complex Problem-Solving.** (Identifying complex problems and reviewing related information to evaluate options and implement solutions.)

3. **Judgment and Decision-Making.** (Considering the costs and benefits of potential actions to choose the most appropriate ones.)[5]

## Why Emotional Reasoning Rules the Day

Earlier in this book, we cited NYU leadership ethics professor and author Jonathan Haidt and his theory about the rider and the elephant.[6] His theory explains how people can be intelligent yet emotional in their decision-making. In his words, he explains, "the rider represents conscious or 'controlled' processes—the language-based thinking that fills our minds and that we can control to some degree. The elephant represents everything else that goes on in our minds, the vast majority of which is outside our conscious awareness."[7]

This metaphor explains how intelligent people—especially young people—can assume they are thinking logically about a choice they've made, but in reality, be driven by realities other than logic and reasoning. For instance, adolescents often make a decision based on a gut feeling they have, then argue for it in a rational way. They think their decision is rational, but in fact, they are rationalizing what they want to embrace. Whether it is gorging on junk food or rebounding after a breakup or binging on video games and Netflix or choosing to try an illegal drug, our gut makes the call and our sense of reason argues to make it feel logical.

Let's face it, we are emotional creatures.

Dr. Haidt would say it appears the rider is whipping the elephant, directing it where to go, but in fact, the elephant is carrying the rider where it wants to go. In fact, the rider often believes he is in control, yet the elephant is vastly stronger and tends to win any conflicts that arises between the two. This is especially true when a student has never been taught to think critically. Dr. Haidt reviewed psychological research showing that the rider generally functions more like the elephant's servant than its master in that the rider is brilliantly skilled at producing "post-hoc justifications for whatever the elephant does or believes."[8]

Psychologists call this emotional reasoning. It is the cognitive distortion that occurs whenever our intellect interprets our decisions in ways that are consistent with our reactive emotional state, without investigating what is true. This distortion prevents us from critical thinking causes us to exaggerate how we feel about ourselves, good or bad; clouds our ability to see all sides of an issue and instead dig our heels in, blinds us from healthy self-awareness, making us defensive and stubborn; and creates a we/they perception on issues, fostering adversarial relationships.

Know any teens like this? I can understand why.

In their adolescent years, students experience raging hormones. Dr. Jeramy Clark writes, "One of the first areas of the teenage brain to be pruned (edited as it matures) is the emotional center of the brain, the limbic system. Teenagers feel high highs and low lows, in part, because the structures of their brains that control emotions undergo serious renovation. Further complicating matters is the fact that while the emotional limbic system is highly aroused early in adolescence the brain's control center—specifically the prefrontal cortex—matures last."[9] Emotions can run high because their executive functioning (forethought, planning, good decision making) are just not keeping up with their emotions. The limbic system precedes the prefrontal cortex.[10]

## THE SIMULTANEOUS REALITIES THAT HAVE REDUCED CRITICAL THINKING

Perhaps this has always been an issue for people, especially teens. My big question is, how in the world can the problem be this bad today when we're more educated than ever? We do not lack education or information, but we tend to divide ourselves into tribes and only seek confirmation of our feelings and beliefs. The challenge is our marvelously educated 21st century culture has simultaneous realities occurring.

### We live in a world of speed and volume.

Information travels faster and faster and comes at us in larger quantities than ever. The name of the game for marketers is get your message to stand out. So, organizations and people produce more content than we've ever produced in the past. To illustrate, consider this fact. Every day the average person produces six newspapers worth of information compared with just two and a half pages 24 years ago—nearly a 200-fold increase.[11] This leaves us in an overwhelmed state, unable to think objectively because we lack the energy. Or, it leaves us seeking only what confirms what we already believe (i.e. politically or socially) as so much comes at us each day.

### We experience significant emotional needs.

Humans have always experienced emotional trauma, loss, death, and despair. But our world of virtual connections (instead of authentic ones) has created social corrosion today, leaving more of us in need of a genuinely supportive community. According to the NPD Group, a marketing research firm, more Americans shop alone, dine alone, and live alone than those who do so with family or friends.[12] BBC online recently featured a restaurant in Amsterdam, Eenmaal, which only has tables for one.[13] A few years ago, a movement even began encouraging people to marry themselves. Marriage for a party of one. It's no joke. It's easier to do life on a screen. Sadly, it is unsatisfying. Because of our unmet emotional needs, we seek to fill those voids any way we can.

### We live in a world of judgment: likes, shares, and views.

Thanks to both media and social media, we are constantly being evaluated by others. Did they "like" my post? Did they share it with others? How many stars did I get from that customer or subscriber? Consequently, we are always looking for affirmation, almost as if we are campaigning all the time for office. It has made us superficial. We go wide but seldom deep. For a typical middle school student in our 2017 focus groups, social media was the primary place they received their sense of identity. Our emotional needs can be so strong they cloud our objectivity and leave us in need of emotional confirmation.

### We become tied to this lifestyle, driven by input from others.

With this new scorecard on life, millions of students develop a lifestyle driven by the affirmation or criticism of others. The ping of a smartphone sends a signal to our brains. When we hear a ding, a ring, or little ping, alerting us to a new text, email, or Facebook post, cells in our brains often release dopamine—one of the chemical transmitters in the brain's reward circuitry. This is why social media can be addictive for our brains. Earlier, I suggested a memorable way to understand what's happened to so many. When our phones had leashes, we were free. Now our phones are free, and we have leashes. We are bonded to a device that controls our behavior.

### We stick to the surface.

Because of each of the above realities, it is now easier to stick to the surface of issues rather than go deep with others. We are victims of prompts, pings, headlines, and other clickbait. Once again, our wealth of information has created a poverty of attention. We move quickly to a new prompt rather than think deeply about any one subject. Several social scientists have called us the distracted generation. Someone who's distracted cannot think critically. One high school student we met put it this way, "Social media on your smartphone is like having someone tap you on your shoulder all day long."

## THE INTERNET'S AGE OF ADULTHOOD IS THIRTEEN

Part of the problem we face today is that kids are exposed to a wealth of information and online content far before their emotions are prepared for that content. *The Wall Street Journal* summarized the challenge well saying, "At 13, kids are still more than a decade from having a fully developed prefrontal cortex, the part of the brain involved in decision-making and impulse control. And yet parents and educators unleash them on the internet at that age—if not before—because they're told children in the U.S. must be at least 13 to download certain apps, create email accounts and sign up for social media."[14]

The internet is essentially declaring adulthood begins at thirteen. You and I both know that just isn't true in a young teen's brain.

Millions of moms and dads view the age thirteen standard as merely a safety precaution, a little like the movie rating PG-13. In reality, this age restriction is the result of a 1998 law called the Children's Online Privacy Protection Act (COPPA), which was intended to protect the privacy of kids ages twelve and under. It was created to keep companies from collecting and posting children's personal information. Sadly, "it has inadvertently caused 13 to become imprinted on many parent's psyche's as an acceptable age of internet adulthood."[15]

Since we see the issue as a movie rating instead of a privacy issue, kids consume content years before their brains are ready to do any critical thinking on it. With so much to stimulate them at such a young age, Generation Z has grown used to reactive thinking, rather than proactive, critical thinking. In short: *We spend more time reacting than reflecting.*

## The PRICE of Social Media

Let's examine a summary of the costs of allowing social media to play such a huge role in our daily lives. We first introduced this idea in *Marching Off the Map.* Millions of people, especially young people, have fallen prey to their portable device. No doubt, there are plenty of positive growth opportunities with social media, but are the costs worth the price tag our youth culture pays for the ubiquitous presence of social media? The columns below capture the realities and outcomes we see.

## The PRICE We Pay for Social Media

Social media offers…

### P—Personal Platform
This has fostered a narcissistic culture of selfies.

### R—Reactionary Opinions
This induces a preoccupation with others' judgments.

### I—Instant Updates
This can make us impulsive with short attention spans.

### C—Constant Information
This has caused angst and depression in users.

### E—External Stimuli
This can lead to addictive lifestyles with our devices.

## Auditing the PRICE We Pay

Let's examine each of these consequences and detail the findings for each of them. As I review, I suggest you consider what you can do to find ways to counter the negative realities that coincide with the emergence of social media.

## 1. A Narcissistic Culture of Selfies

Social media has played an enormous role in the narcissistic tendencies of our population, both young and old. Our phones enable us to both take a selfie and post it in a matter of minutes. According to a survey from Luster Premium White (a teeth whitening brand), the average Millennial will take 25,000 selfies in his lifetime. Ninety-five percent of young adults have taken one. Today, a million selfies are taken every day.[16] I don't believe we'd do this unless we had the ability to post them via social media.

According to Dr. Peggy Drexler, assistant professor of psychology at Weill Medical College and Cornell University, the reasons we take so many selfies vary. "A recent study out of the U.K. found that the selfie phenomenon may be damaging to real-world relationships, concluding that both excessive photo sharing and sharing photos of a certain type—including self-portraits—makes people less likable. The same study found that increased frequency of sharing self-portraits is related to a decrease in intimacy with others. […] The pressure to be 'camera-ready' can also heighten self-esteem issues and increase feelings of competition among friends."[17]

Our work with student athletes reveals a growing number are consumed far more with their own playing time and their personal brand than what happens to the team. It's about me not we.

## 2. Preoccupation with Others' Judgements

Look around you at middle-class teens. Our world is constantly critiquing every word or thought they have. Why? Because social media enables it. This can drive students to be obsessed with how others feel about them, constantly checking comments, likes, dislikes, views, and shares. Sadly, it's like an evaluation of their identity. An increasing number of students are preoccupied and obsessed with others' opinions, even when they're uninformed. It only matters that they've been posted.

Television even imitates social media, as reality TV shows enable viewers to critique and vote on who stays on the show. We've created a population consumed with judging every look, word, and action. It stings to be the receiver.

I should note that criticism and judgmental attitudes go both ways. Our young can get anxious and preoccupied with the critical comments they receive. At the same time, they're proficient at judging others as well, which leads us to the next reality.

## 3. Impulsivity with Short Attention Spans

We live in a time of impulsive behavior. We rant and rave on Twitter, even when we are presidential candidates. We react to information that may diminish our brand, and then we attack the attacker. We cyberbully even if we're celebrities. This tendency may not only lead to addiction, as I will discuss later, but it can also foster an inability to delay gratification. Let's face it. When something is easy to access, the activity can easily become impulsive. Social media fits that criteria.

You've likely heard of the Stanford Marshmallow Experiment by Dr. Walter Mischel, done with four to six-year-old children. The kids were told they could enjoy a marshmallow immediately, or if they'd wait for fifteen minutes, they would receive a second one. Predictably, some were able to wait, and others were not.

Researchers followed up as the children grew into adolescents. They found the kids who could delay gratification were psychologically better-adjusted, more dependable, more self-motivated, and, as high school students, scored significantly higher GPAs. In 2011, the latest study conducted on these same participants showed the characteristics remained with them for life, bad or good.[18] Social media could hinder this ability as they mature. It's far too easy to be impulsive when we can react hiding behind a screen.

When new information constantly streams at adolescents, it's tough to pay attention to any one message very long. Their ability to process information is diminished. Their patience to digest complex information evaporates. A lifestyle full of social media pings can foster superficial thinking rather than deep thinking.

## 4. Angst and Depression in Users

This is the storm on the horizon for which I'm most concerned. The angst that comes with so much information streaming at us 24/7 is overwhelming. As brilliant as I believe our minds are, I don't believe they're hardwired for so much relentless data.

Neuroscientists now report that when we have no margins in our calendar, when information or deadlines are constantly screaming at us, we have less capacity for empathy or creativity.[19] In fact, a noisy, taxing life reduces empathy and raises stress.[20] The noise puts us in survival mode. Life's about coping.

The irony of social media is profound. While many of the messages come from friends we know, the onslaught of information—especially if it appears that the messenger is experiencing a better life than the receiver—can lead to FOMO (Fear of Missing Out) and other such negative emotions. In short, all the happy messages ironically can make us feel sad or anxious.

## 5. Addictive Lifestyles with Their Devices

Because millions of students have social media posts delivered to them with a notification, their psyche becomes conditioned to react to the ping of their phone. Psychologists remind us that dopamine is released as students become expectant of this ping. It can actually be addictive. I've mentioned before a report from Cisco indicates that many college students consider their phones as essential as air and water.[21] It can almost feel as if they're enslaved to the messaging, just like people can be to cigarettes or alcohol. According to research in the 2013 *Journal of Exercise Rehabilitation*, cell phone addiction can negatively impact brain development.[22] Further, the data shows that social media addictions can actually pave the way for other addictive behaviors, such as drug or alcohol abuse. It doesn't stop there. Research by Gwenn Schurgin O'Keeffe and Kathleen Clarke-Pearson, in the *Journal of the American Academy of Pediatrics*, suggest a term for the cumulative challenges accompanying social media: Facebook depression.

Facebook depression is defined as depression that develops when preteens and teens spend a great deal of time on social media sites, such as Facebook, and then begin to exhibit classic symptoms of depression.[23]

## The Bottom Line

Too often, we've not encouraged our young to move beyond the superficial. So much data arrives on their devices, they have little time to process what they access. You can't think critically if you barely have time to think at all. Life is impulsive. Reactionary. Filled with hacks. Our challenge can be summarized this way:

1. **Information requires application.**
   Any time I receive information, I should seek the best way to apply it.

2. **Consumption requires reflection.**
   Any time I consume information, I must find time to process what it means.

Training them to practice critical thinking, we will find, is a balance of life change and mental practice. As we will discuss in the next chapter, it is vital that we address these two needs. You already know why. Critical thinking is the best way to enable the rider to guide the elephant as we journey through life.

# TWENTY-THREE

# *Training Them to Be Critical Thinkers*

Peyton Robertson is a member of Generation Z. When he was eleven years old, Peyton watched Hurricane Sandy wreak havoc across the U.S. coastline in 2012. He was intrigued at how sandbags weren't efficient in stopping the flooding. The sand couldn't prevent the water from getting through. So, what did he do? He invented a new sandbag—with no sand.

Peyton is from Ft. Lauderdale, FL, so he's seen a few storms and floods even as a kid. It's what drove him to design his new protection against floods, hurricanes, and other disasters. He calls it the Sandless Operational Sandbag (SOS). It earned him the title of America's Top Young Scientist in 2013. Here is his flow of thought:

- Conventional sandbags are heavy to transport, and they leave gaps.
- We needed a lighter sandbag that could expand to fill the crevices.
- What if we made a bag with a combination of salt and polymer inside?
- The bag would be doused with water before use, so the polymer expands.
- The mixture makes the bag light, easy to store, and more effective.

It makes sense, doesn't it? What's cool is it also really works. This kid could see layers to a solution that others couldn't because they were bound by the way things have always been done. After all, how many years have we been using sandbags? But in his own way, young Peyton analyzed our current methods, saw why they weren't getting the job done, and invented something more effective.

## The Process of Maker Learning

He likely didn't know it, but Peyton was using a process called maker learning. It's a concept that's as old as education itself, but it has found new life in today's classroom. Due to our rapidly changing world, schools are increasingly trying to empower students to be lifelong learners. It's become one of the most important student traits of the 21$^{st}$ century. Why? A high school student today may likely find a job after college graduation that doesn't even exist today.

Maker learning employs critical thinking to find solutions. Maker learning is both an old and a new idea. It's a relatively new concept to the average person, but the principles of "maker learning" are based on one of the oldest forms of education: self-directed learning. It's how most learning took place centuries ago before we systematized our public schools and began giving lectures. Self-directed learning is the belief that students can and should be active agents in their own discoveries in a classroom. Maker learning utilizes this self-directed, hands-on-learning to push students to think critically and solve real problems, just like Peyton did. It fosters critical thinking.

**Question:** How well and how often do you host critical-thinking conversations?

## How Can We Define Critical Thinking?

Of course, there is no single definition of critical thinking everyone embraces. What people do agree on is it involves analyzing, synthesizing, and applying what you've observed to draw a conclusion. The simplest definition might be:

*Critical thinking is the process of analyzing, evaluating, and applying information as a guide to belief and action.*

If knowledge is possessing information, then critical thinking means knowing how to apply information wisely. In 1597, Francis Bacon was the first to say, "Knowledge is power." If that's true, then critical thinking means having "superpowers." Knowledge becomes wisdom. It requires discipline, objectivity, and corrective thinking so that a solution or judgment can surface. While this sounds rare among people today, especially teens, remember that Peyton did it at eleven years old, and your kids can too.[1]

At our house, we debriefed everything we experienced after we experienced it, from road trips to encounters with new people to Friday night movies. In fact, my kids used to make fun of me for insisting we pick apart the plot and main characters of movies we saw in the cinema. On our drive home or over some dessert, we'd discuss the arch of the story, the conflict, the protagonist and antagonist, and the chief moral of the story. Over the years, my children got very good at recognizing and evaluating stories, situations, and people. Now, as adults, they expect to have a conversation and critically think about what we just experienced. (Especially if I pay for the movie or the trip.) This year, we vacationed in Washington D.C. and processed every museum and memorial we visited.

## How Do We Grow Critical Thinking Skills?

If we have any hope of cultivating critical thinking skills in a new generation of kids, we have got to switch up the way we teach them. Instead of starting with a subject, what if we begin with a problem? Instead of looking to a teacher for answers, what if we turn kids loose to search and find ideas, then bounce them off of a caring adult who could act as a consultant? What if we let them drive the exploration, instead of imposing a static curriculum on those students? I am not saying they need no adults around; I am saying our role must change if they're to

The Enlightenment and the Industrial Revolution accelerated those inventions when people became open to reason instead of mere tradition.

think on their own. Even in our current environments driven by state, county, and national test scores (ACT, SAT), could we create a context that feels student-centered and that teaches them how to think? This issue is far bigger than we can cover in this chapter, but we must begin teaching our kids to analyze and evaluate assumptions.

This is how most inventions have occurred throughout history. The Enlightenment and the Industrial Revolution accelerated those inventions when people became open to reason instead of mere tradition. Today, this is truer than ever, as our communication, our automation, how we travel, and how work gets done changes rapidly. Our current culture demands we think critically. Sadly, too often, we're like the crowd of citizens in the story "The Emperor's New Clothes." Most of us just go along with the majority; few of us are like the boy who looked at the emperor who was stark naked and identified what was happening.

## 3D Glasses

One of our *Habitudes*® is called "3D Glasses." It's a metaphor for critical thinking. Do you remember the last time you went to a movie in 3D? You know the drill. You buy your ticket, and it costs a bit more than a regular movie ticket because you have to rent special 3D glasses to wear while you watch. They are big and strange, but they make the story come alive.

Have you ever tried watching a 3D movie without the glasses? Everyone has taken those glasses off for a minute just to see what it would look like. Everything is fuzzy and distorted. We can still hear the dialogue, but the picture is unclear. That's why they give you the glasses. If you stop and think about it, the 3D lens:

- Helps you to perceive what's happening more clearly.
- Causes the plot and characters to come alive.
- Allows you to experience all three dimensions of the film, instead of just two.

In many ways, these 3D glasses are a picture of what students need today and what employers want in their team members. Critical thinking is like putting on 3D glasses. When students don't wear them, they fail to see all the angles. Things remain fuzzy. Organizations need employees who bring a special lens with them, enabling them to see problems and solutions clearly, a lens that helps them perceive the root of what's really going on, a lens that ultimately allows them to carefully evaluate what to do. The lens aids them in seeing all three dimensions of a situation—height, width, and depth. One manager told me, "I'll pay more for a staff person who can see every situation from all angles and know what to do with it. This skill helps us find solutions more quickly. It's almost priceless."

So, what does this look like in real life?

The outcome is almost always problem-solving. Jodie Wu is a perfect example of what can happen when a student puts 3D Glasses on. Jodie was an engineering student at MIT. One of her classes challenged her to come up with an idea to help a developing nation. She pulled a team of students together and began collaborating with another team in Tanzania. As a result, they identified an efficiency problem in rural villages that had limited or no access to electricity. What those villages did have were bikes. So, they redesigned bicycles to do agricultural tasks such as threshing corn in those limited access areas. It worked brilliantly. She and her team had to think critically to develop the idea, find ways to manufacture and distribute the idea, as well as to fundraise and market the company. She is now the CEO of Global Cycle Solutions in Tanzania. At twenty-four years old, she was named to *Forbes 30 under 30* list in 2011. Because of her ongoing critical thinking around the invention, the Gates Foundation backed the Multi-Crop Thresher in 2013.[2]

## Four Changes that Foster Critical Thinking

We believe the fundamental changes we must help Generation Z kids make are these:

1. **Replace Impulsivity with Delayed Gratification**

   What if you challenged your students to wait on something they really wanted? What if they slowed down their race toward a goal until they considered all angles of the obstacles to a problem, suspending judgment until they did so. Teach them to wait.

2. **Replace Defensiveness with Emotional Security**

   What if your students learned to listen to opposing opinions or views? What if you chose an issue they had strong opinions on and asked them to argue an opposing side of the issue? This would foster both adaptability and fairmindedness in students.

### 3. Replace Complacency with Curiosity

What if your students learned to curiously observe what's going on around them and ask why. Critical thinkers are inquisitive because they question realities rather than assume things must stay the way they are. Teach them to probe and explore.

### 4. Replace Noise with Reflection

What if you held them to two hours a day on their phone? Instead, teach them to analyze and evaluate. Separate the whole into parts to discover their nature, function, and relationships; and learn to listen and think. We must teach them to value solitude.

## ADAPTING TO DEVELOP-DESIGN THINKING

"The single best step I took to get students engaged in my classroom," said one faculty member, "was to move from my typical lesson plan to using design thinking." Earlier, I mentioned maker thinking. Design thinking is a second cousin.

Have you tried design thinking?

It's a practice that's gaining interest among educators, coaches, and even parents across our nation. I have advocated for it for years now, believing it made the difference for me as an instructor, trainer, parent, and leader of students. According to Mary Ellen Flannery of the National Education Association, "At the heart of design thinking are students trying to solve problems that affect people. Those people may be fictional characters in a novel, or they might be their community's very real homeless population. The process requires students to interview others about their needs, or to ask themselves what it's like to be that person, the client or 'end user.'"[3]

Teacher Dan Ryder says, "The secret sauce is the empathy piece. It's the idea that students are attempting to solve problems—real problems—with their brainpower, and that their level of success depends on how well they serve the needs of others."[4]

The root of design thinking goes back centuries, as the best mentors and teachers always began with questions about real-world problems, not merely theories from a textbook. However, its recent popularity stems from Stanford University and its "d.school ." Laura McBain is the director of K12 community and implementation at K12 Lab in

Stanford University's d.school. She says, "The human-centered piece is probably the most profound and important thing we do as educators. It allows students to think about the challenges the world is facing and puts them in the driver's seat to be really engaged to solve those problems to feel empowered to change the world."[5]

I agree. Suddenly, school becomes real for students, not merely hypotheses and facts to be memorized. And it actually prepares them for a well-lived life. Design thinking is a mindset. It begins with empathy and ends with problem solving.

## Five Steps in Design Thinking

So how might you begin to implement design thinking in your work with students? It can begin with students noticing a problem in their school or even their own classroom. Or it may start with observing the property next to the school campus or down the street. It might be a social problem in their city or somewhere in the country, such as the Flint, Michigan (clean water) or Houston, Texas (flooding water problems). In any case, students actually read up and research the problem. Then, they begin to problem-solve as if they were the ones in charge of it. Here is the simple five-step approach popularized at Stanford's d.school.[6]

1. **Choose and define a problem.**

   As a group, students must first decide on what problem most needs to be solved and which ones they are best equipped to address. It can be a campus, local, national, or global issue that captures their attention. Define why it exists. This fosters engagement.

2. **Brainstorm and ideate multiple solutions.**

   This is where the metacognition process begins. Students must stop looking to an adult to come up with the answer and tell them. Instead, they get creative and begin a list of their own potential answers to the question: What does better look like?

3. **Prototype the best solution.**

   Next, they must test one of those solutions to see if it's relevant and helpful. This is a maturing process that forces students to move from idealism to realism. They must think through all the possible outcomes that might happen.

4. **Test the solution once you've tried it.**

Now, they must actually try it out and see if there's any hope that the idea might solve the problem in a beta test. This goes far beyond the story problems our math teachers used to give us. It involves applying knowledge to real life.

5. **Reflect on what worked, what didn't work, and why.**

Finally, critical thinking skills develop as students reflect on why their solutions did or did not work on the problem. In a way, students give themselves their own "exam" on their project and decide how successful they've been.

I love how design thinking makes subjects like math, science, and social studies come alive because they become real, not just facts in a textbook to memorize. Probably the best news is design thinking builds what educators call the four Cs of 21ˢᵗ century skills: creativity, collaboration, communication, and critical thinking. Design thinking cultivates both hard and soft skills students will need as adults, and it frequently beckons students to think and act like leaders. It's a win/win situation.

## The Day Boredom Became a Gift

Ruby Kate Chitsey is only eleven years old. Since she's young and has a working mom, she can't just run off to play the way some of her classmates do after school. So, Ruby Kate often joins her mom at work. Her mother is a nurse practitioner at local nursing homes in Arkansas.

Needless to say, a kid can get bored in a nursing home.

Boredom, however, can lead to positive outcomes. Neuroscience tells us that in times of boredom our brains can develop creativity and empathy.[7] For Ruby Kate, both happened the same day. She was in a sitting room and noticed a resident staring out the window intently, almost as if she was looking for something for someone. The resident sat in a wheelchair, quiet and still. So, Ruby Kate approached her and asked what she was doing. She found out the old woman was watching her dog that she'd owned for twelve years exit with a friend, not knowing if she'd ever see her dog again. For Ruby, it was a sad moment. She knew it was expensive to get a pet sitter to bring a dog by the nursing home each day.

This got Ruby thinking. How many other nursing home residents couldn't afford simple things that brought them joy? In asking this question, she began practicing the ideas we've talked about in this chapter, just like Peyton (and both at eleven years old).

This set Ruby in motion. She took an old notebook and began visiting these elderly folks, asking them what they missed the most from their former world. She called it their Wish List, asking for three wishes they wanted most. She got responses like:

- Fast food
- Paperback books
- Dr. Pepper
- My pet
- A better pillow

- My favorite candy bars
- Magazines
- Vienna sausages
- Fresh fruit
- A cell phone

Once she had some tangible wishes, Ruby Kate was motivated and set in motion.

She launched a Facebook page called Three Wishes for Ruby's Residents. Then, her mother helped her set up a GoFundMe account to help pay for those wishes.[8]

In a relatively short amount of time, she had raised over seventy thousand dollars.

Residents rarely smiled, but Ruby made them melt. There were smiles. Tears. Hugs. Laughter. In fact, GoFundMe took notice and named Ruby Kate Chitsey Kid Hero of the Month. Her mom got emotional watching her daughter take a boring day and turn it into something redemptive in service to others who couldn't do it for themselves. And, then, the idea grew.

Ruby Kate's mother jumped in to help. She recruited a seventy-four-year-old resident, Marilyn Spurlock, who said, "I've been here so long, I no longer felt useful. This gives me something to do. It took away a lot of my depression because I felt worthless and couldn't do anything to help anybody. Now I can."[9]

So, what can we learn from this young leader? I think I spotted a few transferable concepts from Ruby Kate's story:

1. Teach students to view boredom as an ally, not an adversary.

2. As students become bored, enable them to look outward, not inward.

3. As they look outward teach them to look and listen to the needs of others.

4. As they spot a need, coach them to use what they have to meet that need.

5. As they recognize what they have, encourage them to put on 3D glasses.

6. As they pursue meeting needs, help them see their own needs get met.

"I think Ruby's starting a movement—recognizing a need and just doing something about it. This is just about their quality of life—bringing them joy," her mom said.[10] Wow. And to think it all started with some critical thinking on a boring day.

# TWENTY-FOUR

# *Six Experiences That Enable Young People to Mature*

Jim Casey was born in a small town called Pick Handle Gulch, Nevada, in 1888. As a child, Jim's dad passed away, leaving him, his mother Annie, his two brothers, and one sister to survive on their own. They moved to Seattle to find work, and it was there Jim saw the bustling streets of a big city, reacting to the Klondike Gold Rush, which had begun some years earlier in the Northwest.

Annie quickly incentivized her kids to make something of themselves. She spoke to her children about maintaining a strong set of values, about looking for problems to solve, of finding good people to meet, and of serving others with their talents. Her message to her kids was to find a need and fill it. As a teen in 1907, Jim spotted something curious. He saw the increasing demand for telegrams since most people didn't own a phone yet. Thanks to the gold rush, folks were hungry to communicate.

Suddenly, Jim and his friend Claude Ryan had an idea.

With one bicycle between them and one hundred dollars they borrowed from a friend, the two teenagers started their own telegram delivery service, the American Messenger Company. They soon operated out of a tavern basement with Jim and Claude manning the phone requests and Jim's brother George, with a few other teenagers, delivering notes on foot or by bike.

And the idea took off.

A few years later, the young men merged with a rival company, Merchant's Parcel Delivery, and began using a Model-T Ford to deliver not only telegrams but any package that needed delivering. Soon, they added motorcycles and cars to get the job done. By 1919, they were delivering packages to other cities besides Seattle and saw the potential for a nationwide company. It was then they changed the company's name to United Parcel Service (or UPS).

My guess is you've used the services of those teens.

"Casey and Ryan's company that started so humbly is now worth approximately $80 billion with annual revenue at over $50 billion; employing just under half a million workers in 200 countries; delivering over 3.8 billion packages and documents a year. It is the largest postal delivery service in the world. Amazing what $100, some elbow grease, and a bit of ingenuity can do."[1]

And to think it began with a couple of motivated teenagers.

## What Enabled This to Happen?

To his dying day in 1983, Jim Casey credited his mother for keeping him on track and for instilling values in him. He found a need and filled it. In fact, Jim "sought ways to help those who lacked the family life he found to be so crucial. With his brothers George and Harry and his sister Marguerite, Jim created Casey Family Programs in 1966 to help children who were unable to live with their birth parents—giving them stability and an opportunity to grow into responsible adulthood.

"By the time of his death, Mr. Casey left three legacies: UPS, the Annie E. Casey Foundation, and Casey Family Programs."[2]

Jim Casey's story illustrates the experiences Generation Z needs today.

I doubt that his mother fully understood the impact she had in arranging some of Jim's early experiences, but Annie knew what her children would need to be ready for life. Jim is just one example of what can happen in adolescents when certain experiences are inserted into their lives. As we begin to draw some conclusions on how we can best lead the students who make up Generation Z, I'd like to talk about these ideas.

Far too often, we fail to insert these experiences into their lives, and kids become zombies, seated for hours in front of a video game or a portable device. With latent potential inside, we opted for the one-eyed babysitter to keep them occupied, a screen. Sometimes, we even protect them from experiences that may feel intimidating to them. A century ago, a teenager started a company that became the largest delivery service on the planet because the right elements were positioned in his life and he was ready to encounter them. I believe there are more Jim Caseys alive today, and it's our job to prepare them to do what they're capable of doing.

So, how do we do it?

## SIX EXPERIENCES THAT FOSTER MATURITY

Since 1979, I have been committed to mentoring emerging leaders—high school and college students as well as young professionals. Usually, I meet with them in a group, annually for a year. These learning communities are the most rewarding activity in which I participate each year. Over time, I've noticed the experiences that seem to be the most meaningful ones to my mentees. I've recognized how these experiences mature those young leaders as well as build grit and depth in them. Collectively, they serve as a sort of "rite of passage" for the group. I invite you to consider inserting these experiences and encounters as you invest in the young people around you.

### 1. Do something scary.

There is something about stepping out of our comfort zones to attempt a risky act that's unfamiliar and even a little frightening that makes us come alive. Our senses are heightened when we feel we are taking a risk; we don't know what we're doing; we have to trust and even rely on each other. Ideally, these initiatives are intentional and well planned, but they should not be scripted. They must include the element of chance. As a mentor, I have taken my mentees downtown to spend the night with homeless people. Those eighteen-year-old students were wide-eyed as we interacted with an entirely different population of people and found ourselves sleeping on trash bags with newspapers as a blanket. These experiences are unforgettable. A small dose of danger mixed with a large dose of unfamiliar accelerates growth.

When my son was twelve, he and I took a father and son trip to another city. We explored loads of new places, but the scariest event on the four-day trip was when I traded places with him in our car and had him drive it around a parking lot. After explaining the gears and peddles, Jonathan overcame his panic and drove that big automobile. Within moments, he was grinning from ear to ear. The whole experience sparked an extraordinary conversation, comparing that fear to what he'll experience becoming an adult. Adulthood, and particularly manhood, is not for the fainthearted; it is about responsibility, being drivers not passengers in life.

Facing fears is a rite of passage for teens. Doing something that's neither prescribed nor guaranteed unleashes adrenaline and other chemicals in our bodies that awaken us. Fear responses produce endorphins, which can be a sort of natural high. Other feel-good chemicals can also come into play with scary experiences, including dopamine, serotonin, and oxytocin. Part of the reason more teens don't come alive is we've protected them from these rites of passage in the name of safety.

Question: How could you enable your students to do something scary?

## 2. Meet someone influential.

Another challenge for them to rise to is meeting someone they deem significant. Because Generation Z kids feel less at home meeting adults face to face, the encounter itself stretches them. On top of that, meeting significant people invites them to prepare questions to ask and fosters listening skills as well. These can be famous people, but they don't have to be. The key is they're people the students believe to be important due to what they've accomplished. I was invited to participate in a special meeting in Washington D.C. when my daughter, Bethany, was just nine years old. Because I was going to get to meet congressmen, ambassadors, and other civic leaders, I wanted her to experience it with me. Encountering such significant professionals can be intimidating, even to adults like me. But it was fun to introduce her to these people and witness her interacting with them. She eventually felt quite at home, answering their questions, asking them questions, and even raising a few eyebrows. During my son's thirteenth year, he and I joined a group of fathers who introduced our sons to military officers, business owners, professional football coaches, and pastors. I watched my son take notes on what they said, and he still has them to this day.

Over the years, I've mentored students in Atlanta, where I live. I've had the joy of introducing them to key city leaders, such as Truett Cathy, the founder of Chick-fil-A; Ed Bastian, CEO of Delta Airlines; Glen Jackson, the founder of Jackson Spalding; Andy Stanley, founder of North Point Ministries; and others to discuss topics those leaders specialize in and could impart some wisdom about. Those meetings are always growth opportunities for the students, in more ways than one.

I was fortunate for the first twenty years of my career to work for best-selling author John C. Maxwell. My kids knew how important he was to so many and were fortunate enough to build a relationship with John and his wife, Margaret. Interacting with the Maxwell's enabled them to overcome social intimidation and to see noteworthy people as human and approachable. Today, my kids are not star-struck with celebrities and are comfortable interfacing with people of all ages, young and old.

**Question:** How could you introduce your students to someone significant?

### 3. Travel someplace different.

It's been said over and over through the years that travel is an education in itself. While classrooms can be useful learning environments, leaving the classroom and all things familiar is better still. Not only does travel once again push kids out of their comfort zones, but it also exposes them to their need to work at understanding others, at connecting with new contexts, and at problem-solving, since those new environments represent places we cannot default to our subconscious. Consider this, when we are in familiar circumstances, we can shift into "cruise control." We can become numb to reality since we're used to our home turf. We act almost completely from our subconscious mind. This does not occur in a foreign location. These trips stir our curiosity, beg us to research, beckon us to learn, and invite us to grow up. We think new thoughts in new places. Mark Batterson says, "A change of pace plus a change of place equals a change of perspective."[3]

I'll never forget hosting a group of university students on a trip to Budapest, Hungary, in 1987, before the Iron Curtain fell. Central Europe was still under communist rule, which meant our American style had to be tempered and our volume lowered. Most of my students were from Southern California, so Hungary was completely out of the ordinary. We witnessed the residue of bullet holes from past wars and the difficult lives many lived under communism. The next year, I led a team to Romania (still under dictator Nicolae Ceausescu in 1988) and served the people under his brutal tyranny. This trip furnished remarkable perspective for our team, allowing them to see how many people in the rest of the world lived and giving them a deep desire to work for justice and a deep gratitude for the lives they enjoyed in the U.S.

One of my favorite memories, however, was taking my five-year-old daughter, Bethany, to Croatia during the Serbian-Bosnian War in 1993. My goal was to enable her to be comfortable in environments that were both foreign and struggling. Bethany helped to serve clothes, food, and blankets to refugees who had relocated to the area. She saw poverty she'd never seen before and experienced the joy of providing for the needs of those who were displaced and suffering. It was life-changing.

**Question:** Where could you take students that would be different from their norms?

## 4. Chase a meaningful goal.

Earlier in this book, we discussed the idea that teens need adults to let them pursue an objective that has high stakes and give them full control. Past generations matured more effectively because they were given responsibility for jobs and goals that had genuine meaning at a young age. When we lower the stakes or we give kids an artificial purpose to engage in, we end up with artificial maturity. While I believe in the value of academics, it's still a facsimile of a meaningful world, created by our current, contemporary structures. I meet too many students who master the skill of getting a good grade, yet have huge trouble translating those grades into a career, to a marriage, a family, and relationships. Book smarts gain meaning as they cultivate street smarts. Information is meaningful as it becomes application.

When I speak of chasing a big goal, I mean aiming for a target that has deep meaning to the student, one that stretches his capacity and that has high stakes. As a young teen, my son had become heavily involved in community theatre programs and felt he wanted to enter the entertainment industry (he along with millions of other students today). Film and television seemed to be a suitable platform, at least to his adolescent brain at the time. So, my wife and I decided to let Jonathan pursue his big dream at sixteen years old. We met with Jonathan several times to evaluate the seriousness of his ambition. When he convinced us it was real, we all made a big decision. He and his mother moved from Atlanta to Los Angeles for seven months to try his hand at acting.

He got an agent, got some headshots, and did all the work to see if that industry really was his passion. The experience was very revealing, as you might imagine. Living in Burbank at an apartment with hundreds of other kid actors revealed the highly competitive world he planned to enter. He soon recognized that actors do play a role (literally) in that field, but the real influencers are the storytellers. The ones behind the camera, not in front of the camera.

When he moved back home, Jonathan was a different young man—more passionate and clearer about where his talents and passions lay. He later earned a degree in screenwriting and entered a career in storytelling. He's writing scripts every week. I believe the key was allowing Jonathan to chase a big goal. Suddenly, he had ambition.

**Question:** How could you empower students to chase a big goal they desire?

## 5. Wait and work for something you want.

One of the many reasons teens and college students find "adulting" so challenging today is they've grown up in a world where almost everything is instant, at their fingertips, and on-demand. Immature humans expect instant gratification. They find it hard to delay gratification. The opposites of that childish trait are patience and work ethic. Patience and work ethic are signals of maturity because a person has the poise and tenacity to work toward a goal that is still invisible externally. They can work for something because they can envision the outcome.

Let's examine what's happening in their brains. When people are able to envision an outcome before they actually experience it, it can cause the brain to release dopamine and endorphins, which signal pleasure and rewards. Of all the neurotransmitters in the brain, dopamine is the one most associated with pleasure (though endorphins also play a large part). When students experienced learned industriousness ("I keep working because I know it will pay off"), acetylcholine kicks in. Acetylcholine is the brain chemical that appears to play an important role in learning and memory. The neurons producing this neurotransmitter—cholinergic neurons—when stimulated, release their neurotransmitters onto waiting neurons. In short, as teens associate a reward with waiting and working for something, these chemicals seem to be activated closely together and deepen a neuropathway.[4]

One way my wife and I tried to cooperate with this brain develop-ment is slowly requiring our kids to participate in paying for possessions or trips they wanted to experience. When Bethany turned sixteen, she got her driver's license and naturally wanted a car. Many of her friends in Alpharetta instantly got brand new cars on their sixteenth birthdays. We chose a different plan. I made a deal with her that she could pick out whatever car she wanted but she would have to pay for half of it. This encouraged her to choose a previously owned vehicle, which cost less and sped up her saving process. But, she still had to wait. I wasn't being cruel. I was attempting to build a sense of ownership and the ability to delay gratification. The more she matured, the easier it was to wait.

**Question:** How could you position students to work and wait for what they want?

## 6. Practice a new habit

Most would agree that growing up requires people to start new habits and practice new lifestyles. Slowly but surely, we must put away childish things and experience the autonomy and responsibility of adulthood. Adulting is hard for some because they want to retain the rights of childhood while simultaneously gaining the privileges of adulthood. Life in Neverland, as Peter Pan would say, allows you to fly and do whatever you want—and you don't have to grow up.

Unfortunately, that's not how life works.

Fostering the maturation process means encouraging students to take on new habits that prepare them for the future. This means, help-ing them wear "grooves" into their daily schedules that will serve them well as they enter their careers. Whether that's keeping a calendar of priorities, doing their own laundry, washing their car, creating a budget, or sticking to a budget—you name it, new grooves of responsibility are good. Equally important to building new habits is the ability to stop old ones that are unproductive or immature. It is common knowledge that the two go together. Most people cannot quit an old habit until they replace it with a new and better one.

This is the art of making trade-offs.

The late Peter Drucker, management guru for business executives, used to host a workshop on decision-making. With ten minutes left in the day, he would stop and ask his attendees to take out a sheet of paper and list all of the ideas they planned to implement as a result of the workshop. The executives would feverishly jot down dozens of actions they planned to take. It was exhilarating. Then, after five minutes, Drucker instructed them to stop writing. At this point, he surprised them by requesting they turn over their sheet of paper and begin jotting down all the actions they planned to stop taking to make room for the new ones. In short, what old habits would die to allow for new ones? The attendees were often stumped.

Teaching this art to Generation Z kids is imperative. We must enable kids to recognize that growth means change. It means letting go of what you once possessed to enable you to gain something even better. The earlier students learn this the better. As you will remember from earlier in this book, during my son Jonathan's senior year of high school, we looked at five potential colleges he was interested in attending. After making a list of pros and cons, he chose a private university in Southern California. It was expensive, and he knew it. So, I gave him a choice. He could attend this school and I would cover the entire expense, as his father. Or, he could attend a community college for the first two years of general education, then finish his junior and senior year at the more expensive school, and we would split the money I saved. He'd graduate with thousands of dollars in his bank account. He chose the latter, and it served him well. He made a trade-off.

**Question:** How could you enable students to start a new habit and make a trade-off?

## Rites of Passage

In Chapter Nineteen, "Establishing an Identity with Integrity," we discussed rites of passage and what they do for teens as they mature. I enjoy telling the stories of how our children were impacted by their rite of passage experiences. At age thirteen, we arranged for both of our kids to meet with hand-picked people who would be one-day mentors for them. In those liminal experiences with their mentors, they experienced many of these six experiences—traveling, meeting new people, asking questions, doing scary things, you name it.

Both of our kids got to see work environments they were interested in, talk to folks who chose those vocations, and meet influential leaders. At the end of the year, each of our kids enjoyed a post-liminal grand finale, where we celebrated the year and the new chapter in their lives, as they transitioned from childhood to adulthood. We invited all six of the women Bethany met with to our house for a dinner and a time of reflection. Bethany read a personal thank you note out loud to each woman who'd mentored her. Then, as Bethany sat in a chair in the middle of our family room, they knelt down and looking up at our young daughter, they spoke words of affirmation, belief, and vision to her. There was not a dry eye in the room.

Four years later, my son's finale was a gathering of extended family and friends, where five of us dads affirmed our sons and celebrated the year by literally passing a baton to them at the end. It was unforgettable. I detail these rite of passage experiences in the book *Generation iY— Secrets to Connecting with Today's Teens and Young Adults in the Digital Age.*

My favorite outcome from these experiences came years later. My daughter, Bethany, called me when she was twenty-five years old and living two thousand miles from home. She said she called just to talk. When I asked what was on her mind, she replied, "I guess I just called to say thanks."

I said, "Well, every dad loves to hear that from his children—but what drove you to call me like this? Did something happen at work today?"

After collecting her thoughts, she blurted out, "I guess I just noticed that I work with a bunch of young professionals like me, but nobody sees the big picture around here. They act lazy. They're on their phones, and I don't see any work ethic. They're not ready for their jobs!" Then, she paused and concluded, "I guess I got to thinking that you and mom did get me ready. And I just wanted to say thanks."

With tears in my eyes and a smile on my face, I replied, "Bethany, you just made my year."

TWENTY-FIVE

# *Changing Our Ways*

*We must improve the way we lead and develop this generation.*

One of the saddest stories in American history took place when President James Garfield was shot on July 2, 1881. The shooter was Charles Guiteau, a crazy man with a pistol in his pocket at a train station. He stood trial for the assassination of President Garfield months later. The pitiful part of the story is that President Garfield actually didn't die from the gunshot wound. It was due to the misguided treatment of his physician, Dr. Edwin Bliss.

Over an eleven-week period of time, Dr. Bliss dug through Garfield's body, searching for the bullet. During that time, Alexander Graham Bell showed up with a new metal detector he'd just created—suggesting that maybe it could locate the stray bullet. In addition, Joseph Lister had just published his new theory on germs, encouraging doctors to sanitize their hands and instruments before operating on patients. Some of Dr. Bliss' medical team suggested he read this theory as it seemed to be saving lives around the world.

Unfortunately, Bliss wasn't teachable. He limited Alexander Graham Bell's search to the right side of Garfield's back because he stubbornly assumed that's where the bullet was. He was wrong. It was on the left side, and they never found it. Further, Bliss felt Joseph Lister's theory about germs was ridiculous. Consequently, he ignorantly explored Garfield's body with dirty utensils and fingers, causing the infection to grow and eventually killing the president. In effect, it was Dr. Bliss, the very physician assigned to help Garfield recover, who mortally wounded his patient. As one journalist put it, the physician gave new meaning to the phrase: 'ignorance is bliss.'[1]

What's my point in telling this tragic story?

Too often, we have played the role of Dr. Bliss with Generation Z. Too many of us have failed our youngest population. We do it unwittingly. We are not bad people any more than Dr. Bliss was an unqualified physician. He was just blind to what he was doing. He assumed the way he'd always operated was still the right path. In the name of seizing control of a complex and overwhelming situation we, like Dr. Bliss, do too much or perhaps too little to try to fix today's kids. At times, we're part of the problem.

- As parents, we've given them lots of possessions but not much perspective.
- As educators, we've given them plenty of schooling but not plenty of skills.
- As coaches, we've taught them how to win games but not how to win in life.
- As youth workers, we offer lots of explanations but not enough experiences.
- As employers, we've mentored them in profit and loss but not how to profit from loss.

Generation Z will definitely change the world. It is up to us whether they're prepared to change it for the better or for the worse.

In this chapter, we offer a summary of some of the most important changes we must make in order to lead Generation Z students into healthy adulthood and leadership. In some ways, our ideas here represent action steps for many of the challenges we described in earlier chapters.

## Winning the Heart of Generation Z Students

In 1985, educator and culture critic Neil Postman published a book called *Amusing Ourselves to Death*. He observed that popular culture has become tangibly oppressed by its addiction to amusement. We need to be stimulated. Our appetites crave entertainment. And more and more, we suffer from the law of diminishing returns.

This has left our students savvy and aware—and very difficult to "wow."

Many are well-informed, well-entertained and have already traveled to places I never traveled until I was well into my adult life. They scroll through their phones looking for something that will capture their interests. Due to over-exposure to information, some have become jaded. Teachers today compete for their attention against YouTube, Instagram, Netflix, and Snapchat.

So how do we lead a kid who is so difficult to impress? My advice is don't try to "wow" them. Try to win them.

I believe educators and parents can play a unique role in the lives of students. While Hollywood can capture their attention for a few moments, caring adults can engage them in a way that's personal and meaningful. Recently, I had a conversation with a faculty member who said he's taken on the challenge to win the hearts of his students. His report card? Just like students will binge-watch a series on Netflix, he's working to get students to want to binge-watch his classes and other science programs on YouTube or TV. Instead of dazzling them with a show, however, he's engaging and empowering them through a relationship. He gets to know them deeply. He cares for them personally. He discovers what interests them. And they are binging.

## It's Better to Win Students Than to Wow Them

I believe both educators and parents must play a role that no one else plays in the lives of students. This means we don't merely imitate culture; we complement it. We do what only we can do best. To succeed, leaders must understand what Generation Z kids need most from them. Here are four changes we can make to win their hearts:

1. **Shift from playing the hero to playing the guide.**

   According to mythologist, Joseph Campbell, nearly every great story has a hero with a problem who needs a guide to help them solve it. Think Luke Skywalker and Yoda. Think Peter Parker and Uncle Ben. Think Frodo and Gandalf. Too often, adults (teachers, coaches, and parents) position themselves as the hero of the class, the team, or the family, leaving students disengaged. What if you positioned yourself as a guide helping students to become the hero of their own stories? What if you placed the onus on them to search and find the answers, and you gave them clues, hints, and lots of encouragement along the way? People become more engaged when they believe they are the hero of the story. This means your role shifts from supervisor to consultant. You're not a sage on the stage but a guide on the side.

2. **Support the issues that are at the core of what matters most to teens today.**

Instead of always demanding students to "get on board" with your subject and your ideas, what if you enabled them to choose what matters to them (within the confines of your class or topic), and you helped them pursue it? When students believe they get to choose and own the activity, you get a whole new level of engagement from them. In short, students support what they help create. Coaches, what if your student athletes got to run the practice next week? Teachers, what if students got to choose the focal point of an entire week of your course and even help teach it? Or, what if in the midst of your social studies class, you allowed students to choose a meaningful cause to engage in the real world? Suddenly, everything moves from theory to practice. Better yet, students move from apathy to passion.

3. **Present reality, and allow students opportunities to create a unique identity.**

Students today curate their identities from social media and social issues. Because they are often involved in several at a time, they can have multiple personas. What if you presented a current reality in our culture or in the global economy and allowed students to create their identities through involvement in solving a problem? As I see it, most teens are still figuring out who they are. The best way adults can help them is through guiding their involvement with real—rather than virtual—experiences. Students are capable of so much more than we expect of them. If we only give them artificial or hypothetical ways to spend their time, we get artificial young adults. If we let them create their identity through purposeful action, they'll become the best version of themselves. Healthy identity matures through action and reflection.

4. **Utilize various social media platforms to enable them to curate themselves.**

By this, I simply mean we should leverage the mediums and language students find natural and familiar. We must begin where they are, then lead them to where they need to go as mature adults. Social media is their natural habitat. It is their native tongue. What if you leveraged the five biggest social media platforms—YouTube, Instagram, Snapchat, Twitter, and Facebook—to let them curate their identity and their story? I believe we can play a role in helping them become congruent in who they are and what they stand for. What if you engaged them in one of the ways I described above, then give them time to post pictures and tell their story?

Today, the influence of culture—both positive and negative—creeps into our lives from every device imaginable. We must play an active role as their guide, helping students to discover who they are and to play the role they're gifted to play.

It's our move. So, where do we begin?

## LEVERAGING THE PYGMALION EFFECT TO WORK FOR YOU

Too often, teachers, coaches, and parents grow frustrated and impatient with the students they lead. Even when we try to hide it, they can read us like a book. The impact can be negative if for no other reason than the Pygmalion Effect.

Do you remember learning about the Pygmalion Effect?

The term was coined by psychologist Robert Rosenthal and named after the Greek myth of the same name about a sculptor who fell in love with his own sculpture of a beautiful woman. It's about managing the power of expectations. It is a fact that people rise to the expectations others have for them. The Pygmalion Effect is a proven behavioral theory showing how the expectations one person has for another can impact that person's performance. Call it a self-fulfilling prophecy if you like, but the fact is, there is scientific evidence for the fact that people, especially young people, react or respond to the expectations of the adults who lead them. This means they'll live down or up to our expectations. So, what are you expecting of Generation Z?

## Putting This Principle to Work

Earlier in this book, we mentioned the many experiments that have been conducted among teachers and students, which demonstrate the power of expectations. In one experiment by Dr. Rosenthal while at Harvard in 1964, teachers were given a classroom of students and told they were academically high achievers while another classroom full of students was given to a different faculty member who was told the students were low achievers. In reality, both classes were filled with average performers who made average grades. The outcome, however, told a different story. The teacher who was told her students were high achievers actually ended up with measurably higher grades in her classroom while the one who was told she had low performers got exactly what she expected. Low performance.

And that's the point.

Our expectations play a huge role in our outcomes. As Rosenthal did more research, he found that "expectations affect teachers' moment-to-moment interactions with the children they teach in a thousand almost invisible ways. Teachers give the students that they expect to succeed more time to answer questions, more specific feedback, and more approval: they consistently touch, nod and smile at those kids more," according to a report from NPR. "It's not magic, it's not mental telepathy," Rosenthal comments. "It's very likely these thousands of different ways of treating people show up in small ways every day."[2]

Robert Pianta, dean of the Curry School of Education at the University of Virginia, has studied teachers for years. What he learned from his experiments is that it is truly hard for teachers to control their expectations. So, what I'm about to suggest won't be easy for any of us. But—I am challenging you to try.

1. At the beginning of each day, tell yourself that despite what your students may have shown you, they possess an amazing brain, and it's full of untapped potential. This is actually true, but I find I need to say it out loud before I meet up with kids.

2. When you stand in front of someone to teach or encourage them, place an imaginary ten on her forehead. This will remind you that on a scale of one to ten, she has the capacity to fulfill everything you ask of her. (John Maxwell taught me this one.)

3. Each time you look at your students, remind yourself of the strengths they possess. Then, imagine them as adults, using that strength. For instance, if you have students who enjoy science, imagine them as the next Marie Curry or Albert Einstein.

4. Ask yourself: *If I genuinely believe in these students, what one or two actions could demonstrate my belief?* Once you discover your answers, practice them. This will especially help you with the late bloomers under your care.

Generation Z will be the beneficiaries if we leverage the Pygmalion Effect. So, why is this so difficult for us to practice, especially today? I have a theory based on my observations. I suspect it's because we sometimes wish for different kids.

## Leading the Students We Have in Front of Us

There is a subtle and sinister reality facing parents, coaches, and educators today. Its source is invisible but tangible. It can be spotted when we get caught up in the past and begin to resent our present. Let me explain what I mean.

I recently spoke to a group of university faculty who, during a Q and A session, groaned about the students they were teaching today. They expressed some of the sentiments you might have felt yourself.

- Kids today will not get off their phones!
- They don't know how to look you in the eyes when you talk to them.
- Kids have no grit or resourcefulness today.
- Students get stressed out over the smallest of things in their daily lives.
- Their work ethic is not what mine was at their age!
- Today's kids seem like they can't delay gratification.

While all of these statements may be warranted, I began to notice what our attitudes were doing to students. I've seen a shift in their attitudes recently. As I meet with college and high school students, I've begun to recognize how aware they are of our negativity. It is as if they feel our disposition and receive this message:

*"I wish I was teaching different students, like the ones I had in the past, not you."*

They actually walk away from our time with them feeling like we really don't want to be with them—we want to be with students from former times. We wish we could teach our own generation, not theirs. They feel they're not as good as we were.

Believe it or not, I also see this with parents and their teenage kids. I had some high school students tell me they think they got the wrong parent. When I poke around to find out what they mean, they say they can tell their parents don't really like them. They feel like their moms or their dads wished they had different children.

This is a tragic message to relay.

The only way we can begin to address this issue is to fall in love with the students we actually teach, lead, coach, and parent, not the ones we wish we had. Yes, they are anxious and have short attention spans, but our culture has done this to them. They are products of our making.

The fact is, we all feel like the victim here. Parents are afraid they're not measuring up to the perfect parent ideal they're being measured against. Teachers feel they are underpaid and unappreciated. Youth coaches feel they get yelled at when they're actually volunteering their time. Employers feel they're getting young professionals who are unready for the workplace. And Generation Z students? They feel that they've been handed a broken world and are being led by a generation of adults who miss the old days. The moment any of us choose to see ourselves as the victims, everyone else looks like the perpetrators. Others become the enemy. We've got to stop blaming and start assuming responsibility for our part in the equation.

## My Challenge to You

Our work must always begin with a deep respect for those we teach and lead. We must listen and appreciate their realities before we assume we have an answer for them. In fact, let me suggest some simple reminders for you this week.

1. **We must be responsive.**
   This means students feel we listen well and empathize with their situations.

2. **We must be inclusive.**
   This means we work to identify with those who are unlike us, even our own kids.

3. **We must be adaptive.**
   This means we're willing to adjust our methods and styles to reach them.

4. **We must be supportive.**
   This means we see them as humans, not customers, and reach out to meet their needs.

5. **We must be provocative.**
   This means we challenge them to stretch because we believe in their potential.

I recently spoke at an event where I had to work harder than usual to identify with my audience. They were young, minority students in a lower-income part of the city. I did my best to meet members of my audience beforehand, to listen to them and laugh with them (sometimes laughing at myself), and later, communicate with them from the stage. It was as if I was an anthropologist attempting to connect with a cross-cultural audience. And in many ways, that was exactly what was happening.

After my session was over, a young student approached me sheepishly to say thank you. When I smiled and replied that it was my pleasure, she looked at me and said, "I feel like you get me." That was the best affirmation a student could've offered me that day.

Moments like this, where I am able to connect with and understand a member of Generation Z, are one great reason why I do what I do.

## The Nobility of Working with Students

I recently led a workshop for administrators at a university. Attendees were college deans, vice presidents, heads of schools, and high school principals. When I placed them in small discussion groups and posed the question, "What changes do you plan to make this year?" I over-heard one administrator say to his colleagues, "I'm just biding my time until I retire in two years."

In that moment, I attempted to practice a little empathy. I am sure this man was exhausted. He had probably worked for decades in schools and had run out of gas. But his response still saddened me. Clearly, he didn't have it in him to make any effort to understand students today, he didn't have any more vision for creating a better future for his school, and he didn't see the point in preparing the way for tomorrow's leaders.

Far too often, our careers drift in this same fashion. Our work with students begins well. We are passionate about teaching them and building skills inside of them. We work at connecting with them and find creative ways to impart those lessons we know they need. But over time, we get beat up. Our ideas fall on deaf ears. Our effort isn't always rewarded by students who are hungry to learn. In fact, quite the opposite, they appear apathetic. So, we stop trying so hard. We become frustrated and impatient when change happens slowly, and eventually, we may even stop working to make positive change.

## What Happens to Us?

To summarize one of our new resources *Habitudes® for Life-Giving Leaders*, overtime, many of us migrate from a quarterback to a referee. Instead of moving the ball down the field and inspiring teammates, we start looking for people who are out of bounds so we can call fouls. We lose that fire which once burned inside of us. That might be where you are right now.

I simply want to remind you of a poem about the nobility of your work with students. The emerging generation is the best place to invest your time and energy. They represent the future, and while you could find an easier job, you likely won't find a more important one. One of my favorite poems about this simple truth is simply called, "The Builder." I read it often.

*"The Bridge Builder"*

*An old man going a lone highway,*
*Came, at the evening cold and gray,*
*To a chasm vast and deep and wide.*
*Through which was flowing a sullen tide*
*The old man crossed in the twilight dim,*
*The sullen stream had no fear for him;*
*But he turned when safe on the other side*
*And built a bridge to span the tide.*

*"Old man," said a fellow pilgrim near,*
*"You are wasting your strength with building here;*
*Your journey will end with the ending day,*
*You never again will pass this way;*
*You've crossed the chasm, deep and wide,*
*Why build this bridge at evening tide?"*

*The builder lifted his old gray head;*
*"Good friend, in the path I have come," he said,*
*"There followed after me to-day*
*A youth whose feet must pass this way.*
*This chasm that has been as naught to me*
*To that fair-haired youth may a pitfall be;*
*He, too, must cross in the twilight dim;*
*Good friend, I am building this bridge for him!"*[3]

*Will Allen Dromgoole*

Don't ever forget the nobility of your work. You can rest later. Today, those students need what you have to offer. Go build a bridge.

# End Notes

## CHAPTER ONE

1. Powell, Nick. "Dickinson Teen Earns 'Citizen Hero' Award from Medal of Honor Group for Hurricane Harvey Heroics." HoustonChronicle.com. March 16, 2018. Accessed July 01, 2019.

2. Brown, Molly. "From Space to Schools, Elon Musk Takes on the Education System by Starting a New School." GeekWire. May 23, 2015. Accessed July 30, 2019.

3. Stecher, Benjamin. "It's Time to Rethink How We Are Educating Our Children." Futurism. com. March 30, 2017. Accessed July 01, 2019.

4. Editors, History.com. "Wright Brothers." History.com. November 06, 2009. Accessed July 01, 2019.

5. Graser, Marc. "Epic Fail: How Blockbuster Could Have Owned Netflix." Variety. December 08, 2013. Accessed July 02, 2019.

## CHAPTER TWO

1. Mogel, Wendy, Ph.D. "Voice Lessons for Camp." Voice Lessons for Camp | Wendy Mogel PhD. January 2019. Accessed August 19, 2019. https://www.wendymogel.com/press/item/voice_lessons_for_camp_camping_magazine.

2. Growing Leaders. "Nationwide Survey Results Find "Concern" Is Top Emotion Towards Today's Youth." News release, June 2019. Growingleaders.com. Accessed August 19, 2019. https://growingleaders.com/harris-poll-results/.

3. Blad, Evie. "One-Third of Parents Fear for Their Child's Safety at School." Education Week. July 17, 2018. Accessed August 19, 2019. https://www.edweek.org/ew/articles/2018/07/17/school-safety-parents-concerns.html.

4. Lukianoff, Greg, and Jonathan Haidt. The Coddling of the American Mind: How Good Intentions and Bad Ideas Are Setting up a Generation for Failure, 186. New York City: Penguin Press, 2018.

5. Marano, Hara. "A Nation of Wimps." Psychology Today. November 1, 2004. Accessed July 15, 2019

6. Lukianoff, Greg, and Jonathan Haidt. The Coddling of the American Mind: How Good Intentions and Bad Ideas Are Setting up a Generation for Failure, 177. New York City: Penguin Press, 2018.

7. Brown, Brené. Rising Strong. First edition. New York: Spiegel & Grau, an imprint of Random House, 2015.

8. Hari, Johann. Lost Connections: Uncovering the Real Causes of Depression-- and the Unexpected Solutions. New York: 17-23 Bloomsbury, 2018.

9. Ibid.

10. Lukianoff, Greg, and Jonathan Haidt. The Coddling of the American Mind: How Good Intentions and Bad Ideas Are Setting up a Generation for Failure, 14. New York City: Penguin Press, 2018.

11. Fiore, Kristina. "Kids Today Really Are Different." MedPage Today: Medical News and Free CME, MedpageToday, 25 Apr. 2012, www.medpagetoday.com/pediatrics/generalpediatrics/32350.

12. Painter, Kim. "Teens Aren't Grasping 'the Responsibilities of Adulthood,' New Study Says." USA Today. September 19, 2017. Accessed August 19, 2019. https://www.usatoday.com/story/news/2017/09/19/teens-grow-up-slower-study/105758486/.

13. Mlodinow, Leonard. Subliminal: How Your Unconscious Mind Rules Your Behavior, 11-14. New York, NY: Vintage Books, 2013.

14. Ibid.

CHAPTER THREE

1. Graham, Jefferson. "WWDC 2019: Meet Apple's Youngest App Developer, Ayush." USA Today. June 05, 2019. Accessed August 19, 2019. https://www.usatoday.com/story/tech/talkingtech/2019/06/05/apples-youngest-app-developer-wwdc-2019-ayush-kumar/1340131001/.

2. GlobalWebIndex. "Trends 19: THE TRENDS TO KNOW FOR 2019." News release, 2019. GlobalWebIndex. Accessed August 19, 2019. https://www.globalwebindex.com/hubfs/Downloads/Trends-19-report.pdf.

3. Kimberly Holland and Elsbeth Riley | Illustrations by Tony Bueno. "ADHD by the Numbers: Facts, Statistics, and You." Healthline. July 23, 2018. Accessed July 15, 2019.

4. Lee, Lisa. "NIH Study Probes Impact of Heavy Screen Time on Young Brains." Bloomberg.com. December 9, 2018. Accessed August 19, 2019. https://www.bloomberg.com/news/articles/2018-12-10/screen-time-changes-structure-of-kids-brains-60-minutes-says.

5. "Meet Generation Z: Forget Everything You Learned About Millennials." LinkedIn SlideShare. Sparks & Honey, June 17, 2014. https://www.slideshare.net/sparksandhoney/generation-z-final-june-17/26-26They_seek_education_and_knowledgeResearched.

6. Seemiller, Corey. Ohio Speech-Language-Hearing Association. "Motivation, Learning, and Communication Preferences of Generation Z Students." News release, Fall 2017. Accessed August 19, 2019. https://www.ohioslha.org/wp-content/uploads/2017/12/Fall17Issue.pdf.

7. "My name's Blurryface and I care what you think," Twenty One Pilots. Stressed Out. New York: Fueled by Ramen, 2015.

8. "Meet Generation Z: Forget Everything You Learned About Millennials." LinkedIn SlideShare. Sparks & Honey, June 17, 2014. https://www.slideshare.net/sparksandhoney/generation-z-final-june-17/26-26They_seek_education_and_knowledgeResearched.

9. Barkley, INC. and Futurecast, LLC. "Getting To Know Gen Z: How The Pivotal Generation Is Different From Millennials." 2017.

10. Universum. "Building Leaders for the next Decade: How To Support The Workplace Goals of Gen X, Gen Y and Gen Z." News release.

11. Bromwich, Jonah Engel. "We Asked Generation Z to Pick a Name. It Wasn't Generation Z." The New York Times. January 31, 2018. Accessed August 19, 2019. https://www.nytimes.com/2018/01/31/style/generation-z-name.html.

CHAPTER FOUR

1. Griggs, Brandon, and Christina Walker. "In the Year since Parkland There's Been a School Shooting, on Average, Every 12 Days." CNN. February 14, 2019. Accessed August 20, 2019. https://www.cnn.com/2019/02/14/us/school-shootings-since-parkland-trnd/index.html.

2. "Generation Z Is Stressed, Depressed and Exam-obsessed." The Economist. February 27, 2019. Accessed July 16, 2019.

3. Sevits, Kurt. "Student Killed in STEM Shooting 'wasn't Your Average Kid'." KMGH. May 10, 2019. Accessed July 16, 2019.

4. Twenge, Jean M. IGEN: Why Todays Super-connected Kids Are Growing up Less Rebellious, More Tolerant, Less Happy-and Completely Unprepared for Adulthood (and What That Means for the Rest of Us), 139. New York: Atria Books, 2017.

5. Segran, Elizabeth. "Your Guide To Generation Z: The Frugal, Brand-Wary, Determined Anti-Millennials." Fast Company. November 19, 2017. Accessed July 16, 2019.

6. Shahar, David, and Mark G. L. Sayers. "Prominent Exostosis Projecting from the Occipital Squama More Substantial and Prevalent in Young Adult than Older Age Groups." Nature News. February 20, 2018. Accessed July 16, 2019.

7.   Ibid.
8.   "Video Games Boost Visual Attention but Reduce Impulse Control." ScienceDaily. August 04, 2013. Accessed July 22, 2019.
9.   Glass, Brian D., W. Todd Maddox, and Bradley C. Love. "Real-Time Strategy Game Training: Emergence of a Cognitive Flexibility Trait." PLOS ONE. Accessed July 22, 2019.
10.  Pinker, Steven. "Mind Over Mass Media." The New York Times. June 11, 2010. Accessed July 22, 2019.
11.  Sutter, John D. "Trouble Sleeping? Maybe It's Your iPad." CNN. May 13, 2010. Accessed July 22, 2019.
12.  Ducharme, Jamie. "More Than 90% of Generation Z Is Stressed Out." Time. October 30, 2018. Accessed July 22, 2019.
13.  "Studies Show Normal Children Today Report More Anxiety than Child Psychiatric Patients in the 1950's." American Psychological Association. December 14, 2000. Accessed July 16, 2019.
14.  Thompson, Clive. "Your Outboard Brain Knows All." Wired. September 25, 2007. Accessed August 20, 2019. https://www.wired.com/2007/09/st-thompson-3/.
15.  "The Aftermath of Calculator Use in College Classrooms." ScienceDaily. November 12, 2012. Accessed July 22, 2019.
16.  Carr, Nicholas. "Is Google Making Us Stupid?" The Atlantic. June 13, 2018. Accessed July 22, 2019.
17.  Hiscott, Rebecca. "8 Ways Tech Has Completely Rewired Our Brains." Mashable. March 14, 2014. Accessed July 22, 2019.
18.  Andrews, Sally, David A. Ellis, Heather Shaw, and Lukasz Piwek. "Beyond Self-Report: Tools to Compare Estimated and Real-World Smartphone Use." PLOS ONE, 2015. Accessed July 30, 2019.
19.  "Video Games Boost Visual Attention but Reduce Impulse Control." ScienceDaily. August 04, 2013. Accessed July 22, 2019.
20.  DeLisi, Matt, Michael G. Vaughn, Douglas A. Gentile, Craig A. Anderson, and Jeffrey J. Shook. "Violent Video Games, Delinquency, and Youth Violence: New Evidence." SAGE Journals, 2013. Accessed August 13, 2019.

## CHAPTER FIVE

1.   Coloroso, Barbara. Kids Are worth It!: Giving Your Child the Gift of Inner Discipline, 15. William Morrow Paperbacks, 2002.
2.   Bacon, John. "Parkland Resource Officer Scot Peterson Stayed outside as Bullets Flew. Is He Negligent or a Scapegoat?" USA Today. June 05, 2019. Accessed July 30, 2019.

## CHAPTER SIX

1.   Kircher, Madison Malone. "Even If Your GPS Says Turn Left, If Left Is a Lake ... Maybe Don't Do It." Intelligencer. June 30, 2017. Accessed August 21, 2019. http://nymag.com/intelligencer/2017/06/massachusetts-man-drives-into-pond-following-gps-directions.html.
2.   "Man Reenacts "Frogger," Gets Hit by Car." CBS News. December 29, 2010. Accessed August 21, 2019. https://www.cbsnews.com/news/man-reenacts-frogger-gets-hit-by-car/.
3.   Faccio, Mara and McConnell, John J., Death by Pokémon GO: The Economic and Human Cost of Using Apps While Driving. February 2, 2018. https://ssrn.com/abstract=3073723
4.   Rizzo, Cailey. "More People Have Died from Selfies than Shark Attacks This Year." Mashable. September 21, 2015. Accessed August 21, 2019. https://mashable.com/2015/09/21/selfie-deaths/.
5.   "Yearly Worldwide Shark Attack Summary." Florida Museum. February 15, 2019. Accessed August 21, 2019. https://www.floridamuseum.ufl.edu/shark-attacks/yearly-worldwide-summary/.

6.   "List of Selfie-related Injuries and Deaths." Wikipedia. August 17, 2019. Accessed August 21, 2019. https://en.wikipedia.org/wiki/List_of_selfie-related_injuries_and_deaths.

7.   Twenge, Jean M., and W. Keith Campbell. "Associations between Screen Time and Lower Psychological Well-being among Children and Adolescents: Evidence from a Population-based Study." Preventive Medicine Reports12 (2018): 271-83. doi:10.1016/j.pmedr.2018.10.003.

8.   OFCOM. "Children and Parents: Media Use and Attitudes Report." November 29, 2017. OFCOM.ORG.UK. Accessed August 20, 2019. https://www.ofcom.org.uk/__data/assets/pdf_file/0020/108182/children-parents-media-use-attitudes-2017.pdf.

9.   "Children Consuming Online Time 'like Junk Food'." BBC News. August 06, 2017. Accessed August 21, 2019. https://www.bbc.com/news/uk-40840823.

10.  Burns, Judith. "Social Media Harms Moral Development, Parents Say." BBC News. July 18, 2016. Accessed August 21, 2019. https://www.bbc.com/news/education-36824176.

11.  Common Sense Media. "Zero to Eight: Children's Media Use in America 2013." News release, October 28, 2013. Common Sense Media. Accessed August 20, 2019. https://www.commonsensemedia.org/research/zero-to-eight-childrens-media-use-in-america-2013/key-finding-2:-kids'-time-on-mobile-devices-triples.

12.  Boyd, Robert S. "Researchers Study Why Teenagers Can Be so Difficult to Get along with." Mcclatchydc. December 18, 2006. Accessed August 21, 2019. https://www.mcclatchydc.com/latest-news/article24460156.html.

13.  Ibid.

14.  Vedantam, Shankar, Laura Kwerel, Tara Boyle, and Jennifer Schmidt. "Close Enough: The Lure Of Living Through Others." NPR. February 11, 2019. Accessed August 21, 2019. https://www.npr.org/2019/02/05/691697963/close-enough-the-lure-of-living-through-others.

15.  Oettingen, Gabriele. Rethinking Positive Thinking: Inside the New Science of Motivation. New York, NY: Current, 2015.

16.  Twenge, Jean M. IGEN: Why Todays Super-connected Kids Are Growing up Less Rebellious, More Tolerant, Less Happy-and Completely Unprepared for Adulthood (and What That Means for the Rest of Us), 17-40. New York: Atria Books, 2017.

17.  Twenge, Jean M. "Have Smartphones Destroyed a Generation?" The Atlantic. September 2017. Accessed August 21, 2019. https://www.theatlantic.com/magazine/archive/2017/09/has-the-smartphone-destroyed-a-generation/534198/.

18.  Beck, Julie. "The Decline of the Driver's License." The Atlantic. January 22, 2016. Accessed August 21, 2019. https://www.theatlantic.com/technology/archive/2016/01/the-decline-of-the-drivers-license/425169/.

19.  Morisi, Teri. "Teens Trends." U.S. Department of Labor Blog. March 9, 2017. Accessed August 21, 2019. https://blog.dol.gov/2017/03/09/teens-trends.

20.  Fry, Richard. "For First Time in Modern Era, Living With Parents Edges Out Other Living Arrangements for 18- to 34-Year-Olds." Pew Research Center. May 24, 2016. Accessed August 21, 2019. https://www.pewsocialtrends.org/2016/05/24/for-first-time-in-modern-era-living-with-parents-edges-out-other-living-arrangements-for-18-to-34-year-olds/.

21.  "Long Island Middle School Bans Footballs, Other Recreational Items." CBS New York. October 07, 2013. Accessed August 21, 2019. https://newyork.cbslocal.com/2013/10/07/long-island-middle-school-bans-footballs-other-recreational-items/.

22.  Robert Green Ingersoll Quotes. BrainyQuote.com, BrainyMedia Inc, 2019. https://www.brainyquote.com/quotes/robert_green_ingersoll_104886, accessed August 20, 2019.

CHAPTER SEVEN

1.   "School ditches rules and loses bullies." TVNZ. January 26, 2014. http://tvnz.co.nz/national-news/school-ditches-rules-and-loses-bullies-5807957

2. "CHILD NEGLECT AMENDMENTS." Utah State Legislature. March 15, 2018. Accessed August 21, 2019. https://le.utah.gov/~2018/bills/static/SB0065.html.

3. "Why Utah Now Has First 'free-range' Parenting Law." BBC News. May 06, 2018. Accessed August 21, 2019. https://www.bbc.com/news/world-us-canada-43997862.

4. Ibid.

5. "A DIVIDED AND PESSIMISTIC ELECTORATE." Pew Research Center. November 10, 2016. Accessed August 21, 2019. https://www.people-press.org/2016/11/10/a-divided-and-pessimistic-electorate/3-11/.

CHAPTER EIGHT

1. Lukianoff, Greg, and Jonathan Haidt. The Coddling of the American Mind: How Good Intentions and Bad Ideas Are Setting up a Generation for Failure, 188-189. New York City: Penguin Press, 2018.

2. Gray, Peter. (2011). The Decline of Play and the Rise of Psychopathology in Children and Adolescents. Am J Play. 3.

3. Center for Collegiate Mental Health. (2017, January). 2016 Annual Report (Publication No. STA 17-74). https://sites.psu.edu/ccmh/files/2017/01/2016-Annual-Report-FINAL_2016_01_09-1gc2hj6.pdf.

4. Gray, Peter. (2011). The Decline of Play and the Rise of Psychopathology in Children and Adolescents. Am J Play. 3.

5. Ibid.

6. Siegel, Daniel J. Brainstorm. the Power and Purpose of the Teenage Brain. New York: Jeremy P. Tarcher/Penguin, 2013.

7. Ibid.

8. Brown, Trice. "NYU Social Psychologist Speaks on the Usefulness of Adversity to Kick off Critical Conversations Speaker Series." The Auburn Plainsman, October 7, 2018. https://www.theplainsman.com/article/2018/10/nyu-social-psychologist-speaks-on-the-usefulness-of-adversity-to-kick-off-critical-conversations-speaker-series.

9. "Moral Hazard." Policonomics. Accessed August 21, 2019. https://policonomics.com/moral-hazard/.

10. Yogman, Michael, Andrew Garner, Jeffrey Hutchinson, Kathy Hirsh-Pasek, and Roberta Michnick Golinkoff. "The Power of Play: A Pediatric Role in Enhancing Development in Young Children." Pediatrics142, no. 3 (September 2018). https://doi.org/10.1542/peds.2018-2058.

11. Korn, Melissa. "Failure 101: Colleges Teach Students How to Cope With Setbacks." The Wall Street Journal. Dow Jones & Company, December 19, 2018. https://www.wsj.com/articles/failure-101-colleges-teach-students-how-to-cope-with-setbacks-11545129000.

12. Brown, Trice. "NYU Social Psychologist Speaks on the Usefulness of Adversity to Kick off Critical Conversations Speaker Series." The Auburn Plainsman, October 7, 2018. https://www.theplainsman.com/article/2018/10/nyu-social-psychologist-speaks-on-the-usefulness-of-adversity-to-kick-off-critical-conversations-speaker-series.

13. Yogman, Michael, Andrew Garner, Jeffrey Hutchinson, Kathy Hirsh-Pasek, and Roberta Michnick Golinkoff. "The Power of Play: A Pediatric Role in Enhancing Development in Young Children." Pediatrics142, no. 3 (September 2018). https://doi.org/10.1542/peds.2018-2058.

14. Anderson, Jenny. "Kids Are so over-Scheduled That Doctors Are Being Told to Prescribe Play." Quartz. Quartz, August 21, 2018. https://qz.com/1363294/the-american-academy-of-pediatrics-is-telling-doctors-to-start-prescribing-play/.

15. Anderson, Jenny. "If You Want Your Kid to Get a Good Job, Let Them Play More." Quartz. Quartz, February 28, 2018. https://qz.com/1217146/child-development-kids-that-play-more-often-are-better-prepared-for-employment/.

CHAPTER NINE

1.  Christensen, Tanner. "Looking for the Right Idea Will Cause You to Overlook the Creative Ones." Creative Something. Creative Something, April 23, 2015. https://creativesomething. net/post/117169083856/looking-for-the-right-idea-will-cause-you-to.

2.  "Good Intentions, Gap in Action: The Challenge of Translating Youth's High Interest in Doing Good into Civic Engagement." University of Maryland, March 2018. https://spp. umd.edu/sites/default/files/2019-07/Good Intentions, Gap in Action_Do Good Institute Research Brief.pdf.

3.  1980 December, Reader's Digest, Volume 117, Quotable Quotes, Quote Page 172, The Reader's Digest Association. (Verified on microfilm)

CHAPTER TEN

1.  Butler, Gavin. "An Indian Man Is Suing His Parents for Conceiving Him Without His Consent." Vice. Vice, February 11, 2019. https://www.vice.com/en_ca/article/9kpk4v/an-indian-man-is-suing-his-parents-for-conceiving-him-without-his-consent.

2.  Immordino-Yang, Mary Helen, Joanna A. Christodoulou, and Vanessa Singh. "Rest Is Not Idleness: Implications of the Brain's Default Mode for Human Development and Education." Perspectives on Psychological Science7, no. 4 (June 29, 2012): 352–64. https:// doi.org/10.1177/1745691612447308.

3.  Fink, Jenni. "Teacher Claims She Was Fired for Violating 'No Zero' Policy When She Refused to Grade Projects That Weren't Turned In." Newsweek, September 25, 2018. https:// www.newsweek.com/teacher-claims-she-was-fired-violating-no-zero-policy-not-giving-students-who-1137573.

4.  Lapin, Tamar. "Teacher Says She Was Fired for Ignoring School's 'No Zero' Policy." New York Post. New York Post, September 26, 2018. https://nypost.com/2018/09/26/teacher-says-she-was-fired-for-ignoring-schools-no-zero-policy/.

5.  Morisi, Teri. "Teens Trends." U.S. Department of Labor Blog. March 9, 2017. Accessed August 21, 2019. https://blog.dol.gov/2017/03/09/teens-trends.

6.  Twenge, Jean M. IGEN: Why Todays Super-connected Kids Are Growing up Less Rebellious, More Tolerant, Less Happy-and Completely Unprepared for Adulthood (and What That Means for the Rest of Us), 31. New York: Atria Books, 2017.

7.  Ibid.

8.  Ibid, 34.

9.  Fry, Richard. "For First Time in Modern Era, Living With Parents Edges Out Other Living Arrangements for 18- to 34-Year-Olds." Pew Research Center. May 24, 2016. Accessed August 21, 2019. https://www.pewsocialtrends.org/2016/05/24/for-first-time-in-modern-era-living-with-parents-edges-out-other-living-arrangements-for-18-to-34-year-olds/.

10. Alsop, Ron. "The 'Trophy Kids' Go to Work." The Wall Street Journal. Dow Jones & Company, October 21, 2008. https://www.wsj.com/articles/SB122455219391652725.

11. "Gratitude Is Good Medicine." UC Davis Health, November 25, 2015. https://health. ucdavis.edu/medicalcenter/features/2015-2016/11/20151125_gratitude.html.

CHAPTER ELEVEN

1.  Tennant, Don. "Entitlement-Minded Workers More Likely to See Bosses as Abusive, Study Finds." itbusinessedge, September 26, 2013. https://www.itbusinessedge.com/blogs/from-under-the-rug/entitlement-minded-workers-more-likely-to-see-bosses-as-abusive-study-finds.html.

2.  Ibid.

3.  Harvey, Paul, and Mark J. Martinko. "An Empirical Examination of the Role of Attributions in Psychological Entitlement and Its Outcomes." Journal of Organizational Behavior30, no. 4 (May 2009): 459–76. https://doi.org/10.1002/job.549.

4.    Moore, Brian. "The Worst Generation?" New York Post. New York Post, May 10, 2010. https://nypost.com/2010/05/10/the-worst-generation/.

5.    Standring, Suzette. "Matthew McConaughey: Gratitude Reciprocates." HuffPost. HuffPost, May 7, 2014. https://bit.ly/2KR3Mus.

6.    Watkins, Philip C., Kathrane Woodward, Tamara Stone, and Russell L. Kolts. "Gratitude And Happiness: Development Of A Measure Of Gratitude, And Relationships With Subjective Well-Being." Social Behavior and Personality: an International Journal31, no. 5 (January 2003): 431–51. https://doi.org/10.2224/sbp.2003.31.5.431.

7.    Grubbs, Joshua B., and Julie J. Exline. "Trait Entitlement: A Cognitive-Personality Source of Vulnerability to Psychological Distress." Psychological Bulletin142, no. 11 (2016): 1204–26. https://doi.org/10.1037/bul0000063.

8.    MacMillan, Amanda. "Entitled People More Likely to Be Disappointed in Life." Time. Time, September 21, 2016. https://time.com/4500437/entitled-disappointment-personality/.

9.    MacMillan, Amanda. "Entitled People Are More Likely to Be Disappointed by Life." Health.com, September 15, 2016. https://www.health.com/depression/entitlement-disappointment.

10.   Ibid.

11.   Brooks, David. The Road to Character. New York: Random House, 2016.

## CHAPTER TWELVE

1.    McLaughlin, Katy. "Wealthy Parents Help Child Athletes Go Pro in Their Own Backyards." The Wall Street Journal. Dow Jones & Company, August 16, 2018. https://www.wsj.com/articles/wealthy-parents-help-child-athletes-go-pro-in-their-own-backyards-1534429841.

2.    Alini, Erica. "Kids Activities: When Too Many Extracurriculars Lead to Anxiety." Global News, September 5, 2017. https://globalnews.ca/news/3706356/kids-activities-anxiety-back-to-school-2017/.

3.    "Meet Generation Z: Forget Everything You Learned About Millennials." LinkedIn SlideShare. Sparks & Honey, June 17, 2014. https://www.slideshare.net/sparksandhoney/generation-z-final-june-17/26-26They_seek_education_and_knowledgeResearched.

4.    "More Young Children with ADHD Could Benefit from Behavior Therapy." CDC Newsroom. Center for Disease Control, May 3, 2016. https://www.cdc.gov/media/releases/2016/p0503-children-ADHD.html.

5.    Beurkens, Nicole. "Children with Mental Health Symptoms Are Overmedicated and Under-Researched." Nicole Beurkens, March 6, 2018. https://www.drbeurkens.com/children-with-mental-health-symptoms-are-overmedicated-and-under-researched/.

6.    Gray, Peter. Free to Learn: Why Unleashing the Instinct to Play Will Make Our Children Happier, More Self-Reliant, and Better Students for Life. New York: Basic Books, 2015.

7.    Ibid.

8.    Center for Collegiate Mental Health. (2017, January). 2016 Annual Report (Publication No. STA 17-74). https://sites.psu.edu/ccmh/files/2017/01/2016-Annual-Report-FINAL_2016_01_09-1gc2hj6.pdf.

9.    Leahy, Robert L. "How Big a Problem Is Anxiety?" Psychology Today. Sussex Publishers, April 30, 2008. https://www.psychologytoday.com/us/blog/anxiety-files/200804/how-big-problem-is-anxiety.

10.   Twenge, J., et al., (2010). "Birth cohort increases in psychopathology among young Americans, 1938-2007: A cross-temporal meta-analysis of the MMPI." In press, Clinical Psychology Review 30, 145-154. http://www.personal.umich.edu/~daneis/symposium/2012/readings/Twenge2010.pdf.

11.   Schrobsdorff, Susanna. "Teen Depression and Anxiety: Why the Kids Are Not Alright." Time. Time, October 27, 2016. https://time.com/magazine/us/4547305/november-7th-2016-vol-188-no-19-u-s/.

12.  "Data and Statistics on Children's Mental Health | CDC." Centers for Disease Control and Prevention. Centers for Disease Control and Prevention, April 19, 2019. https://www.cdc.gov/childrensmentalhealth/data.html.

13.  Mclean, Carmen P., Anu Asnaani, Brett T. Litz, and Stefan G. Hofmann. "Gender Differences in Anxiety Disorders: Prevalence, Course of Illness, Comorbidity and Burden of Illness." Journal of Psychiatric Research45, no. 8 (2011): 1027–35. https://doi.org/10.1016/j.jpsychires.2011.03.006.

14.  "Any Anxiety Disorder." National Institute of Mental Health. U.S. Department of Health and Human Services, November 2017. https://www.nimh.nih.gov/health/statistics/any-anxiety-disorder.shtml.

15.  "Child Mind Institute Children's Mental Health Report Finds an Estimated 17.1 Million Young People in the U.S. Have or Have Had a Diagnosable Psychiatric Disorder." Child Mind Institute, May 4, 2015. https://childmind.org/news/child-mind-institute-childrens-mental-health-report-finds-an-estimated-17-1-million-young-people-in-the-u-s-have-or-have-had-a-diagnosable-psychiatric-disorder/.

## CHAPTER THIRTEEN

1.  Garcia-Navarro, Lulu. "The Risk Of Teen Depression And Suicide Is Linked To Smartphone Use, Study Says." NPR. NPR, December 17, 2017. https://www.npr.org/2017/12/17/571443683/the-call-in-teens-and-depression.

2.  "Meet Generation Z: Forget Everything You Learned About Millennials." LinkedIn SlideShare. Sparks & Honey, June 17, 2014. https://www.slideshare.net/sparksandhoney/generation-z-final-june-17/26-26They_seek_education_and_knowledgeResearched.

3.  Lagorio-Chafkin, Christine. "What You Need to Know About Generation Z." Inc.com. Inc., June 19, 2014. https://www.inc.com/christine-lagorio/entrepreneurial-generation-z.html.

4.  Lipp, Kathi. "Cheri Gregory - Be Longing." Kathi Lipp, January 12, 2015. https://www.kathilipp.com/2015/01/cheri-belonging/.

5.  Hoge, Elizabeth A., Eric Bui, Luana Marques, Christina A. Metcalf, Laura K. Morris, Donald J. Robinaugh, John J. Worthington, Mark H. Pollack, and Naomi M. Simon. "Randomized Controlled Trial of Mindfulness Meditation for Generalized Anxiety Disorder." The Journal of Clinical Psychiatry74, no. 08 (2013): 786–92. https://doi.org/10.4088/jcp.12m08083.

6.  Wesch, Michael. "A Vision of Students Today." YouTube video, 4:44. October 12, 2007. https://www.youtube.com/watch?v=dGCJ46vyR9o.

7.  Levitin, Daniel J. "Why the Modern World Is Bad for Your Brain." The Guardian. Guardian News and Media, January 18, 2015. https://www.theguardian.com/science/2015/jan/18/modern-world-bad-for-brain-daniel-j-levitin-organized-mind-information-overload.

8.  Kim, Larry. "Multitasking Is Killing Your Brain." Inc.com. Inc., July 15, 2015. https://www.inc.com/larry-kim/why-multi-tasking-is-killing-your-brain.html.

9.  Bradberry, Travis. "Emotional Intelligence (EQ): The Premier Provider - Tests, Training, Certification, and Coaching." TalentSmart. Accessed August 24, 2019. https://www.talentsmart.com/articles/Multitasking-Damages-Your-Brain-and-Your-Career,-New-Studies-Suggest-2102500909-p-1.html.

10.  Kim, Larry. "Multitasking Is Killing Your Brain." Inc.com. Inc., July 15, 2015. https://www.inc.com/larry-kim/why-multi-tasking-is-killing-your-brain.html.

11.  Ibid.

12.  Mindfulness: the New Science of Health and Happiness. New York, NY: Time Books, an imprint of Time Inc. Books, 2018.

13.  Ibid.

14.  Lester-Coll, Gabby. "You're Probably Low on This Essential Mineral." Coveteur. Coveteur, August 21, 2018. http://coveteur.com/2018/08/21/how-to-avoid-magnesium-deficiency-nutritionist-tips/.

15. Lee, J., Park, B.-J., Tsunetsugu, Y., Kagawa, T., Miyazaki, Y. (2009). Restorative effects of viewing real forest landscapes, based on a comparison with urban landscapes. Scandinavian Journal of Forest Research. 24(3): 227-234. http://www.tandfonline.com/doi/abs/10.1080/02827580902903341#preview.

16. Csikszentmihalyi, Mihaly. Flow: the Psychology of Optimal Experience. New York: Harper Row, 2009.

17. Bilton, Nick. "Steve Jobs Was a Low-Tech Parent." The New York Times. The New York Times, September 10, 2014. https://www.nytimes.com/2014/09/11/fashion/steve-jobs-apple-was-a-low-tech-parent.html.

18. Hellmich, Nanci. "Go to School and Just Dance." USA Today. October 11, 2010, 11 edition, sec. Life.

19. Mozes, Alan. "Excess Cellphone Use May Mean Anxiety, Depression." WebMD. WebMD, March 15, 2016. https://www.webmd.com/depression/news/20160315/could-too-much-cellphone-time-signal-anxiety-depression#1.

20. Markham, Laura. "How to Stay Calm? The Same Way You Get to Carnegie Hall." Psychology Today. Sussex Publishers, June 9, 2015. https://www.psychologytoday.com/us/blog/peaceful-parents-happy-kids/201506/how-stay-calm-the-same-way-you-get-carnegie-hall.

## CHAPTER FOURTEEN

1. Fernandez, Manny, Richard Pérez-peña, and Azam Ahmed. "Ethan Couch, 'Affluenza' Teenager, Had Last Party Before Fleeing, Officials Say." The New York Times. The New York Times, December 29, 2015. https://www.nytimes.com/2015/12/30/us/affluenza-ethan-couch-mexico.html?_r=0.

2. Noman, Natasha. "Study Reveals Most People Don't Feel Like an Adult Until the Age of 29." Mic, September 2, 2015. https://www.mic.com/articles/124772/study-reveals-most-people-don-t-feel-like-an-adult-until-the-age-of-29#.eQ7LQ8aD2.

3. Nesterak, Max, Chris Benderev, Shankar Vedantam, Jennifer Schmidt, and Maggie Penman. "Me, Me, Me: The Rise Of Narcissism In The Age Of The Selfie." NPR. NPR, July 12, 2016. https://www.npr.org/2016/07/12/485087469/me-me-me-the-rise-of-narcissism-in-the-age-of-the-selfie.

4. Burnett, Jane. "Survey: 13% of Millennials Started Their First Job after 20 Years Old." Ladders, August 22, 2018. https://www.theladders.com/career-advice/survey-13-of-millennials-started-their-first-job-after-20-years-old.

5. Fry, Richard. "More Young Adults Are Living at Home, and for Longer Stretches." Pew Research Center, May 5, 2017. https://www.pewresearch.org/fact-tank/2017/05/05/its-becoming-more-common-for-young-adults-to-live-at-home-and-for-longer-stretches/.

6. "Historical Marital Status Tables." Historical Marital Status Tables. US Census Bureau, November 14, 2018. https://www.census.gov/data/tables/time-series/demo/families/marital.html.

7. Mathews, T.J., and Brady E. Hamilton. "Mean Age of Mother, 1970–2000." National Vital Statistics Report51, no. 1 (December 11, 2002). https://www.cdc.gov/nchs/data/nvsr/nvsr51/nvsr51_01.pdf.

8. Leonard, Kimberly. "Moms Are Older Than They Used to Be." U.S. News & World Report. U.S. News & World Report, January 14, 2016. https://www.usnews.com/news/blogs/data-mine/2016/01/14/cdc-the-median-age-of-first-time-motherhood-is-increasing.

9. Koch, Kathy. Screens and Teens: Connecting with Our Kids in a Wireless World. Chicago: Moody Publishers, 2015.

10. Lukianoff, Greg, and Jonathan Haidt. The Coddling of the American Mind: How Good Intentions and Bad Ideas Are Setting up a Generation for Failure, 58. New York City: Penguin Press, 2018.

11. Ibid, 58.

12. Paul, Pamela. "From Students, Less Kindness for Strangers?" The New York Times. The New York Times, June 25, 2010. https://www.nytimes.com/2010/ 06/27/fashion/27StudiedEmpathy.html?mtrref=www.nytimes.com&gwh=F9A355CF98F5D41BBAA864B-D54044337&gwt=pay&assetType=REGIWALL.

13. Denizet-Lewis, Benoit. "Why Are More American Teenagers Than Ever Suffering From Severe Anxiety?" The New York Times. The New York Times, October 11, 2017. https://www.nytimes.com/2017/10/11/magazine/why-are-more-american-teenagers-than-ever-suffering-from-severe-anxiety.html.

14. Rosin, Hanna, and Alix Spiegel. "Flip the Script." NPR. NPR, July 15, 2016. https://www.npr.org/programs/invisibilia/485603559/flip-the-script.

15. Foley, Katherine Ellen, and Akshat Rathi. "Researchers Say One of the Most Powerful Tools to Diffuse Hate Is the Hardest to Master: Genuine Empathy." Quartz. Quartz, July 21, 2016. https://qz.com/736618/researchers-have-found-that-one-of-the-most-powerful-tools-to-diffuse-hate-is-also-the-hardest-to-master-genuine-empathy/.

## CHAPTER FIFTEEN

1. Brooks, David. The Road to Character. New York: Random House, 2016.

2. Niebuhr, Reinhold. Human Nature. London: Nisbet, 1946.

3. Brooks, David, "Should you Live for Your Resume… or Your Eulogy?," March, 2014. TED video, 4:50, https://www.ted.com/talks/david_brooks_should_you_live_for_your_resume_or_your_eulogy?language=en.

4. Twenge, Jean M. IGEN: Why Todays Super-connected Kids Are Growing up Less Rebellious, More Tolerant, Less Happy-and Completely Unprepared for Adulthood (and What That Means for the Rest of Us), 214-215. New York: Atria Books, 2017.

5. Little, Becky. "How Martin Luther King Jr. Took Inspiration From Gandhi on Nonviolence." Biography.com. A&E Networks Television, June 24, 2019. https://www.biography.com/news/martin-luther-king-jr-gandhi-nonviolence-inspiration.

6. Ibid.

7. Ibid.

8. Lukianoff, Greg, and Jonathan Haidt. The Coddling of the American Mind: How Good Intentions and Bad Ideas Are Setting up a Generation for Failure, 61. New York City: Penguin Press, 2018.

9. King, Martin Luther. "'Pilgrimage to Nonviolence.'" The Martin Luther King, Jr., Research and Education Institute. Stanford University, April 13, 1960. https://kinginstitute.stanford.edu/king-papers/documents/pilgrimage-nonviolence.

10. Wiltons, Rebbekah. "Middle School Football Players Execute a Life-Changing Play." KiwiReport, November 9, 2017. http://www.kiwireport.com/road-middle-school-football-players-execute-life-changing-play/.

## CHAPTER SIXTEEN

1. Kelly, Kevin. The Inevitable: Understanding the 12 Technological Forces That Will Shape Our Future. New York: Penguin Books, 2017.

2. Harari, Yuval Noah. Sapiens: A Brief History of Humankind. London: Vintage, 2019.

3. McNamee, Roger. "I Mentored Mark Zuckerberg. I Loved Facebook. But I Can't Stay Silent About What's Happening." Time. Time, January 17, 2019. https://time.com/magazine/us/5505429/january-28th-2019-vol-193-no-3-u-s/.

4. Buchmann, Bryce. "Cheating In College: Where It Happens, Why Students Do It and How to Stop It." HuffPost. HuffPost, February 20, 2014. https://www.huffpost.com/entry/cheating-in-college-where_b_4826136.

5. "Age Distribution - Religion in America: U.S. Religious Data, Demographics and Statistics." Pew Research Center's Religion & Public Life Project. Accessed August 27, 2019. https://www.pewforum.org/religious-landscape-study/age-distribution/.

6. Teasley, Deborah. "What Is a Moral Decision?" Study.com. Study.com. Accessed August 27, 2019. https://study.com/academy/lesson/what-is-a-moral-decision-definition-examples-quiz.html#/lesson.

7. "The End of Absolutes: America's New Moral Code." Barna Group, May 25, 2016. https://www.barna.com/research/the-end-of-absolutes-americas-new-moral-code/.

8. Ibid.

9. Barna. Gen Z: the Culture, Beliefs and Motivations Shaping the next Generation. Ventura, CA: Barna Group, 2018.

10. Tompkins, Chris, Don Posterski, and John McAuley. Elastic Morality: Leading Young Adults in Our Age of Acceptance. Bloomington, IN: West Bow Press, 2011.

11. Smith, Christian. Lost in Transition: the Dark Side of Emerging Adulthood. New York: Oxford University Press, 2011.

12. Ibid.

13. Ibid.

14. Ibid.

15. Ibid.

16. Vedantam, Shankar. "Hookup Culture: The Unspoken Rules Of Sex On College Campuses." NPR. NPR, September 25, 2017. https://www.npr.org/templates/transcript/transcript.php?storyId=552582404.

## CHAPTER SEVENTEEN

1. Schweitzer, Albert, and C. T. Campion. Civilization and Ethics. London: Unwin Books, Published in association with A. & C. Black, 1969.

2. Wallace, Kelly. "Can Babies Tell Right from Wrong? Inside Yale's 'Baby Lab'." CNN. Cable News Network, February 14, 2014. https://www.cnn.com/2014/02/13/living/what-babies-know-anderson-cooper-parents/index.html.

3. Teasley, Deborah. "What Is a Moral Decision?" Study.com. Study.com. Accessed August 27, 2019. https://study.com/academy/lesson/what-is-a-moral-decision-definition-examples-quiz.html#/lesson.

4. Haidt, Jonathan. The Righteous Mind: Why Good People Are Divided by Politics and Religion. New York: Vintage Books, a division of Random House, 2013.

## CHAPTER EIGHTEEN

1. Twenge, Jean M. "Have Smartphones Destroyed a Generation?" The Atlantic. Atlantic Media Company, September 2017. https://www.theatlantic.com/magazine/archive/2017/09/has-the-smartphone-destroyed-a-generation/534198/.

2. Standage, Tom, and Seth Stevenson. "What Happens the First Time People See Themselves in Photos?" Slate Magazine. Slate, October 10, 2018. https://slate.com/technology/2018/10/the-birth-of-photography-and-the-age-of-the-selfie.html.

3. Ibid.

4. Madrigal, Alexis C. "When the Revolution Was Televised." The Atlantic. Atlantic Media Company, April 1, 2018. https://www.theatlantic.com/technology/archive/2018/04/televisions-civil-rights-revolution/554639/.

5. Taylor, Adam. "47 Percent of the World's Population Now Use the Internet, Study Says." The Washington Post. WP Company, November 22, 2016. https://www.washingtonpost.com/news/worldviews/wp/2016/11/22/47-percent-of-the-worlds-population-now-use-the-internet-users-study-says/.

6. Leswing, Kif. "62% Of All Apps Downloaded Last Month Were Owned by Facebook." Business Insider. Business Insider, June 8, 2016. https://www.businessinsider.com/more-facebook-apps-are-downloaded-than-all-other-companies-combined-2016-6.

## CHAPTER NINETEEN

1. Kohlstedt, Kurt. "Tsunami Stones: Ancient Japanese Markers Warn Builders of High Water." 99% Invisible, August 15, 2016. https://99percentinvisible.org/article/tsunami-stones-ancient-japanese-markers-warn-builders-high-water/.

2. Rohr, Richard. Adams Return: the Five Promises of Male Initiation. New York: Crossroad Pub., 2004.

3. Gennep, Arnold van. The Rites of Passage, 11. London: Routledge, 2004.

4. Ibid, 28.

5. Ibid, 75.

6. Ibid, 99.

7. Ibid, 9.

8. Ibid, 75.

9. Nylon. "Roll Call: Meet 25 Gen Z'ers Changing The World." NYLON. NYLON, May 1, 2018. https://nylon.com/articles/roll-call-gen-z-list-nylon-may-2018-cover.

10. Kohlstedt, Kurt. "Tsunami Stones: Ancient Japanese Markers Warn Builders of High Water." 99% Invisible, August 15, 2016. https://99percentinvisible.org/article/tsunami-stones-ancient-japanese-markers-warn-builders-high-water/.

## CHAPTER TWENTY

1. Hanford, Emily. "Angela Duckworth and the Research on 'Grit'." APM Reports. American Radio Works. Accessed August 27, 2019. http://americanradioworks.publicradio.org/features/tomorrows-college/grit/angela-duckworth-grit.html.

2. Ibid.

3. Lukianoff, Greg, and Jonathan Haidt. The Coddling of the American Mind: How Good Intentions and Bad Ideas Are Setting up a Generation for Failure, 21. New York City: Penguin Press, 2018.

4. Gopnik, Alison. "Should We Let Toddlers Play With Saws and Knives?" The Wall Street Journal. Dow Jones & Company, August 31, 2016. https://www.wsj.com/articles/should-we-let-toddlers-play-with-saws-and-knives-1472654945.

5. "Time for Parents to Power down: Why Coddling Children Can Harm Them." The Chronicle of Higher Education. University of Warwick. Accessed August 27, 2019. https://www.chronicle.com/paid-article/time-for-parents-to-power-down/212.

6. Taleb, Nassim Nicholas. Antifragile: Things That Gain from Disorder. New York: Random House, 2016.

7. "You Tell Us: Which Are the Words That Sum up 2016?" Financial Times. Financial Times, December 21, 2016. https://www.ft.com/content/fc1bea28-b7cb-11e6-ba85-95d1533d9a62.

8. Bhunjun, Avinash. "What Is the Snowflake Generation?" Metro. Metro.co.uk, January 10, 2018. https://metro.co.uk/2018/01/10/what-is-the-snowflake-generation-7218112/.

9. Thompson, Sonia. "Kids Who Stick to This Activity for 2 Years Have Higher Self-Esteem, According to Science." Inc.com. Inc., July 11, 2017. https://www.inc.com/sonia-thompson/research-shows-kids-who-do-this-earn-better-grades.html.

10. Beck, Julie. "When Do You Become an Adult?" The Atlantic. Atlantic Media Company, January 5, 2016. https://www.theatlantic.com/health/archive/2016/01/when-are-you-really-an-adult/422487/.

11. Yeager, David Scott, Valerie Purdie-Vaughns, Julio Garcia, Nancy Apfel, Patti Brzustoski, Allison Master, William T. Hessert, Matthew E. Williams, and Geoffrey L. Cohen. "Breaking the Cycle of Mistrust: Wise Interventions to Provide Critical Feedback across the Racial Divide." Journal of Experimental Psychology: General143, no. 2 (2014): 804–24. https://doi.org/10.1037/a0033906.

12.  Lai, Alexis. "Blind Student Learns to Read Braille with Lips." CNN. Cable News Network, September 4, 2014. https://www.cnn.com/2013/07/17/world/asia/hong-kong-blind-student-braille-lips/index.html.

## CHAPTER TWENTY-ONE

1.  Seligman ME, Maier SF. Failure to escape traumatic shock. Journal of Experimental Psychology. 1967; 74:1–9.
2.  Nakazawa, Donna Jackson. "7 Ways Childhood Adversity Can Change Your Brain." Psychology Today. Sussex Publishers, August 7, 2015. https://www.psychologytoday.com/us/blog/the-last-best-cure/201508/7-ways-childhood-adversity-can-change-your-brain.
3.  Ibid.
4.  Dweck, Carol. Mindset. London: Robinson, 2017.
5.  "What the United States Can Learn From Singapore's World-Class Mathematics System (and what Singapore can learn from the United States): An Exploratory Study." American Institutes for Research. U.S. Department of Education Policy and Program Studies Service (PPSS), January 28, 2005. https://www.air.org/sites/default/files/downloads/report/Singapore_Report_Bookmark_Version1_0.pdf.
6.  Maxwell, John. Twitter Post. May 3, 2016, 10:57 am. https://twitter.com/JohnMaxwellTeam/status/727557639488544768.
7.  Medina, J. Brain Rules: 12 Tips for Surfing and Thriving at Work, Home, and School. Pear Press, 2008.
8.  "Meet Generation Z: Forget Everything You Learned About Millennials." LinkedIn SlideShare. Sparks & Honey, June 17, 2014. https://www.slideshare.net/sparksandhoney/generation-z-final-june-17/26-26They_seek_education_and_knowledgeResearched.
9.  Varty, Boyd. Cathedral of the Wild: an African Journey Home. Place of publication not identified: Thorndike Press, 2015.
10. Pratt, Casey. "TBT: After Losing His Arm and Career, Dave Dravecky Had to Find Himself." Field of Teams. NBC Sports, August 15, 2013. http://fieldofteams.csnbayarea.com/2013/08/15/tbt-dave-dravecky-delivers-his-final-pitch-learns-how-to-cope-with-tragedy/.

## CHAPTER TWENTY-TWO

1.  "World Economic Forum." World Economic Forum. World Economic Forum, January 2016. http://reports.weforum.org/future-of-jobs-2016/?doing_wp_cron=1565570080.1260941028594970703125.
2.  Ibid.
3.  Paul, Richard. "The State of Critical Thinking Today." The State of Critical Thinking Today. Foundation for Critical Thinking, 2004. https://www.criticalthinking.org/pages/the-state-of-critical-thinking-today/523.
4.  Casserly, Meghan. "The 10 Skills That Will Get You Hired In 2013." Forbes. Forbes Magazine, December 10, 2012. https://www.forbes.com/sites/meghancasserly/2012/12/10/the-10-skills-that-will-get-you-a-job-in-2013/#5f27988d633d.
5.  Ibid.
6.  Haidt, Jonathan. The Righteous Mind: Why Good People Are Divided by Politics and Religion. New York: Vintage Books, a division of Random House, 2013.
7.  Lukianoff, Greg, and Jonathan Haidt. The Coddling of the American Mind: How Good Intentions and Bad Ideas Are Setting up a Generation for Failure, 35. New York City: Penguin Press, 2018.
8.  Ibid.
9.  Clark, Jeramy. Your Teenager Is Not Crazy: Understanding Your Teens Brain Can Make You a Better Parent, 24. Grand Rapids, MI: Baker Books, 2016.

10.  Ibid.

11.  Alleyne, Richard. "Welcome to the Information Age - 174 Newspapers a Day." The Telegraph. Telegraph Media Group, February 11, 2011. https://www.telegraph.co.uk/news/science/science-news/8316534/Welcome-to-the-information-age-174-newspapers-a-day.html.

12.  "Consumers Mainly Eat Alone - Food Trends." The NPD Group. The NPD Group/National Eating Trends®, August 6, 2014. https://www.npd.com/wps/portal/npd/us/news/press-releases/consumers-are-alone-over-half-of-eating-occasions-as-a-result-of-changing-lifestyles-and-more-single-person-households-reports-npd/.

13.  Balfour, Barbara. "Tables for One - the Rise of Solo Dining." BBC News. BBC, July 24, 2014. https://www.bbc.com/news/business-28292651.

14.  Jargon, Julie. "How 13 Became the Internet's Age of Adulthood." The Wall Street Journal. Dow Jones & Company, June 18, 2019. https://www.wsj.com/articles/how-13-became-the-internets-age-of-adulthood-11560850201.

15.  Ibid.

16.  Glum, Julia. "Millennials Selfies: Young Adults Will Take More Than 25,000 Pictures Of Themselves During Their Lifetimes: Report." International Business Times, September 22, 2015. https://www.ibtimes.com/millennials-selfies-young-adults-will-take-more-25000-pictures-themselves-during-2108417.

17.  Drexler, Peggy. "What Your Selfies Say About You | Psychology Today New Zealand." Psychology Today. Sussex Publishers, September 16, 2013. https://www.psychologytoday.com/nz/blog/our-gender-ourselves/201309/what-your-selfies-say-about-you?amp.

18.  Casey, B. J., et al. (2011). Behavioral and neural correlates of delay of gratification 40 years later. Proceedings of the National Academy of Sciences, 108(36), 14998–15003.

19.  British Psychological Society (BPS). "Boredom can be good for you, scientists say." ScienceDaily. www.sciencedaily.com/releases/2015/03/150324205940.htm.

20.  Smith, Jeremy Adam. "What Is the Relationship Between Stress and Empathy?" Greater Good. University of California Berkeley, August 13, 2015. https://greatergood.berkeley.edu/article/item/what_is_the_relationship_between_stress_and_empathy.

21.  "2011 Cisco Connected World Technology Report." Cisco, 2011. https://www.cisco.com/c/dam/en/us/solutions/enterprise/connected-world-technology-report/2011-CCWTR-Chapter-3-All-Finding.pdf.

22.  Kim, Hyunna. (2013). Exercise rehabilitation for smartphone addiction. Journal of exercise rehabilitation. 9. 500-505. 10.12965/jer.130080.

23.  "Clinical Report—The Impact of Social Media on Children, Adolescents, and Families." aappublications.org. American Academy of Pediatrics, April 2011. https://pediatrics.aappublications.org/content/pediatrics/127/4/800.full.pdf.

## CHAPTER TWENTY-THREE

1.  Alban, Deane. "Why Critical Thinking Is Important (& How to Improve It)." Be Brain Fit, July 6, 2018. https://bebrainfit.com/critical-thinking/.

2.  "Jodie Wu." Echoing Green. Accessed August 12, 2019. https://www.echoinggreen.org/fellows/jodie-wu.

3.  Flannery, Mary Ellen. "Design Thinking: Connecting Students to the Larger World." NEA Today. National Education Association, April 19, 2018. http://neatoday.org/2018/04/19/design-thinking-in-the-classroom/.

4.  Ibid.

5.  Ibid.

6.  Plattner, Hasso. "An Introduction to Design Thinking PROCESS GUIDE." dschool. stanford.edu. Institute of Design at Stanford University. Accessed August 11, 2019. https://dschool-old.stanford.edu/sandbox/groups/designresources/wiki/36873/attachments/74b3d/ModeGuideBOOTCAMP2010L.pdf.

7.  British Psychological Society (BPS). "Boredom can be good for you, scientists say." ScienceDaily. www.sciencedaily.com/releases/2015/03/150324205940.htm (accessed August 9, 2019).

8.  "Three Wishes for Ruby's Residents." Facebook. Accessed August 12, 2019. https://www.facebook.com/3wishesforrubysresidents/.

9.  Chillag, Amy. "A 5th Grader's Boredom While Visiting Her Mom's Job Led to $70,000 for the Elderly in Need." CNN. Cable News Network, February 7, 2019. https://www.cnn.com/2019/01/29/health/iyw-5th-grader-nursing-home-mission-trnd/index.html.

10. Ibid.

## CHAPTER TWENTY-FOUR

1.  "Jim Casey: The Unknown Entrepreneur Who Built the Great UPS." Archbridge Institute. Archbridge Institute, July 29, 2019. https://www.archbridgeinstitute.org/2018/05/23/jim-casey-the-unknown-entrepreneur-who-built-the-great-ups/.

2.  Running Deer. "James E. Casey (1888-1983)" Find A Grave. Accessed August 9, 2019. https://www.findagrave.com/memorial/51490184/james-e_-casey.

3.  Batterson, Mark. Twitter Post. January 3, 2015, 3:06 pm. https://twitter.com/MarkBatterson/status/551514907212914689

4.  "The Chemicals of the Brain." Big Picture, November 2017. https://bigpictureeducation.com/chemicals-brain.

## CHAPTER TWENTY-FIVE

1.  Rosen, Fred, and Hank Garfield. Murdering the President: Alexander Graham Bell and the Race to Save James Garfield. University of Nebraska Press, 2016. http://www.jstor.org/stable/j.ctt1d4v00p.

2.  Spiegel, Alix. "Teachers' Expectations Can Influence How Students Perform." NPR. NPR, September 17, 2012. https://www.npr.org/sections/health-shots/2012/09/18/161159263/teachers-expectations-can-influence-how-students-perform.

3.  Dromgoole, Will Allen. "The Bridge Builder by Will Allen Dromgoole." Poetry Foundation. EP Dutton & Company (1931). Accessed August 8, 2019. https://www.poetryfoundation.org/poems/52702/the-bridge-builder.

# Acknowledgments

At this point in my journey—every book I am a part of is a joint venture. I am surrounded by good people, at Growing Leaders, and include several team members in each project. Each one of them is a learning experience. In this space, I'd like to offer a "shout out" to those who participated in this book:

**Andrew McPeak** collaborated with me on this book as a co-author. He was a part of every chapter and wrote a few of the chapters himself. He oversaw the project from soup to nuts and insured we finished with a resource that was helpful and relevant. Thanks Andrew.

**Matt Litton** served as a chief editor, helping us with content and flow. Matt believes in our cause of preparing the emerging generations for life and leadership so he was perfect for this role. Thanks, Matt, for your tough but helpful feedback and your belief in the project.

**Makenzie Skinner** served as our editor for grammar and punctuation. She got in the weeds and made sure the words were right and clear for readers. It was tedious work. Thanks Makenzie for your attention to detail and for your desire to help create this resource.

**Jim Woodard** oversaw the layout and production of this manuscript. He insured that the content you read in this book is appealing to the eye and is as easy as possible to follow. Jim figures out a way to accomplish anything that needs to be done, which makes him invaluable.

**Chris Harris** helped us formulate the original idea for this book. He saw the benefit of my books, Generation iY and Marching Off the Map and believed a book was needed that not only offered data on Generation Z, but also practical solutions to meet their challenges.

**Cameron Turner** dug into the minutia of insuring the sources for our research were accurate. As a college student at the University of Michigan, Cam understands the importance of sourcing information well. Cam is a leader in the making and will be writing his own books one day.

**Emma Smith** sat in on our original meetings at Growing Leaders helping us create a resource that was different and that complimented other books on the market. She offered us a sounding board for her generation and is a quick learner and tireless worker. Thanks Emma.

**Cody Braun** and **Gabby Williams** lead our marketing team at Growing Leaders. They always have great ideas on how to creatively say what needs to be said. These two are a dynamic duo who find a way to get any job done. I am very grateful for the role you both played.

**B.T. Harman** who helped us launch this book well. B.T. is tremendously creative and finds ways for a message to stand out and get noticed. He's a marketing specialist who believes in our cause and participated in countless meetings this year. Thanks B.T. for loaning your gifts.

**Evan Donoho** researched primary sources on several of the biggest challenges facing Generation Z. He found some studies that helped us pinpoint what those challenges are. Evan cares about the students who are growing up just behind him. Thanks for the data Evan.

**Vanna Farley** is last, but certainly not least. Vanna created the cover design for this book. She studied and formed several iterations until we landed on the one you hold in your hands. Vanna, thanks for the extra hours you invested and for believing in kids.

# About the Authors

**Dr. Tim Elmore,** Founder & CEO of Growing Leaders, is a best-selling author and international speaker who uses his expertise on generations to equip educators, coaches, leaders, parents, and other adults to impart practical life and leadership skills to young adults that will help them navigate through life.

He educates adults to help them understand the challenges and experiences today's generation faces and connect with them in a way that resonates. Dr. Elmore believes, by cultivating leadership ability in young adults and encouraging the adults who guide then, Growing Leaders can be the catalyst for emerging generations that will truly change the world.

Tim Elmore teaches leadership courses and speaks at schools, universities, businesses, and athletic programs. He has trained thousands of leaders in partnership with nationally renowned schools and organizations like the Kansas City Royals, Stanford University, University of Alabama, National Football League, Ohio State University's Athletic Department, Chick-fil-A, and more.

Dr. Elmore has authored more than 30 books including: *Habitudes®: Images that Form Leadership Habits and Attitudes, Marching Off the Map: Inspire Students to Navigate a Brand New World, Generation iY: Secrets to Connecting with Today's Teens & Young Adults in the Digital Age, 12 Huge Mistakes Parents Can Avoid,* and *Artificial Maturity: Helping Kids Meet the Challenge of Becoming Authentic Adults.*

**Andrew McPeak** is a next gen researcher, speaker and curriculum designer for Growing Leaders. Along with Dr. Tim Elmore, he co-authored *Marching Off the Map: Inspire Students to Navigate a Brand New World.* He works with schools, universities, and sports teams on implementing *Habitudes* as a teaching tool for life and leadership skills. He excels at helping these leaders craft their message to connect with students in Generation Z.

# GENERATION Z **UNFILTERED** Events

Bring GENERATION Z UNFILTERED to your organization or campus. Hear Dr. Tim Elmore, Andrew McPeak, or one of our other amazing speakers share the insights, ideas, and strategies from GENERATION Z UNFILTERED at your next event.

While it's true that today's students present a host of new challenges for those who mentor and lead them, we have hope that they can succeed in life, and like you, we are determined to help them fulfill their potential.

Available as a customized 90-minute, half-day, or full-day presentation, our GENERATION Z UNFILTERED in-person event will further educate your team on the unique characteristics of Generation Z and provide you with practical strategies to connect with and lead today's young adults.

We have previously brought Growing Leaders concepts to:

- Schools
- Organizations
- Athletic Departments
- Businesses
- Churches

With the right resources to help educate, lead, and parent young adults better, we can all be a catalyst for emerging generations that will truly change the world.

So, while we all love a good book, this discussion-based workshop can be the catalyst to spark long-term change with your group. We're building a community of leaders to help Generation Z achieve their ultimate potential. Will you join us?

## Contact: Speakers@GrowingLeaders.com

# GROWING LEADERS
## *Ready for Real Life*

Imagine a world improved—even transformed—by millions of young influencers who solve problems and serve people in their communities. That's our vision at Growing Leaders.

Founded in 2003 by Dr. Tim Elmore, Growing Leaders is a global non-profit that encourages and equips young adults to take on real-life opportunities and challenges in the classroom, in their careers, and in the community.

We do this by partnering with organizations like yours to teach practical life and leadership skills using real stories, intriguing images, and engaging experiences that are relatable and memorable.

Our process and resources are grounded in research and a unique understanding of the emerging generations, and recognize that leading others at any level begins with learning how to lead yourself.

**These tools include:**

- Life and leadership skills curriculum to educators and trainers
- Leadership resources for mentoring communities
- Speakers that can travel to your organization or campus

**Some of the organizations that use our training resources include:**

- National FFA Organization
- Kansas City Royals Baseball Club (minor league affiliates)
- University of Alabama
- Pepperdine University
- Nebraska Department of Education
- The Ohio State University
- Chick-fil-A Restaurants

Tim Elmore and the Growing Leaders team are available to help you invest wisely in the next generation. For more information, please visit:

## GrowingLeaders.com

# HABITUDES®
## IMAGES THAT FORM LEADERSHIP HABITS & ATTITUDES

Every person is faced with unique obstacles and possibilities throughout his or her life. What makes someone a leader is how they manage them and leverage those experiences to positively influence others.

*Habitudes* is a curriculum and training system that combines images, relatable stories and experiences into leadership lesson plans that resonate with today's young adults, equipping them to navigate through life's challenges and opportunities.

Grounded in established research, they are a fun, creative, and engaging way that helps young adults:

- Take initiative and set the pace to influence others in positive ways.
- Overcome complex problems through creative persistence.
- Capitalize on personal strengths to be career-ready after graduation.
- Develop critical thinking skills that produce better life choices, such as choosing healthy friends, improving study habits, and setting meaningful goals.

*Habitudes* has been used in over 10,000 schools and organizations across the world for:

- Secondary School Advisement Periods
- Athletic Programs (High School, College, and Professional)
- College Freshmen Programs
- Corporate On-boarding Programs for Young Professionals
- Leadership Classes
- Youth Groups

*"Habitudes has it all. It has the implementation of why we're doing this and the why behind 'you should have integrity.' We found something that the kids are hooked on immediately."*

*- Julie Diaz, Principal of Travis High School*

## For a Free Sample visit GrowingLeaders.com/Habitudes